Oracle VM Manager 2.1.2

Manage a flexible and elastic data center with
Oracle VM Manager

Tarry Singh

[PACKT]
PUBLISHING

BIRMINGHAM - MUMBAI

Oracle VM Manager 2.1.2

First published: July 2009

Production Reference: 1090709

Published by Packt Publishing Ltd.
32 Lincoln Road
Olton
Birmingham, B27 6PA, UK.

ISBN 978-1-847197-12-2

www.packtpub.com

Cover Image by Parag Kadam (paragvkadam@gmail.com)

Credits

Author
Tarry Singh

Reviewer
Hans Forbrich

Acquisition Editor
James Lumsden

Development Editor
Dilip Venkatesh

Technical Editors
Mehul Shetty
Rakesh Shejwal

Indexer
Monica Ajmera

Editorial Team Leader
Akshara Aware

Project Team Leader
Priya Mukherji

Project Coordinator
Leena Purkait

Proofreader
Angie Butcher

Production Coordinator
Dolly Dasilva

Cover Work
Dolly Dasilva

About the Author

Tarry Singh, an Oracle OCP, has been a Sr. DBA and has worked with
Oracle technologies starting from Oracle database version 7.3 through 11g.
An industry veteran, whose career spans several industries such as Oil & Gas sector,
Maritime, and currently IT. He has worked for several Fortune 500 companies.
He is currently working for a large French multi-national SI vendor, Atos Origin,
as a Strategic Business Executive. Tarry spends his time talking to customers and
offering cost-effective solutions. He also monitors the emerging trends and is a
renowned industry veteran when it comes to Virtualization and Cloud Computing.

Tarry is also involved in several NGO projects across the world, the latest being
a €2 million technology project in Uganda which he leads as a Chief Technology
Consultant together with Hanze University in The Netherlands. Tarry has also
co-authored a research paper for IEEE called "Smart Metering the Clouds" where he
discusses the vision of developing a consolidated metering solution from a utility
perspective. This was published in June where he co-chaired the IEEE workshop and
is being read by millions across the world.

Tarry holds a Nautical Science graduate degree from India's LBS of Advanced
Research and Studies in Mumbai and holds many IT and non-IT related certifications
such as GMDSS, Firefighter, and so on. Having worked with more than 40
nationalities and having worked across the globe, Tarry has been able to develop
deep multi-cultural skills and has handled virtual teams with great passion and
tremendous control.

Tarry is a Dutch citizen based in the Netherlands. In his free time, Tarry conducts
market research and analysis with tremendous zest and is very well connected
with the investor community across the globe. Tarry has advised several firms in
executing their strategy and has helped them in M&A, product development, and
other areas. He also runs his popular Cloud Computing blog called "Sustainable
Global Clouds" at http://ideationcloud.com and writes passionately about
Mergers and Acquisitions, Business Strategies, Emerging Trends around Sustainable,
and Environmental-friendly technologies. Tarry has spoken at many large
international events and has been quoted by The Economist and several other
leading magazines.

Acknowledgement

To my loving wife and dearest friend, Foke, without you I couldn't have achieved this hurdle. You are truly the crystal clear water that cleanses my soul. Also, I am thankful to my kids who have been patient while daddy was busy writing the book, even during Easter!

James Lumsden and other technical staff at Packt publishing for their patience, perseverance, and continued guidance in this journey of bringing to you all a collection of thoughts around a technology as I see it. James helped me in packaging it so you all could read comfortably without getting lost in the complex verbiage that I am sometimes prone to indulge in. The same also goes to the technical reviewers who helped me stay on track.

About the Reviewer

Hans Forbrich has been around computers for 40 years. Indeed, while studying for his BSc EE in the 70s he worked as a Contract Programmer to help pay for school. Hans has been working with Oracle product since 1984, while at Nortel in the field service group when he met Oracle Database version 4. He joined Oracle, Canada to work in the Communications vertical from 1996 to 2002.

In 2003, Hans started Forbrich Computer Consulting Ltd., which has become a successful international Oracle consultancy and Oracle training partner based in St. Albert, near Edmonton, Alberta, Canada.

As an Oracle ACE Director and OCP, Hans frequently responds in various Oracle forums, teaches for Oracle University, consults with Oracle customers on maximizing value from Oracle licenses, and speaks at Oracle User Group conferences around the world. He holds a strong belief that Oracle products provide significant value and the key to extracting that value—and reducing the effective cost of the product—is in understanding the product and using the right tool for the job.

I thank my wife for the 27 years of her patience, especially while I experiment in the lab. And also I thank my two sons for their patience, their assistance at computer setups, and help with those same experiments. And I am proud to note that Son number one, also known as Employee number two, also known also Chief Network & Systems Administrator, has achieved his MSc EE this past year. Finally, I thank Edmonton Opera and my colleagues there, for allowing me to break away from computers and unwind on stage with the Edmonton Opera Chorus.

Table of Contents

Part 2 – Looking into the Architecture and Management

Preface

Oracle VM Manager is a management product developed by Oracle that complements Oracle Grid Control and fits into Oracle's Cloud Computing strategy. Oracle VM Manager is a rather new product and is gaining popularity within the Oracle community, especially within groups that have been testing Oracle products in sandbox environments using alternate Virtualization products or tools. Since Oracle provides its own version of Oracle EL **jeOS (Just Enough OS)**, and its own VM stack (or platform as they call it), Oracle VM Manager, Oracle VM Server, and Oracle VM agent become an essential part of the Oracle Virtualization platform; the "one-stop-shop" approach allows Oracle customers to rely on a consolidated support. This could also fit very well into their strategy where Oracle will eventually launch its own Cloud Services and will fully manage and support its offerings via the Cloud.

Oracle entered the virtualization market in 2007 by releasing Oracle VM Server and Oracle VM Manager. Oracle has also been shipping Oracle EL, or Oracle Enterprise Linux products, recently calling Oracle jeOS. Do note that they are separately downloadable from Oracle's e-delivery. Oracle's entry into the virtualization arena is a validation of the fact that virtualization is going mainstream and also that it is increasingly becoming an enabler to Cloud Computing and Cloud Applications.

Oracle VM Manager is a powerful web application, based on **ADF (Application Development Framework)**, and its purpose is, as you may have guessed, to manage multiple Oracle VM Servers. This means that it does the **VMLM (Virtual Machine Lidecycle Management)**, adds virtual machines (whether from completely built templates or from installation media), live migration, deployment, and relocation, among others.

Oracle VM Manager also manages resources such as ISO files, VM templates, and shared disk resources. In the new release, 2.1.2, there are several cool features such as the Server Pool Wizard, HA for Server Pools and VM Servers, VM conversions, Rate Limit of **VIF (Virtual Network Interface)**, and Priority Class of Virtual Disk.

Oracle's virtualization play may seem to encounter a lot of resistance and skepticism, but Oracle is gradually treading a path where it will continue to develop its product to match enterprise class maturity as the market further evolves. Clearly with the latest Oracle VM 2.1.2, many new features have come about indicating that Oracle is more than serious.

What this book covers

The book is designed so that you can dive into chapters on your own, as the chapters will be written independently of each other. You can use them both as reference as well as detailed guidance, purely based on you current focus. So for instance, you may want to do a quick installation of the Oracle VM Server, and then jump to Chapter 3 directly. My intention is to keep this book both conversational as well as provide screenshots to satisfy your needs.

I would recommend beginners to read the book chapter by chapter, increasing the pace as you move ahead with your installations. As the chapters progress, while not necessarily complex, they may require you to dig into some of skills in Linux, Virtualization, and so on. But like I said in the beginning, you need to have some sort of understanding on virtualization and a bit of experience as well. The latter part of the book concentrates on the VM management, a more fun part after you are done with installing and understanding the architecture of the Oracle VM platform.

I have divided the book into two parts, **Getting Started** and **Looking into the Architecture and Management**. In the first section, you will learn a little bit about the Oracle VM platform and the components of the Oracle VM platform. In the next part, you will get into the fun part of managing the VMs across a typical high-availability Oracle VM platform by using the Oracle VM Manager.

Part I: Getting Started

The first few chapters introduce the Oracle VM platform. Then we will go about installing Oracle VM manager and Oracle VM Server. You will carefully select the hardware and/or software platforms to carry out these installations.

I have typically chosen two environments and both happen to be hardware platforms. I will explain in detail the architecture that I have chosen for the purpose of writing this book, and also why.

Chapter 1: Introduction to Oracle VM

In this section we provide general information about Oracle VM Manager, Oracle VM Server, and Oracle VM Agent. We will explain how Oracle's VM Manager, a typical ADF web application, can act as a frontend in a typical Cloud architecture, and why Oracle VM Server (which is derived from XEN Hypervisor, a rather popular Hypervisor used by Amazon EC2 type of installations) complements the Cloud services architecture in the backend of the Data Center.

We will go about explaining what Oracle VM Manager is, what is new in the Oracle VM platform 2.1.2, where you can find it, how to install it, and how to get started. And obviously we will end with the "why you should choose Oracle VM Server and Oracle VM Manager" above other virtualization solutions.

Chapter 2: Installing Oracle VM Manager

Here you go about configuring the Oracle VM Manager and go through the regular pre-installation checklists. What kind of hardware requirements you could best use, and which type of Operating Systems could be used to install the Oracle VM Manager upon.

We will get into details here and go ahead with successfully installing Oracle VM Server.

Chapter 3: Installing Oracle VM Server

The Oracle VM Server is based upon Xen Hypervisor, a very small Linux-based management Operating System.

Here we explore installing Oracle VM Server via the CD-ROM and other shared and accessible sources such as NFS, HTTP, and so on.

Part II: Looking into the Architecture and Management

These chapters are intended for all Data Center administrators, architects, and system builders, just about anyone who is interested in knowing and managing Virtual Machines on Oracle's VM platform.

There are no really advanced features such as testing Oracle RAC on a typical multiple-Oracle VM Server node, but it will have enough meat to not only do things through the feature rich VM Manager web application, but also to get your hands dirty with the console.

The main purpose of this section of the book is to see what really happens on the Oracle VM platform and how we can manage multiple Virtual Machines.

Chapter 4: Oracle VM Management

Here we will get into the management of the Oracle VM servers such as the addition of nodes, removing nodes, editing nodes, and starting and shutting down the nodes.

We will manage the Oracle VM server pool, explore the principles of designing the server pool, and creating and enabling the HA—all of the meaty stuff is explained here. This chapter will be interesting for anyone who wants to learn about managing the Oracle VM Manager.

Chapter 5: Managing VMs with Oracle VM Manager – Part 1

In this part, we will go about explaining what VMs are, how we create them, how to startup-shutdown those VMs, typical console based actions required to manage the VMs, and basic configuration tasks around VM management.

We will discuss what Guest VMs are supported on Oracle VM Servers and do a quick install of one of them.

Chapter 6: Managing VMs with Oracle VM Manager – Part 2

Continuing from the previous chapter we will go about managing the VMs and exploring the VMs through the Oracle VM Manager, such as viewing VM information or details, editing configurations, and other advanced functions such as Live VM Migration.

Chapter 7: Managing VMs with Oracle VM Manager – Part 3

In the final part, we shall be performing some typical VM resource management tasks, such as importing VMs via several methods such as templates, VM Images, ISO files, and so on. We will also look briefly at creating shared storage.

Chapter 8: Troubleshooting and Gotchas

Like any other tool, this platform will not be completely free from problems and here we will explain briefly about the problems you can run into, and what steps you must take to remediate them.

Appendix: Command Line Tools

We cover some essential command line tools in the Appendix. We will explore some of the important ones and the rest will be an exercise.

What you need for this book

Unless otherwise stated, the environment used in the examples and referred to throughout the book is Oracle VM Manager 2.1.2, installed on hardware. I have chosen two scenarios – the first is a two box HP DL 360 Dual CPU, 2 GB RAM configuration and the other is a two box Dell 2900 Quad-core, 32GB RAM each. We'll use the shipped Oracle templates where necessary, so as to do exciting things such as Server pool creation, live migration, and so on, but we will also go about creating custom templates where necessary.

All Oracle VM platform and tools are available on Oracle's virtualization site and we will use them for the purpose of understanding this book.

Who this book is for

This book is meant for all virtualization fans, not just the ones who have been playing with Oracle databases or other Oracle applications but just about anyone who wishes to test and create sandboxes, and test their applications and eventually deploy them in production. Oracle has recently won some new customers, so Oracle VM platform is also being deployed in production environments.

But like I said, VM is also meant for the regular virtualization enthusiast who wishes to run and deploy multiple flavors of Operating Systems. You can also create Windows VMs! In the later chapters we will look into the supported OSes and it will surprise you that you can do a lot with Oracle VM platform. Don't expect this book to answer all your problems, it should be treated more as an introductory book where we will test the waters and get you up and running. If you do happen to like this book then I will be tempted to write a more advanced book that will take a deep dive into advanced concepts, but for now let's get you up and running with the basics.

It is also very handy to be a little inclined towards Oracle applications such as databases. I myself have been an Oracle DBA, and knowing a little bit about SQL might help as we might test Oracle jeOS + 11g DB VMs, but it is not a must by any means.

On the whole you will definitely benefit a lot more if you are aware of Linux commands, Oracle SQL, PL/SQL, and so on. To get that information please feel free to dig into Oracle's rich documentation manuals, both in PDF as well as downloadable media sets to run locally at your end.

What you will find in the book

This book intends to provide you with in depth detail about all aspects of using Oracle VM Manager and installing Oracle VM server, and then touching lightly all aspects of Oracle VM Management aspects. We will go about by installing Oracle VM platform and managing it. This will help you get more productive with your time and you will learn techniques to manage your VMs both effectively and efficiently.

What you won't find

This book will not teach you SQL, PL/SQL, Linux, or any other languages here. We will also not delve too deeply into the concept of virtualization either. We expect you to know a bit about virtualization and expect you to have used other virtualization products already.

Neither will we get into all forms of virtualization such as clustering, hardware-assist, host- based, full, or Para virtualization. We will also not get into the security part of the book, something which is increasingly becoming a hot topic among the virtualization industry. We will first concentrate on getting you started.

Conventions

In this book, you will find a number of styles of text that distinguish between different kinds of information. Here are some examples of these styles, and an explanation of their meaning.

Code words in text are shown as follows: "The OC4J log file can also be investigated and can be located at /opt/oc4j/dump-timestamp.dmp."

A block of code is set as follows:

```
[default]
exten => s,1,Dial(Zap/1|30)
exten => s,2,Voicemail(u100)
exten => s,102,Voicemail(b100)
exten => i,1,Voicemail(s0)
```

Any command-line input or output is written as follows:

```
# mkdir mnt-pt
# mount -o loop,ro OracleVM-Manager-2.1.2.iso mnt-pt
```

New terms and **important words** are shown in bold. Words that you see on the screen, in menus or dialog boxes for example, appear in the text like this: "When the Installation screen appears, choose **Next**".

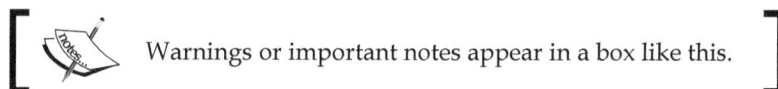

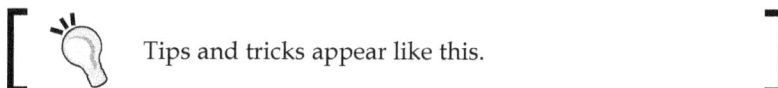

> Warnings or important notes appear in a box like this.

> Tips and tricks appear like this.

Reader feedback

Feedback from our readers is always welcome. Let us know what you think about this book—what you liked or may have disliked. Reader feedback is important for us to develop titles that you really get the most out of.

To send us general feedback, simply send an email to feedback@packtpub.com, and mention the book title via the subject of your message.

If there is a book that you need and would like to see us publish, please send us a note in the **SUGGEST A TITLE** form on www.packtpub.com or email suggest@packtpub.com.

If there is a topic that you have expertise in and you are interested in either writing or contributing to a book on, see our author guide on www.packtpub.com/authors.

Customer support

Now that you are the proud owner of a Packt book, we have a number of things to help you to get the most from your purchase.

Errata

Although we have taken every care to ensure the accuracy of our content, mistakes do happen. If you find a mistake in one of our books—maybe a mistake in the text or the code—we would be grateful if you would report this to us. By doing so, you can save other readers from frustration and help us to improve subsequent versions of this book. If you find any errata, please report them by visiting http://www.packtpub.com/support, selecting your book, clicking on the **let us know** link, and entering the details of your errata. Once your errata are verified, your submission will be accepted and the errata added to any list of existing errata. Any existing errata can be viewed by selecting your title from http://www.packtpub.com/support.

Piracy

Piracy of copyright material on the Internet is an ongoing problem across all media. At Packt, we take the protection of our copyright and licenses very seriously. If you come across any illegal copies of our works, in any form, on the Internet, please provide us with the location address or website name immediately so that we can pursue a remedy.

Please contact us at copyright@packtpub.com with a link to the suspected pirated material.

We appreciate your help in protecting our authors, and our ability to bring you valuable content.

Questions

You can contact us at questions@packtpub.com if you are having a problem with any aspect of the book, and we will do our best to address it.

Part 1

Getting Started

Introduction to Oracle VM

Installing Oracle VM Manager

Installing Oracle VM Server

Introduction to Oracle VM

1

As stated in the Preface, Oracle VM Manager is a management product developed by Oracle that complements the Oracle Grid Control. Oracle VM Manager is increasingly popular within the Oracle community. In addition, firms that weren't Oracle customers are now adopting it, due to its low cost high-end support. This is clearly good news for Oracle as it really needs to find its place in this new and emerging market.

At the time of writing this book, Oracle has joined the Xen.org advisory board, thus joining the companies IBM, HP, Sun, and others who understand the need of Open Source hypervisors in this increasingly commoditizing market. This is great news as Oracle's VM is derived from the Open Source project Xen. This is a very important development for the Open Source Virtualization revolution and Oracle is poised to benefit from it tremendously.

In this chapter we will be covering the following topics:

- **Virtualization**: A general introduction
- **Oracle VM components**: This will comprise of Oracle VM Manager, Oracle VM Server, and Oracle VM Agent
- **Xen hypervisor**: Domains, VMs, and much more.

Virtualization: What is it?

I have assumed that you know what virtualization is and now want to explore Oracle's version of virtualization. Still we feel that a quick introduction and a brief history of virtualization can never hurt. It is very hard to compact the past 50 years of IT achievements about virtualization, but I will attempt to cover it (very) briefly.

Brief history of virtualization

To take a look at x86 virtualization—a concept that often confuses a lot of IT Managers (even today) when they are confronted by consultants, vendors, or even internal staff, we have to go back to the 60's when IBM first introduced "Time sharing". Time sharing is basically sharing resources of expensive machines among several users, something we also call multi-tasking. Back then the machines were so expensive that it was necessary to come up with something creative. Fast forwarding 50 years we have come a full circle with the re-introduction of virtualization—only this time it has come to dominate the x86 servers. This was done, or should we say initiated, by VMware, which went on to create this huge ecosystem around it. Then came Xen, an Open Source project that began its subtle penetration into the ASP space and hosting providers, and which was later to be acquired by Citrix. Microsoft, not to be left behind in the process, carried on to acquire Connectrix, and after conducting several rebranding exercises on its hypervisor, later introduced Hyper-V.

Oracle worked on Xen's Open Source technology and introduced its Xen-flavored virtualization software as well. The list is quite exhaustive as the virtualization market has become rather huge. You might even say that in the drive to battle the oversubscription monster, the mushroom effect of all of the start-ups has created the over-subscription dilemma for themselves.

The introduction of virtualization is definitely the most significant event in the history of IT. It can drive down the costs dramatically and provides several open and public platforms to general public in the form of "public clouds". VMware, Microsoft, and several other firms are constantly fighting for the "private cloud" space where the mother-of-all virtualization, IBM, is also fighting. There has been a huge data center build-up across the world where all IT firms are battling to spread their wings and go after the Cloud Computing space.

What forms of virtualization do we have?

There are several forms of virtualization and let's briefly go through a few of them (for the sake of brevity we will stick to server virtualization):

- **Emulation**: A trick to copy a resource and make it look like some other resource can be called emulation.
- **Partitioning**: Segmenting a resource so it looks like many resources.
- **Clustering**: Aggregating many resources so they look like one. Think of the Oracle RAC VIP, where all you need is one IP which is a Virtual IP.

However exciting it sounds, we won't go too deep into the partitioning and clustering part and instead we'll have a look at the forms of emulation. They are—full virtualization, para-virtualization, and hardware-assist virtualization.

Full virtualization uses a concept of **Binary Translation (BT)** to provide a typical runtime re-write method which is required for this method to work. Here each instruction is read from the machine's binary and helps place the machine in a similar state to where the VM would be, after it has carried out that specific function. However, there are discussions about the "accuracy of emulation" as to how accurate the instruction modifications are. There are five types of accuracies, from datapath accuracy to HLE. But we won't delve into these deeper as we might have to get scientists from Intel and AMD to do the explanation.

Para-virtualization took birth from the Xen project originated at Cambridge University. It is the Open Source answer to the ring privileging solution. Simply said, instead of capturing the whole IA32 instruction set, it just captures the parts that are altered, thus increasing the performance of the VMs against the full-virtualization methods.

Finally, hardware-assist virtualization rests on the newer families of chips such as Intel VTx and AMD V chipsets. This enables unmodified VMs to execute on more enhanced **VMMs (Virtual Machine Monitors)**. They might be faster than the above mentioned two methods but a lot of mixing occurs where both full and para-virtualization solutions are taking full advantage of the VTx and AMD V technologies.

Why should we virtualize?

Every time we look at a virtualization opportunity within a data center, customers are often exposed to fear, uncertainty, and doubt. It is a new technology; it aggregates everything and poses a challenge, not only to the siloed environment but also the siloed mentality. As the convergence takes place inside the cores, the "people and process convergence" needs to happen as well. The benefits of virtualization are simply irresistible.

Virtualization is a golden opportunity for organizations to do a technology refresh, providing a means to deliver IT in variety of ways to a highly aspirational consumer. Another major opportunity is towards **Corporate Social Environmental Responsibility (CSER)**, especially energy, which helps organizations reduce their carbon footprints. But still the biggest advantage is—it saves a lot of money!

It helps organizations to:

- Smart meter power and energy consumption as against the siloed approach where everything is always "turned on"
- Redeploy resources as and when the demand is generated
- Reduce and even contain the risk and cost of legacy applications on legacy hardware, which can now run seamlessly on state-of-the-art hardware
- Always be available—there is a growing demand for continuous availability without increasing costs, and virtualization can adequately address both, the pain and the pleasure here

There are a lot more arguments, but keeping the focus simple we can safely say that with virtualization you can increase your productivity while reducing costs of operations.

Oracle VM

Oracle VM is a platform, and its various components are discussed briefly in the subsequent sections. As we work through the rest of the book, we will install and configure these components.

Oracle VM Manager

Oracle VM Manager is installed on a physical machine which is eventually used to manage the Oracle VM Server pools. This is the WebUI interface, developed with Oracle's ADF. We will be using it to manage our Oracle VM platform. So this management console, which we can access in the cloud, is essentially the interface we will use to administer our Oracle VM platform for tasks such as:

- Creating VMs from media, template, and other resources
- Importing and exporting ISO files
- Performing live migration
- Creating and managing VMs and VM templates
- Creating and managing (shared) storage
- Other admin tasks such as shut down, restart, and so on

Oracle VM Server

VM Server is a physical server which is installed with a very thin layer of Linux, and complemented with the Xen hypervisor technology. The VMs are then installed on this layer, thus effectively consolidating and aggregating multiple platforms, such as Windows and Linux on Oracle VM Server.

Oracle VM Agent

This is installed with Oracle VM Server and essentially communicates with the Oracle VM Manager to manage the VMs in variety of ways. Now let's take a quick look at the Oracle VM Architecture in the following illustration:

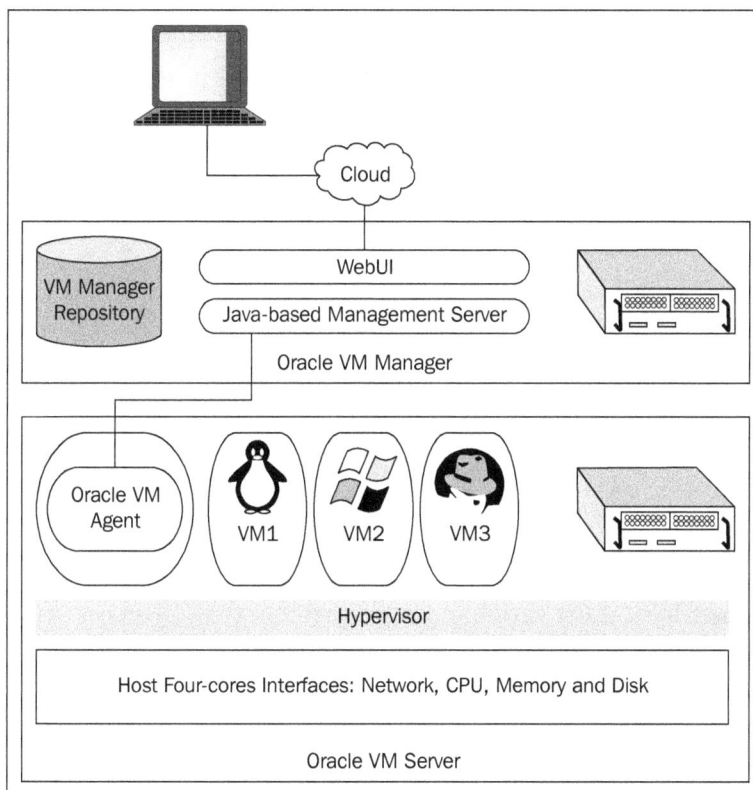

Oracle VM Manager configuration

In this section, we will see some of the configuration possibilities of Oracle VM Manager. The deployment of Oracle VM can be done in several ways. The server pools within Oracle VM platform is the best way to go about when setting up the Oracle VM farm. The following diagram will make it a bit easier to understand how the pools are built:

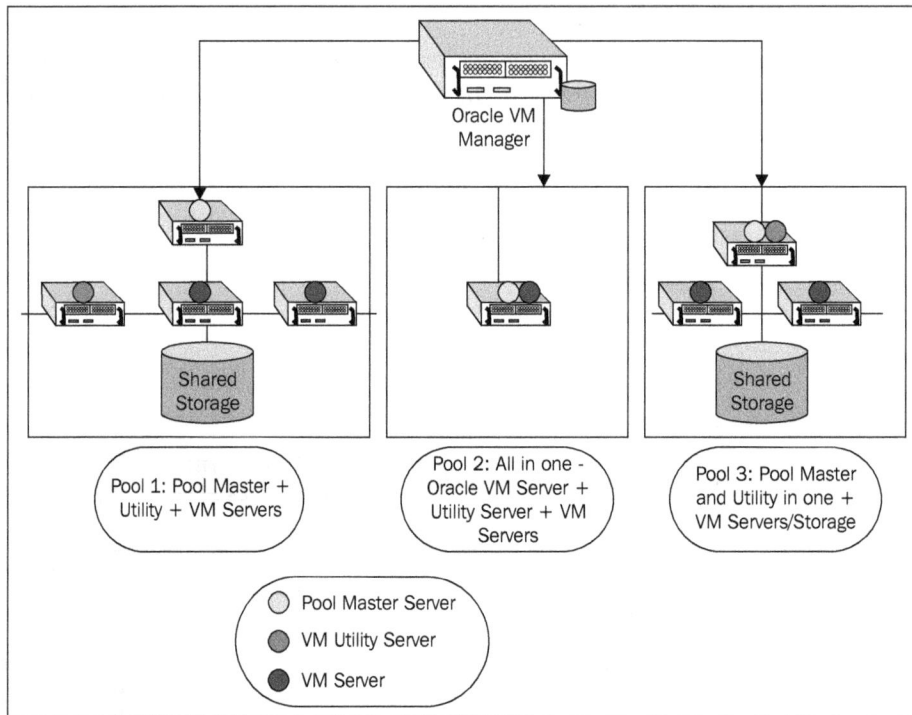

Let's take a closer look at the various components that play a key role in defining what type of Oracle Cloud farm we can build with Oracle's VM platform:

- **Oracle VM Manager Host**: This machine will typically have Oracle's VM Manager installed. This is the place for us to be in order to carry out all of the administrative tasks. This can be done locally or can be done remotely depending on customer requirements.

- **Oracle VM Servers**: These are typically the servers that come embedded with a Xen hypervisor installation. A typical server can perform three different functions—the Server pool master function, the Utility function, or merely the VM Server function. The VM Agent is responsible for interacting with those functions and the VM Manager, thus notifying the user of the role(s) of the specific server.

- ° **Server Pool Master role**: This role is special for the server and interfaces with the outside world by communicating with the utility and VM servers. It also provides the load balancing capabilities by assigning the VM a VM Server that has the maximum resources available. We can only have one Server Pool Master in a pool.

- ° **Utility Server role**: This server will carry out heavy I/O tasks such as copy, move, and so on. A typical Virtual Data Center can have loads of ISO files and templates that are deployed across VM Servers. We will see more of this in the *Oracle VM Management* chapter. We can have several Utility Servers. The Pool Master Server chooses the Utility Server with maximum available CPU resources to carry out the intensive tasks, thus balancing the load.

- ° **VM Server role**: The main role of these servers is to host VMs. The Oracle VM agent installed on these servers communicates with the Utility Servers, Pool Master Server, and other VM Servers, thus aggregating all of the resources within the machines as a **Single Logical Unit (SLU)** to form a Sustainable Global Cloud Center.

- **Server Pools**: Multiple Server Pools can be created within a Data Center. For instance, Pool 1 could be a pool for a typical production environment for an enterprise customer, Pool 2 could be a typical production pool for an SMB customer, and Pool 3 can be a SMB+ customer's delight. The pools act and function as logical units within a Data Center.

- **Storage**: Storage could be local as well as part of a **storage area network (SAN)**. Shared storage such as iSCSI or FC is necessary in order to perform live migration of VMs between VM Servers.

What about roles in Oracle VM Manager?

As an Oracle VM Manager user, we can have the following roles—User, Manager, or Administrator.

- **User**: This is a typical operator role where a user can carry out tasks such as creating and managing VMs and resources within those VMs.

- **Manager**: With this role one can manage Server Pools, Servers, and resources. This user typically has all of the privileges of the User role as well.

- **Administrator**: Besides managing user accounts, resources, and so on, this user has all of the permissions to manage Server Pools, Resources, and Virtual Machines.

As we go about the chapters in part II of this book, we will see in detail where these roles can be used.

Oracle VM Manager a **Virtual Machine Lifecycle Management (VMLM)** tool that helps us monitor the complete life cycle of a VM until its decommissioning. It covers other tasks such as importing, cloning, migrating, creating, and configuring server pools. It also covers management of VM Servers, resource management of templates, media, shared storage, and finally Oracle VM Manager Users and groups.

Oracle VM Manager is a feature rich tool and hopefully Oracle will continue its push into Cloud Computing by providing WebUIs for mobile applications where one can manage the Oracle VM platform with ease.

Throughout the book we will provide in depth detail about all aspects of using Oracle VM Manager, installing Oracle VM Server, and touch lightly all aspects of Oracle VM Management. We will go about installing the Oracle VM platform and managing it. Now let's take a look at Oracle VM Server.

Oracle VM Server

The Oracle VM Server uses the Xen hypervisor technology and Oracle VM Agent. It includes a Linux kernel with support for devices, file systems, and so on. The Linux kernel runs as a **dom0** and manages other DomU or VMs, called domains in Xen, the para-virtualization terminology. So essentially dom0 is the first guest booted and typically represents the physical machine by functioning as the supervisor module. Here the DomU could be a Linux, Solaris, or a Windows VM as we can see in the following image.

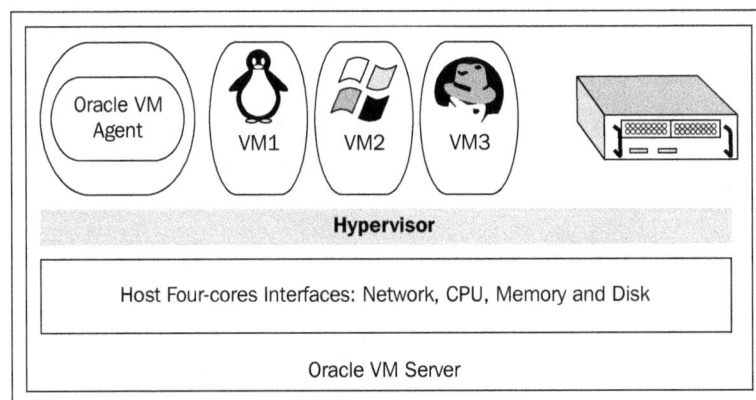

Xen hypervisor, Domains, and Virtual Machines

Oracle VM Server is designed so that the only entity that has full control of the system is the hypervisor or so called **VMM**. It is thin and is constructed using extremely well written code which basically handles your resources and interrupts.

In Xen terminology, we will see Domains, Guests, and VMs are often used interchangeably but they do have their differences. Simply said — Domain, with its virtual four-cores allows a VM to run on it, whereas a Guest is an operating system that runs within a Domain in para-virtualized or hardware virtualized mode (as explained earlier in the modes). A VM or to make it even more stylish, a **Virtual Appliance** is an operating system with the associated application running inside it.

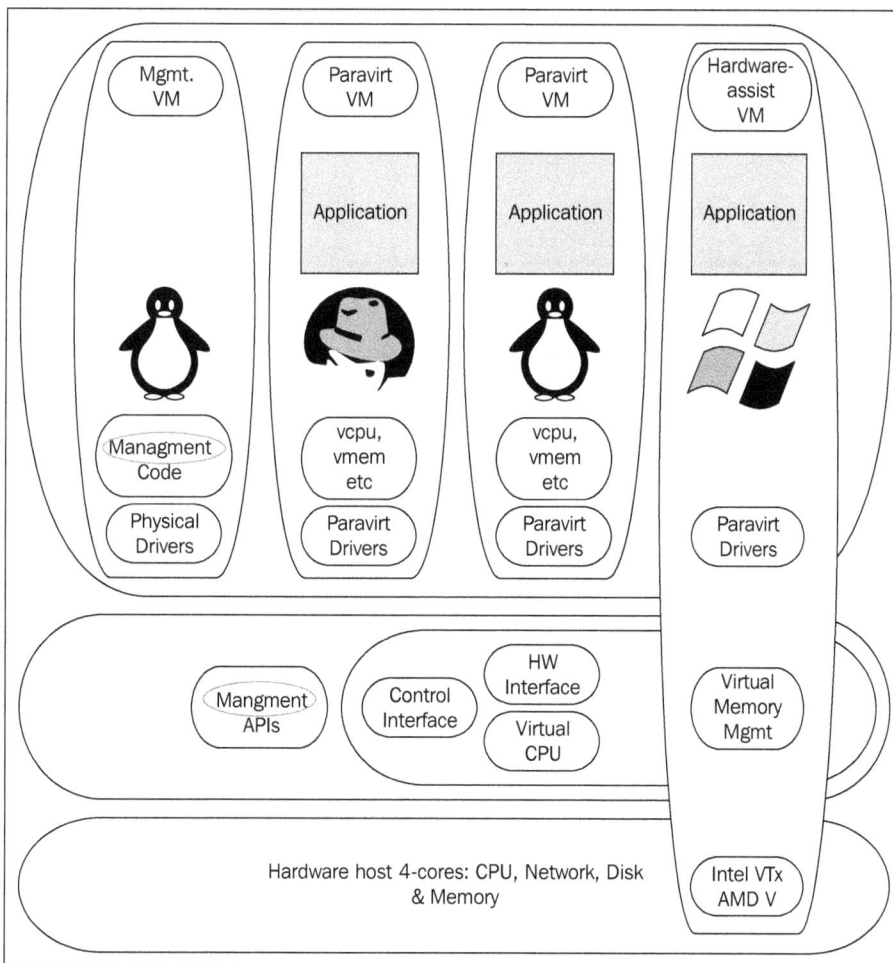

VMs within an Oracle VM platform that run in para-virtualized modes need the necessary kernel modification and run at near-native speeds. Should the VMs run on hardware-assist virtualization, they run completely unmodified. Such hardware-assisted VMs are carefully monitored for instruction set changes and manipulations. The good part is that Operating Systems such as Microsoft Windows run fine as hardware-assisted VMs.

A lot of work, such as hardware detection in an Oracle VM Server, is performed by the Management domain also referred to as dom0. The VMs are often referred to as DomU. The dom0 is a complete kernel with a vast array of drivers and provides extensive support for file systems, volume management, and much more.

Looking quickly at the big picture, we get an idea of the basic Oracle Cloud Farm that could be built when the consumer starts using Oracle's VM Server and Oracle VM Manager on a large scale.

The following diagram is a high level view of how a typical Oracle Cloud farm can be built with Oracle VM Servers placed in various data centers and Oracle VM Manager managing the farms.

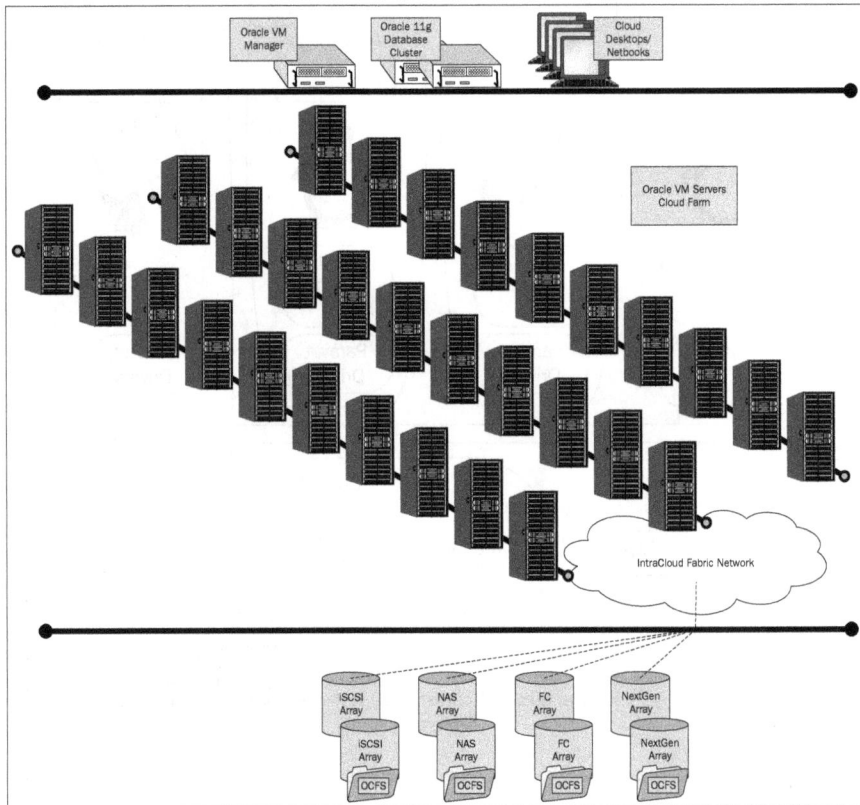

Summary

Clearly the advantages and the excitement of virtualization are hard to ignore. Besides the obvious fact that virtualization is an excellent business and technology convergence enabler, it is something that businesses have long strived for.

In the next chapter, we will install the VM Server. I hope that with this brief introduction of the Oracle VM platform and its components I was able to excite you to move ahead to the next chapter. Also, in the upcoming chapter we will explore the management of Domains, as well as the configuration and management of Oracle VM Manager and VM Server.

Installing Oracle VM Manager
2

In the previous chapter, we moved ahead and explored the whole virtualization phenomena and how Oracle's VM platform attempts to fill in the void by using the internal Cloud which we will refer to as **IntraCloud** environment. An IntraCloud is nothing but our internal data center which is elastic enough to cope with flexible demand within the physical perimeters of our enterprise. In this chapter, we will install the Oracle VM Manager. In particular we will cover the following:

- Oracle EL U2 installation
- Installing Oracle VM Manager
- Upgrading existing Oracle VM Manager

What's new in Oracle VM Manager 2.1.2

Let's quickly go through the latest features of Oracle VM Manager 2.1.2:

- **Server pool wizard**: With this easy to use wizard we can create pools in a matter of seconds
- **HA for pools**: This is inline with the Continuous Availability of Oracle Cloud Farm, where we can make **HA (High Available)** pools upon creation
- **P2V and V2V conversions**: Convert machines seamlessly to Oracle format
- **Rate limit of VIF**: Set limits to the Virtual Network Interface and customize network traffic per VM
- **Prioritize storage usage with Priority Class option for disk**: This way we can define levels of **QoS (Quality of Service)** per disk, assigning 0 as highest priority and 7 as lowest priority

Clearly Oracle is slowly and gradually working towards the commoditization path of Virtual Infrastructure with Xen, where features such as HA, On-Demand Usage, and Smart Metering make perfect sense for a Cloud Computing model.

What are the hardware requirements?

This section is quite easy to follow. All we need is a machine with the following minimums:

- **Memory**: 2 GB RAM
- **CPU**: 1.8 Ghz
- **Swap space**: 2 GB
- **Hard Disk**: 4 GB

For testing purposes, we can also choose to pick up any desktop virtualization software such as Sun's VirtualBox, VMware's Workstation 6.5, VMware's Fusion (for Mac OSX), or any other forms. Eventually we can migrate the VM to our Oracle platform and put it in the HA pool. In practical life, I have seen many production environments using **VMM (Virtual Machine Management)** Consoles products also as VMs, although it is advisable to use a separate piece of hardware to install VM Management Servers.

Getting the software

Going to the Oracle's VM site (`http://www.oracle.com/technologies/virtualization/index.html`) will lead us directly to Oracle's e-delivery center (`http://edelivery.oracle.com/linux`). For more information, go to Oracle's Linux portal: `http://www.oracle.com/technology/tech/linux`.

All we need to do is to read the EULA carefully and we can go ahead and download the software of our choice. There are Oracle VM templates, Oracle Enterprise Linux Servers, and of course Oracle VM Manager and Oracle VM Servers packages.

Oracle has been working hard and keeping the e-delivery center pretty much up-to-date. The Oracle Enterprise Linux 5 UPDATE 2 has been recently made available and can be downloaded the minute we acknowledge and accept the legal agreement and fill in the details. Here, we can choose to download the 32 bit version of Oracle Enterprise Linux 5 Update 2. It has been built from Open Source Linux source code. We will go ahead and perform installation on the 64 bit platform. We will even perform Windows 2003 64 bit installations to demonstrate that Oracle VM Servers can run all Windows flavors.

I will quickly sketch out two configurations that I will be using for the Oracle VM platform.

Oracle VM Manager works fine with both Oracle Enterprise Linux 4 Update 5 upwards and **RHEL 4 (Red Hat Enterprise Linux Release 4)**. We will download the latest media pack, a DVD ISO file of approximately 2.6 GB. I have chosen to do the installation of my VMware Fusion on my Mac Book Pro, which has 4 GB memory and a dual core Intel processor. I intend to build a VM and use it to communicate with the two Oracle VM Servers which I will build on two physical servers.

Following are the Quick VM Manager software minimums and checks that we need to perform:

- OS: Oracle EL 4 Update 5 and upwards OR RHEL Release 4 and upwards
- Web Browser: Firefox 1.5 and upwards, Microsoft IE 6.x and upwards
- Check on `libaio.rpm` file
- Port check on 8888 and 8899

Before we get to that, we need to do a quick installation of the Oracle Enterprise Linux 5 Update 2 that we have just downloaded. So let's get on with the installation.

Installing Oracle EL 5 Update 2

Now that we have downloaded the DVD, it's time to install it.

1. The following screenshot shows the first installation screen:

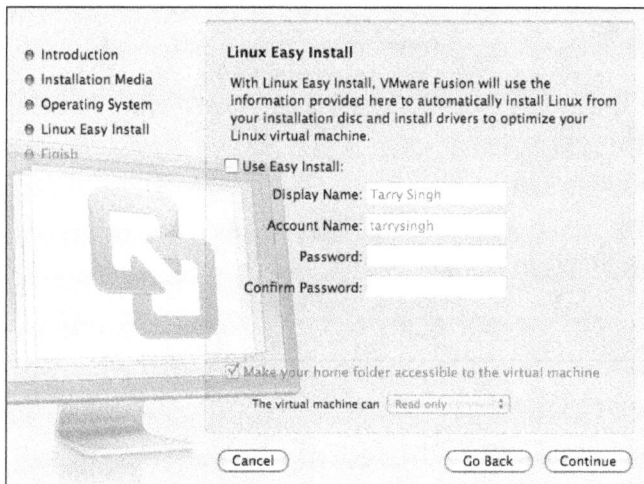

2. Point to the DVD ISO image to start the installation as shown in the following screenshot:

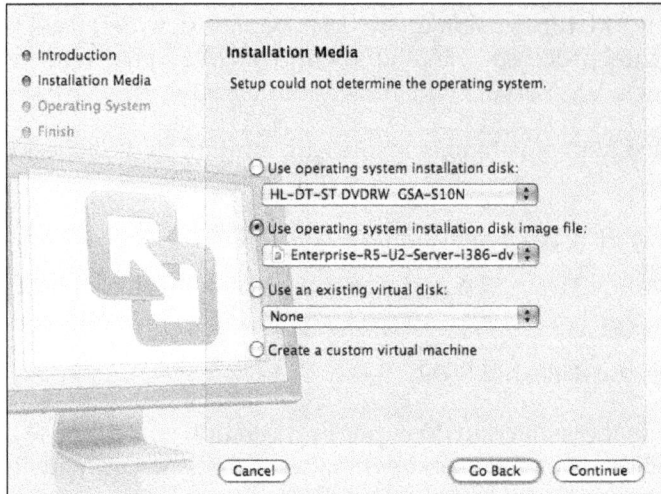

3. Choose the platform and version.

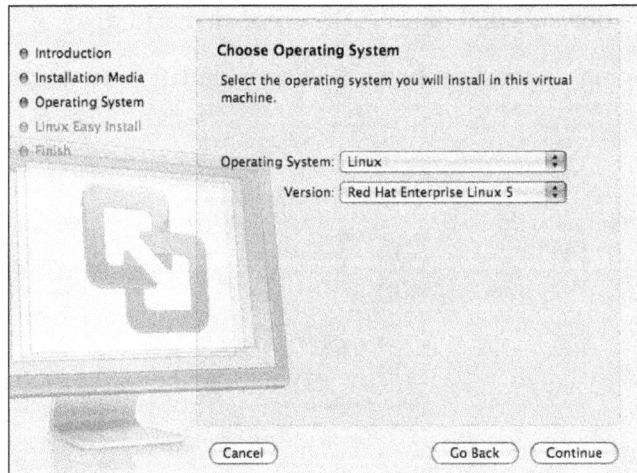

4. Choose **Custom Installation** and edit the settings to match the hardware requirements:

5. For instance, we shall choose 20 GB for the hard disk here:

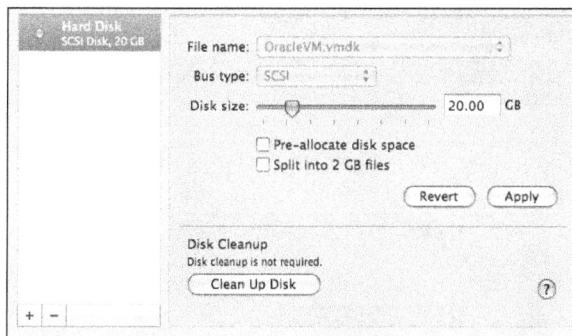

6. Now let's start the machine and ensure that the ISO image is selected and the station is connected:

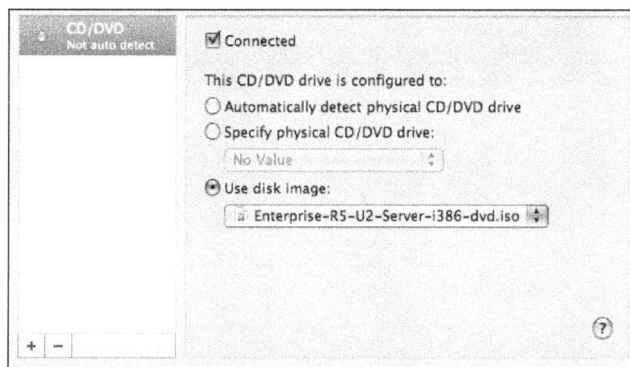

7. We'll get the following Oracle splash screen. Just press *Enter*:

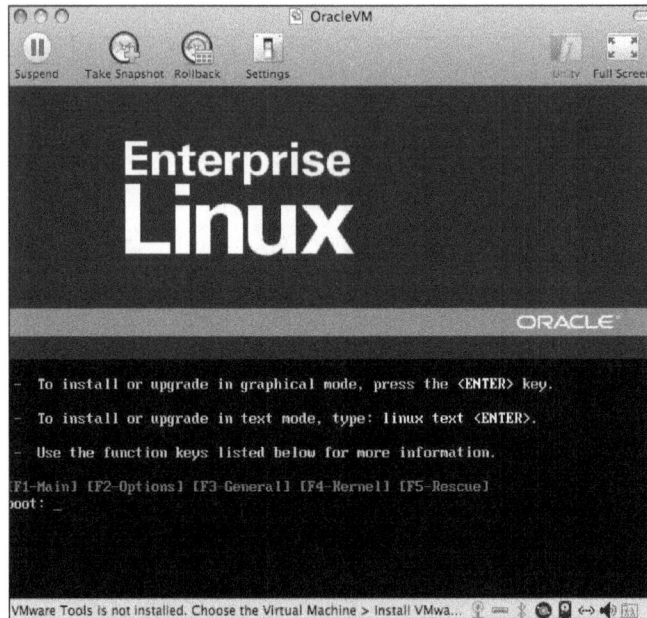

8. We can choose to test the DVD ISO, but let's choose to skip it:

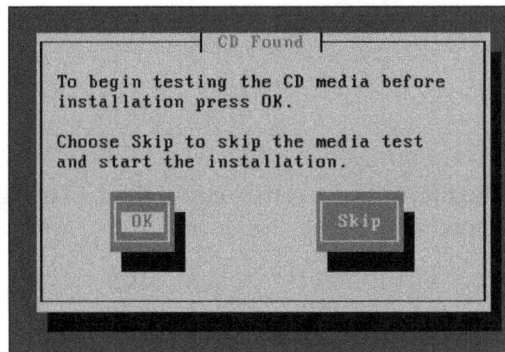

9. When the installation screen appears, choose **Next**:

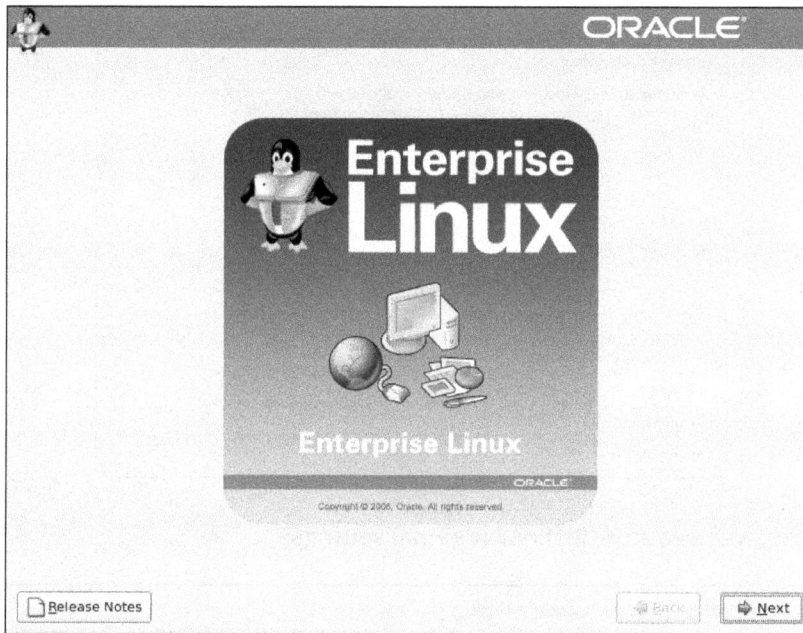

10. Choose **English** on both occasions unless of course some other language is preferred:

11. We need to change the IP address to static, and make sure that it is on the same LAN segment as our Oracle VM Servers:

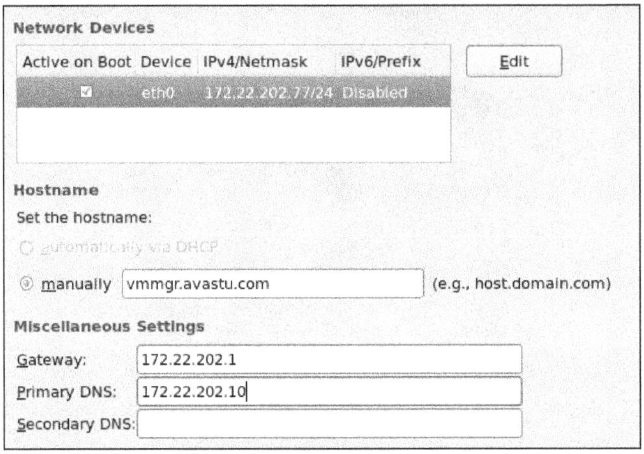

Network Devices

Active on Boot	Device	IPv4/Netmask	IPv6/Prefix	Edit
☑	eth0	172.22.202.77/24	Disabled	

Hostname

Set the hostname:

○ automatically via DHCP

◉ manually `vmmgr.avastu.com` (e.g., host.domain.com)

Miscellaneous Settings

Gateway: `172.22.202.1`

Primary DNS: `172.22.202.10`

Secondary DNS:

12. Now, we need to adjust our regional settings:

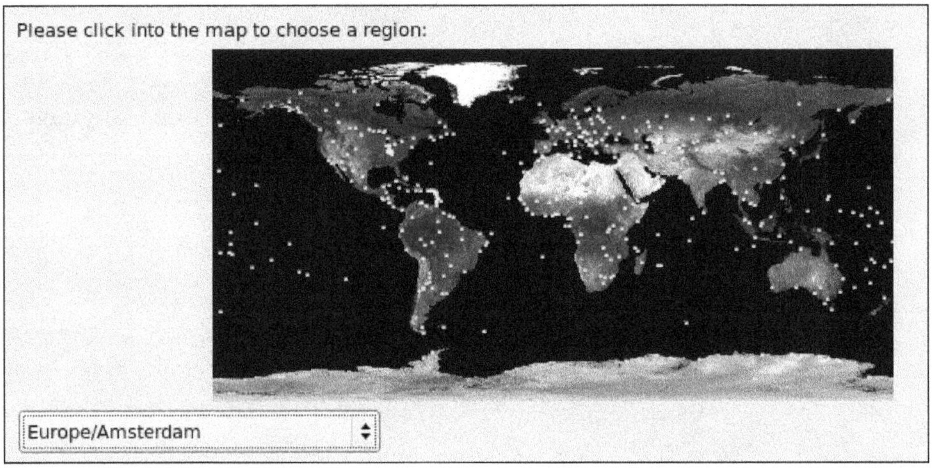

Please click into the map to choose a region:

Europe/Amsterdam

13. Choose a strong, unbreakable password for `root`:

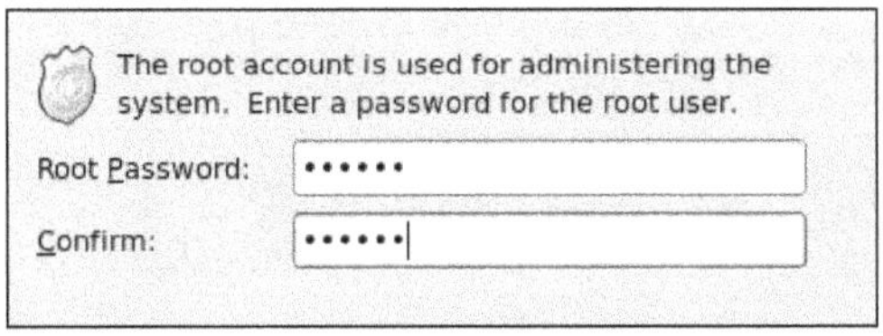

The root account is used for administering the system. Enter a password for the root user.

Root Password: `••••••`

Confirm: `••••••`

14. Next up, select **Software Development** and choose the **Customize now** radio button:

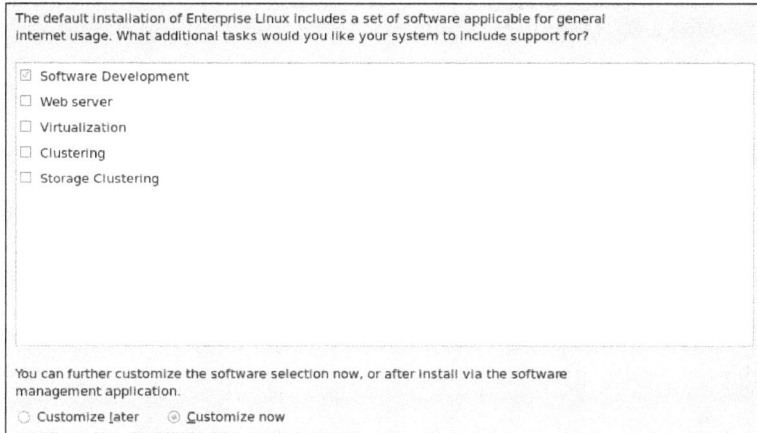

> The default installation of Enterprise Linux includes a set of software applicable for general internet usage. What additional tasks would you like your system to include support for?
>
> ☑ Software Development
> ☐ Web server
> ☐ Virtualization
> ☐ Clustering
> ☐ Storage Clustering
>
> You can further customize the software selection now, or after install via the software management application.
> ○ Customize later　◉ Customize now

15. In **Desktop Environments**, we can either select **GNOME Desktop Environment** or **KDE (K Desktop Environment)**. I will be using GNOME as I am more comfortable with it; one can feel free to use the environment of his or her choice.

> **Desktop Environments**　　　☐ **GNOME Desktop Environment**
> Applications　　　　　　　　　☐ **KDE (K Desktop Environment)**
> Development
> Servers

16. Next, click on **Applications** and choose **Editors** and **Graphical Internet**:

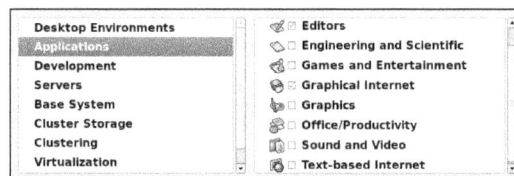

> Desktop Environments　　　☑ Editors
> **Applications**　　　　　　　☐ Engineering and Scientific
> Development　　　　　　　　☐ Games and Entertainment
> Servers　　　　　　　　　　☑ Graphical Internet
> Base System　　　　　　　　☐ Graphics
> Cluster Storage　　　　　　☐ Office/Productivity
> Clustering　　　　　　　　　☐ Sound and Video
> Virtualization　　　　　　　☐ Text-based Internet

17. Click **Development** and choose **Java Development** and **Legacy Software Development**:

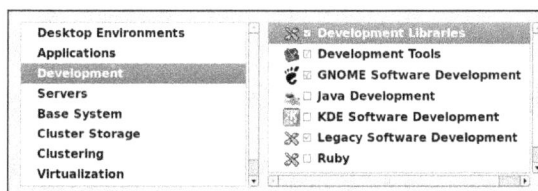

> Desktop Environments　　　☐ **Development Libraries**
> Applications　　　　　　　　☐ Development Tools
> **Development**　　　　　　　☐ GNOME Software Development
> Servers　　　　　　　　　　☑ Java Development
> Base System　　　　　　　　☐ KDE Software Development
> Cluster Storage　　　　　　☑ Legacy Software Development
> Clustering　　　　　　　　　☐ Ruby
> Virtualization

18. Deselect **Printing Support** in the **Servers** section as that will not be the primary function of this server, thus making the **Servers** section totally deselected.

19. Now, click on **Base System** and select **Java** (I often select **Administration Tools** for troubleshooting purposes):

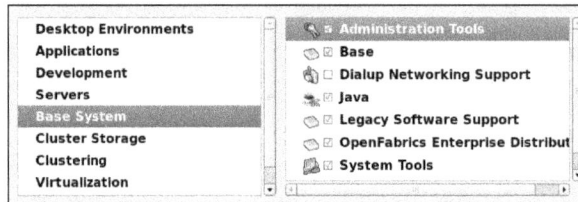

20. Leave **Cluster Storage**, **Clustering**, and **Virtualization** unchecked and continue with the installation.

21. After the installation is complete, the system reboots itself and we will get the following screen:

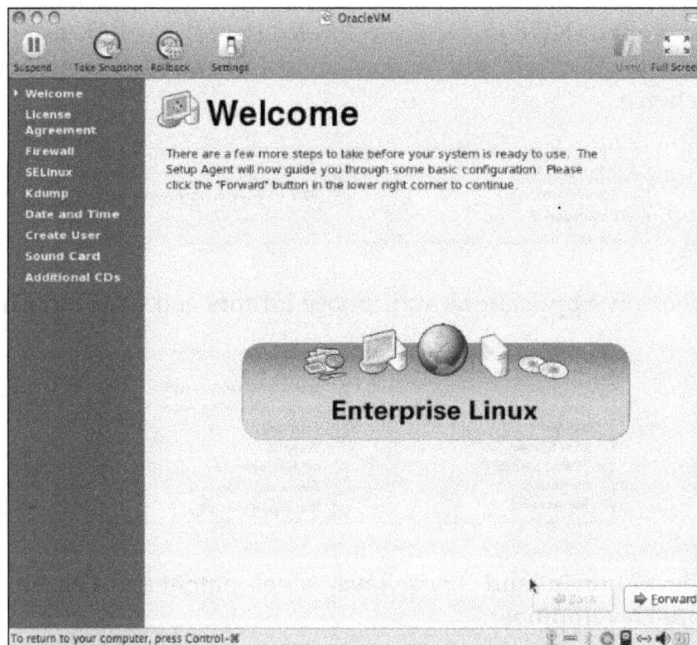

22. Now, go ahead and create a user, and continue logging in to the system:

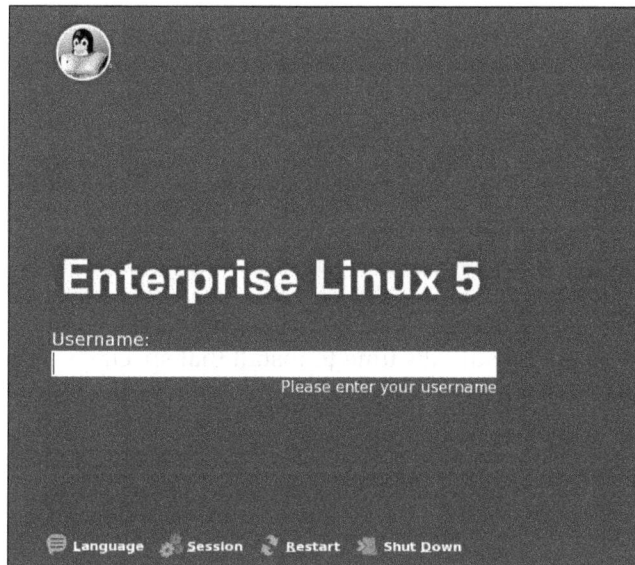

Final checks before installing Oracle VM Manager

We need to carry out some final checks before the installation process.

Port test

Make sure that ports 8888 and 8899 are free. If, upon entering the following commands, we don't get any response, then it means that these ports are available.

```
# netstat -na |grep 8888
# netstat -na |grep 8899
```

If we do get responses, then we must release these ports and allow them through the firewall by entering the following:

```
# /usr/bin/system-config-securitylevel
```

Select **Enabled** for Security Level and choose **customize.** In **Others** add the two ports 8888 and 8899 respectively as follows:

```
8888:tcp,8899:tcp
```

Libaio check

The libaio differs for numerous versions. For our chosen OS we should get the following results:

```
# /bin/rpm -q libaio.i386
libaio-0.3.106-3.2
```

If we don't get the desired result, it's time to install that specific version of the libaio. We can get it from sites such as `rpmfind`, and others. Enter the following to install the required libaio version.

```
# rpm -ivh libaio-0.3.105-2.i386.rpm
```

Other checks: Passwords and ports

The following checks need to be performed:

- **1521**: A fresh installation may not really pose a problem with ports such as 1521 (Oracle DB Express Edition that is installed on the system) but if we are carrying out the installation again, we might want to check it once more.
- **8080**: Default HTTP port for Oracle Database 10g Express Edition.
- **Passwords**: We will be asked to fill passwords for SYS, SYSTEM, **OVS (Oracle VM Manager Schema)**, OC4J (admin password required), SMTP address for our mail server (we can use google.com for test purposes), and email address and password for the admin account for Oracle VM Manager.

What comes packaged with the Oracle VM Manager ISO file?

The ISO which we will now use has the following components:

- Oracle Database 10g Express Edition
- Oracle VM Manager package
- Data Collector
- Server performance information
- Realtime VM information

- OVS DataCollector log
- Oracle Containers for J2EE (OC4J)
- XML RPC 3.0

Installing Oracle VM Manager

Now that we are done with the preparatory work of installing the OS and have conducted our formal checks on ports and libraries, we can go ahead and install the VM Manager.

Oracle VM Manager installation goes rather fast and we should be done in about 5-15 minutes depending on how well we have installed the Operating System.

1. Insert the Oracle VM 2.1.2 ISO (if using a desktop virtualization tool) or CD in the CD/DVD ROM drive.

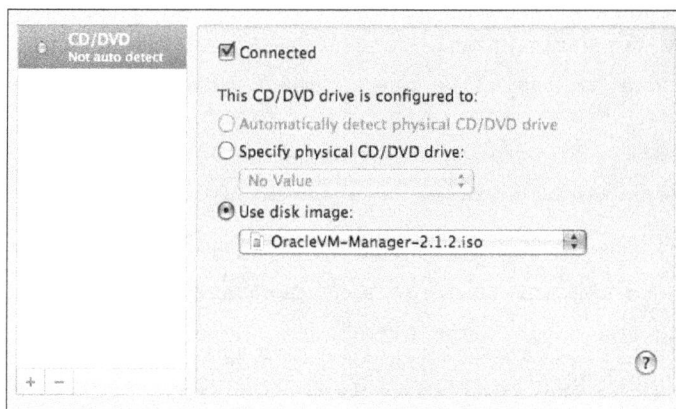

2. Now, enter the following as the `root` user to mount it in our Oracle EL OS:

   ```
   # mkdir mnt-pt
   # mount /dev/cdrom mnt-pt
   ```

3. Here, `mnt-pt` is the directory where we mount the ISO file. Mounting from a hard drive would go like this:

   ```
   # mkdir mnt-pt
   # mount -o loop,ro OracleVM-Manager-2.1.2.iso mnt-pt
   ```

4. Next, run the following command from `mnt-pt` directory:

   ```
   # sh runInstaller.sh
   ```

5. The following installation run is self-explanatory:

```
[root@vmmgr ~]# cd mnt-pt/
[root@vmmgr mnt-pt]# sh runInstaller.sh
Welcome to Oracle VM Manager 2.1.2
```

6. Now enter **1** to install Oracle VM Manager.

```
Please enter the choice: [1|2|3]
1. Install Oracle VM Manager
2. Uninstall Oracle VM Manager
3. Upgrade Oracle VM Manager
1

Starting Oracle VM Manager 2.1.2 installation ...
```

7. We need to choose **1** if we are carrying out a fresh Oracle 10g installation. We need to choose **2** if we want to point the Oracle VM Manager to an existing database. We shall choose **1** here as this is a fresh install:

```
Do you want to install a new database or use an existing one?
[1|2]
1. Install a new Oracle XE database on localhost
2. Use an existing Oracle database in my network
1

Prepare to install the Oracle XE database ...
Checking the supported platforms ... Done

Checking the prerequisite packages are installed ... Done

Checking the available disk space ... Done

Installing the oracle-xe-univ package (rpm) now ...
 Done


Oracle Database 10g Express Edition Configuration
-------------------------------------------------
This will configure on-boot properties of Oracle Database 10g
Express
Edition.  The following questions will determine whether the
database should
be starting upon system boot, the ports it will use, and the
passwords that
```

```
will be used for database accounts.  Press <Enter> to accept the
defaults.

Ctrl-C will abort.
```

8. Simply press enter to choose port 8080.

    ```
    Specify the HTTP port that will be used for Oracle Application
    Express [8080]:
    ```

9. Simply press enter to choose port 1521, the standard Oracle listener port:

    ```
    Specify a port that will be used for the database listener [1521]:
    ```

10. Choose a typical unbreakable password here:

    ```
    Specify a password to be used for database accounts.  Note that
    the same

    password will be used for SYS and SYSTEM.  Oracle recommends the
    use of

    different passwords for each database account.  This can be done
    after

    initial configuration:

    Confirm the password:
    ```

11. This option ensures that our database instance is started upon booting, and we would certainly want that:

    ```
    Do you want Oracle Database 10g Express Edition to be started on
    boot (y/n) [y]:

    Starting Oracle Net Listener...Done

    Configuring Database...Done

    Starting Oracle Database 10g Express Edition Instance...Done

    Installation Completed Successfully.

    To access the Database Home Page go to "http://127.0.0.1:8080/
    apex"

    Checking the availability of the database ...

    Set default database schema to 'OVS'.

    Please enter the password for account 'OVS':

    Confirm the password:

    Creating the Oracle VM Manager database schema ...Done

    Installing the ovs-manager package (rpm) ...

    Done
    ```

```
Installing the oc4j package (rpm) ...
Done

Please enter the password for account 'oc4jadmin':
Confirm the password:

Starting OC4J ... Done.
To access the OC4J Home Page and change the password go to
http://127.0.0.1:8888/em

Deploying Oracle VM Manager application to OC4J container.
Creating connection pool ... Done
Creating data source ... Done
Deploying application ... Done
Deploying application help ... Done

Configuring Oracle VM Manager DataCollector ... Done

Please enter the password for the default account 'admin':
Confirm the password:

Configuring SMTP server ...
Please enter the outgoing mail server (SMTP) hostname: smtp.
google.com
Mail server checking, may need some time, please wait ...
Setting the SMTP hostname server to smtp.google.com ...
Done

Please enter an e-mail address for account 'admin': tarry.singh@
gmail.com

Confirm the e-mail address: tarry.singh@gmail.com

Updating e-mail address for account 'admin' to 'mymail@mymail.com'
...
Done

The console feature is not enabled by default.
For detailed setup, refer to Oracle VM Manager User's Guide

Installation of Oracle VM Manager completed successfully.

To access the Oracle VM Manager home page go to:
  http://vmmgr:8888/OVS

To access the Oracle VM Manager help page go to:
  http://vmmgr:8888/help/help
[root@vmmgr mnt-pt]#
```

Upgrading Oracle VM Manager from 2.1 or 2.1.1 to 2.1.2

Upgrading the Oracle VM Manager from older versions is also an easy procedure:

1. Again, enter the following as the `root` user to mount it in our Oracle EL OS:

   ```
   # mkdir mnt-pt
   # mount /dev/cdrom mnt-pt
   ```

2. Here `mnt-pt` is the directory where we mount the ISO file.

3. Mounting from a hard drive would go like this:

   ```
   # mkdir mnt-pt
   # mount -o loop,ro OracleVM-Manager-2.1.2.iso mnt-pt
   ```

4. Next, running the installer from the `mnt-pt` directory:

   ```
   # sh runInstaller.sh

   [root@vmmgr ~]# cd mnt-pt/
   [root@vmmgr mnt-pt]# sh runInstaller.sh
   Welcome to Oracle VM Manager 2.1.2
   ```

5. This time, enter **3** to upgrade Oracle VM Manager

   ```
   Please enter the choice: [1|2|3]
   1. Install Oracle VM Manager
   2. Uninstall Oracle VM Manager
   3. Upgrade Oracle VM Manager
   ```

6. The upgrade process starts:

   ```
   Starting Oracle VM Manager 2.1.2 upgrade ...
   ```

7. Enter **y** when prompted:

   ```
   Are you sure you want to upgrade Oracle VM Manager from version
   current_version
   to new_version ? [y|N]: y
   ```

8. Enter the required passwords for **OVS** and **oc4jadmin**:

   ```
   Please enter the password for database account 'OVS':
   Please enter the password for account 'oc4jadmin':
   ```

9. Enter **y** to accept the Oracle VM Manager backup option:

```
Would you like to back up the Oracle VM Manager database ? [Y|n]
(default=y)
```

10. Upgrade is completed when the following message is displayed:

```
Upgrade Oracle VM Manager sucessfully.
```

Now, login to the Oracle VM Manager and check if it has upgraded to version 2.1.2. The OC4J log file can also be investigated and can be located at /opt/oc4j/ dump-timestamp.dmp. Any upgrade issues can also be investigated by checking the upgrade_oldversion_newversion.log in the /var/log/ovm-manager directory.

Uninstalling Oracle VM Manager

Uninstallation may be required if something has gone awry in our installation. The following steps will perform a complete uninstall. It is a simple procedure:

1. Again, enter the following as the root user to mount it in our Oracle EL OS:

```
# mkdir mnt-pt

# mount /dev/cdrom mnt-pt
```

2. Here mnt-pt is the directory where we mount the ISO file.

3. Mounting from a hard drive would go like this:

```
# mkdir mnt-pt

# mount -o loop,ro OracleVM-Manager-2.1.2.iso mnt-pt
```

4. Then run the following:

```
# sh runInstaller.sh

[root@vmmgr ~]# cd mnt-pt/

[root@vmmgr mnt-pt]# sh runInstaller.sh

Welcome to Oracle VM Manager 2.1.2
```

5. Here enter **2** to uninstall Oracle VM Manager.

```
Please enter the choice: [1|2|3]

1. Install Oracle VM Manager

2. Uninstall Oracle VM Manager

3. Upgrade Oracle VM Manager
```

6. Enter **y** to confirm the uninstallation:

```
Are you sure you want to uninstall Oracle VM Manager ? [y|N]
(Default=N) :y
```

7. A message stating that the Oracle VM Manager was uninstalled will be displayed:

```
Oracle VM Manager was removed.
```

Logging into WebUI: Oracle VM Manager, Oracle Database, and OC4J homepages

Now that we have successfully installed everything, the Application Server homepage should look like the following:

The Database homepage should look like the following:

And finally our Oracle VM Manager homepage:

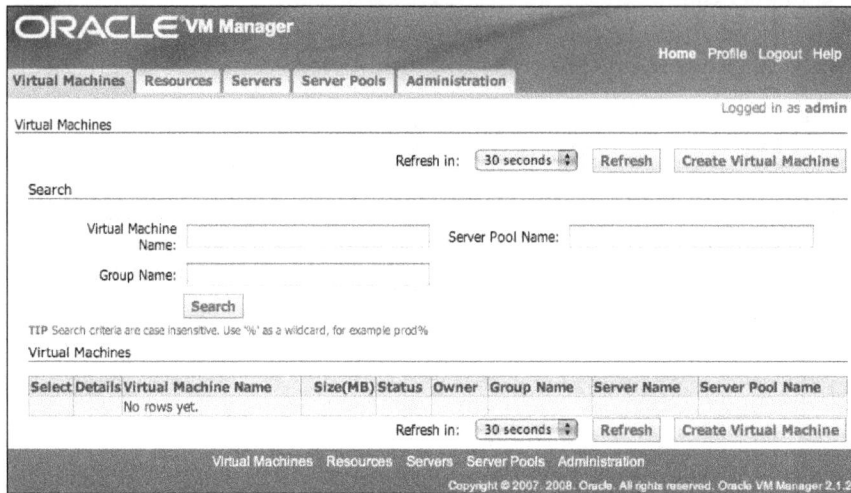

Summary

Clearly the installation of Oracle VM Manager 2.1.2 is a breeze. However, it should be noted that taking a snapshot at some critical stages can help us revert back to a particular scenario, in case of a faulty installation where we are forced to perform a reinstall. After all, the purpose of the virtualization ball game is that we don't have to spend endless hours in mundane operational tasks, right?

In the next chapter we will go ahead and install Oracle VM Servers on two of our HP DL 360 Servers.

3
Installing Oracle VM Server

In the last chapter, we covered the detailed installation of Oracle VM Manager. In this chapter we will explore the installation of the backbone of the Oracle's IntraCloud or Private Cloud farm, the Oracle VM Server. In particular, we will be covering:

- Guest OS support in the Oracle VM Server 2.1.2 Release
- Hardware and software requirements
- Installation of Oracle VM Server from CD ROM
- Installation of Oracle VM Server from other sources
- Upgrading the Oracle VM Server

What is supported in Oracle VM Server

We can quickly examine the guest Operating Systems that are supported and tested on Oracle VM Server. Here's a list of supported guest OSes.

For 64 bit Hypervisor:

Guest OS	Paravirtualized	Hardware Virtualized
64 bit Hyper visor	32bits | 64 bits	32 bits | 64 bits
Red Hat EL 3.x	Yes | No	Yes | Yes
Red Hat EL 4.x	Yes | Yes	Yes | Yes
Oracle EL 4.x	Yes | Yes	Yes | Yes
Red Hat EL 5.x	Yes | Yes	Yes | Yes
Oracle EL 5.x	Yes | Yes	Yes | Yes

And in the list of tested guest operating systems, we can see all of the Microsoft Windows flavors:

Guest OS	Hardware Virtualized
	32 bits | 64 bits
Microsoft Windows™ 2000	Yes | Yes
Microsoft Windows™ 2003	Yes | Yes
Microsoft Windows™ XP Pro	Yes | Yes
Microsoft Windows™ Vista	Yes | Yes
Microsoft Windows™ 2008 Service Pack 1	Yes | Yes

Clearly this is an impressive list by any standards. As we move ahead with Windows 7 and Windows 2008 R2 Servers, we will see that these machines too will be tested and eventually supported by Oracle VM platform. Can you imagine that? Oracle supporting Microsoft Windows! This is what Virtualization and Cloud Computing are doing to the industry where consumers triumph—no matter what.

> Please go to Oracle's site for technical information regarding support and licensing: http://www.oracle.com/technologies/virtualization/technical.html.

What are the hardware requirements?

Oracle VM Server runs fine on both x86 and x86_64 processors. All we need is a machine with the following minimum requirements:

- **Memory**: 1 GB RAM (Recommend at least 2 GB for good performance)
- **Intel Pentium 4 or AMD Athlon CPU**: 1.8 Ghz
- **Swap space**: 2 GB
- **Hard disk**: 72 GB

Obviously we will also run the Oracle VM Server on some supercharged Dell PowerEdge servers that have 8 cores, 32 GB RAM and some NetApp storage in the backend to provide some excellent performance.

Our goal is obviously a lot higher. Later in the book, we will run CloudApps on the lean and mean **JeOS (Just Enough Operating System)**, which we also fondly call CloudOS, that fire up in milli-seconds to serve the consumer instantaneously.

Getting the software

Going to the Oracle's VM site (http://www.oracle.com/virtualization.html) will lead you directly to Oracle's e-delivery center (http://edelivery.oracle.com/linux). For more information you need to go to Oracle's Linux portal: http://www.oracle.com/technology/tech/linux .

As mentioned in the previous chapter, we can get the latest Oracle VM Server ISO file there. Download it and burn it to CD as we will be using it to install on our HP DL 360 boxes.

So let's get on with the installation of Oracle VM Server with the CD ROM.

On-premise Cloud installation: Installing Oracle VM Server 2.1.2 with a CD ROM

Now that we have downloaded the ISO and burned it to a CD, it's time to install it.

Here we are going to install the Oracle VM Server operating system—a rather small Linux. We will get the Oracle VM Server up and running and ready to communicate with the **VMM** (**Virtual Machine Monitor**) on specific ports. The fun part is that we won't be allocating space as this will be used by the VMs themselves.

Do remember to assign **static IP addresses** to your Oracle VM Servers and not DHCP. The reason is simple, we don't want our Oracle VM Server to end up displaying undefined behavior when the DHCP lease time expires. Also, it is a good practice to just assign static IP address for servers.

1. Start the server and wait for the screen. Upon prompt, press *Enter*.

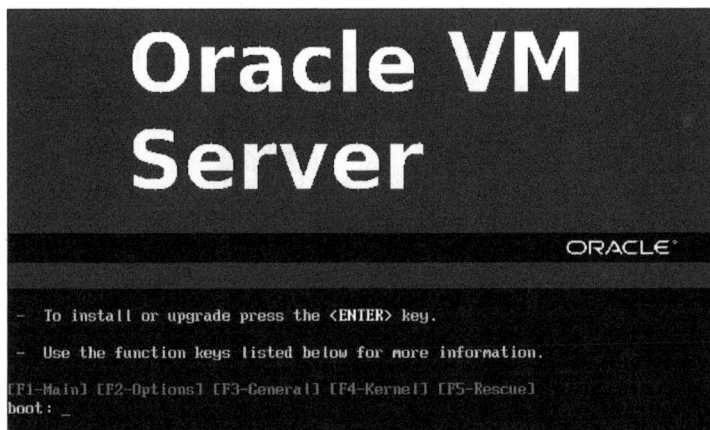

2. We choose the **Skip** option to skip the CD ROM test, although is is advisable to test the CD/DVD at least once to check if the download was clean.

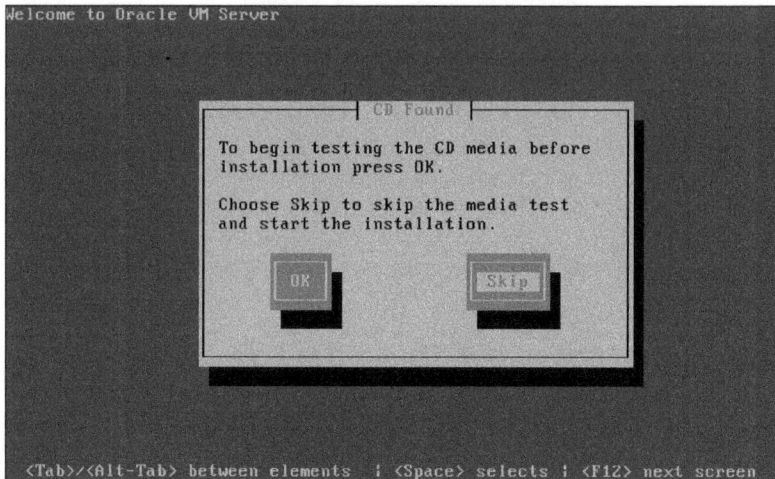

3. We can choose the keyboard type; in this case we have chosen the **us** option and then clicked on the **OK** button.

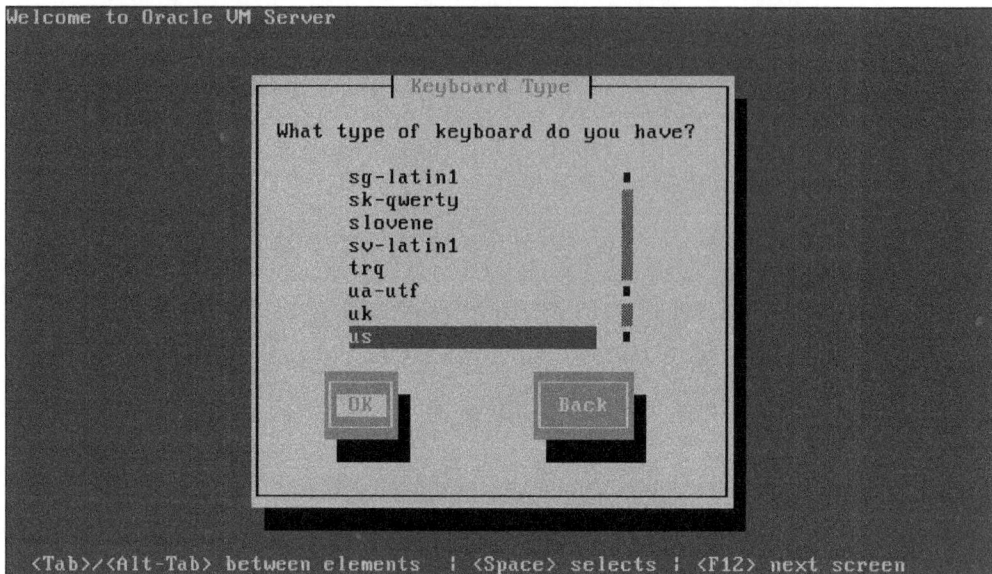

4. Since this is a fresh installation, we get the following message screen requesting to delete all data on that disk. As we don't have anything on that disk, we choose the option **Yes**:

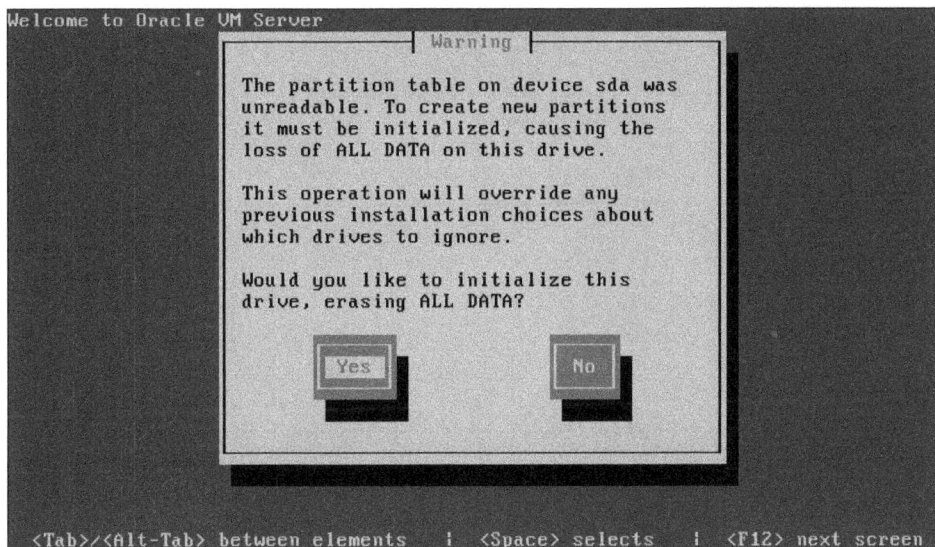

```
Welcome to Oracle VM Server
                    ┤ Warning ├

        The partition table on device sda was
        unreadable. To create new partitions
        it must be initialized, causing the
        loss of ALL DATA on this drive.

        This operation will override any
        previous installation choices about
        which drives to ignore.

        Would you like to initialize this
        drive, erasing ALL DATA?


              Yes              No




  <Tab>/<Alt-Tab> between elements  ¦  <Space> selects  ¦  <F12> next screen
```

5. We choose the R**emove all partitions on selected drives and create default layout.** option. We choose our **sda** disk and click on the **OK** button to jump to the next screen:

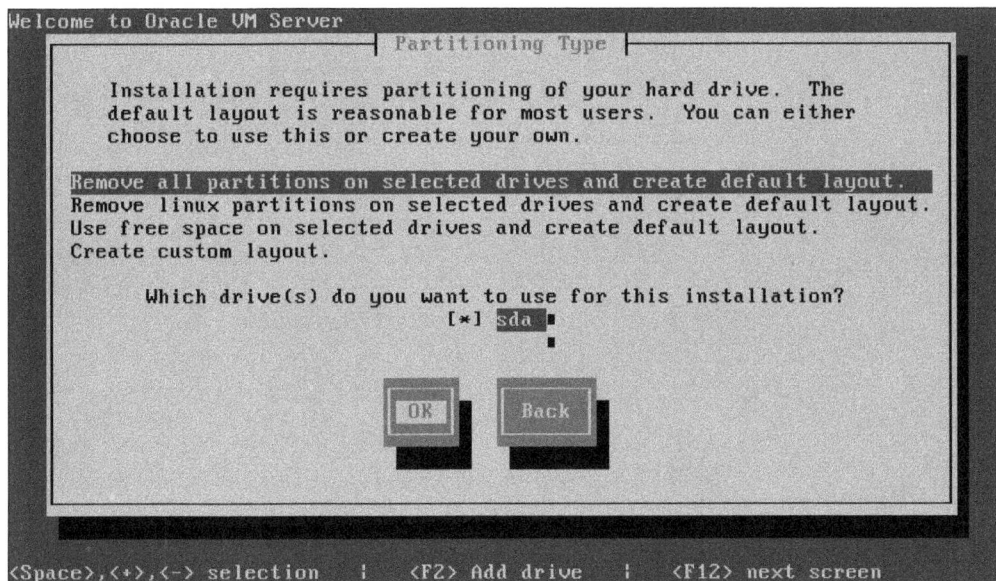

```
Welcome to Oracle VM Server
                    ┤ Partitioning Type ├

     Installation requires partitioning of your hard drive.  The
     default layout is reasonable for most users.  You can either
     choose to use this or create your own.

    Remove all partitions on selected drives and create default layout.
    Remove linux partitions on selected drives and create default layout.
    Use free space on selected drives and create default layout.
    Create custom layout.

         Which drive(s) do you want to use for this installation?
                        [*] sda



              OK          Back




<Space>,<+>,<-> selection  ¦   <F2> Add drive  ¦   <F12> next screen
```

6. This is yet another screen asking for a confirmation whether you're really sure what you are doing. We choose **Yes** to move ahead:

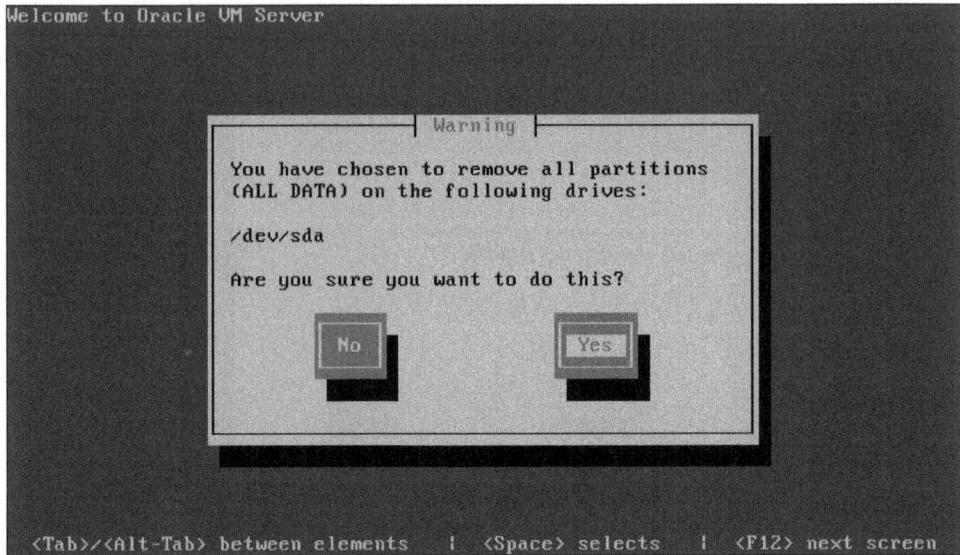

```
Welcome to Oracle VM Server

                    ┤ Warning ├
       You have chosen to remove all partitions
       (ALL DATA) on the following drives:

       /dev/sda

       Are you sure you want to do this?

              ┌─────┐              ┌─────┐
              │ No  │              │ Yes │
              └─────┘              └─────┘


 <Tab>/<Alt-Tab> between elements   |   <Space> selects   |   <F12> next screen
```

7. Click **Yes** to review the partitioning layout:

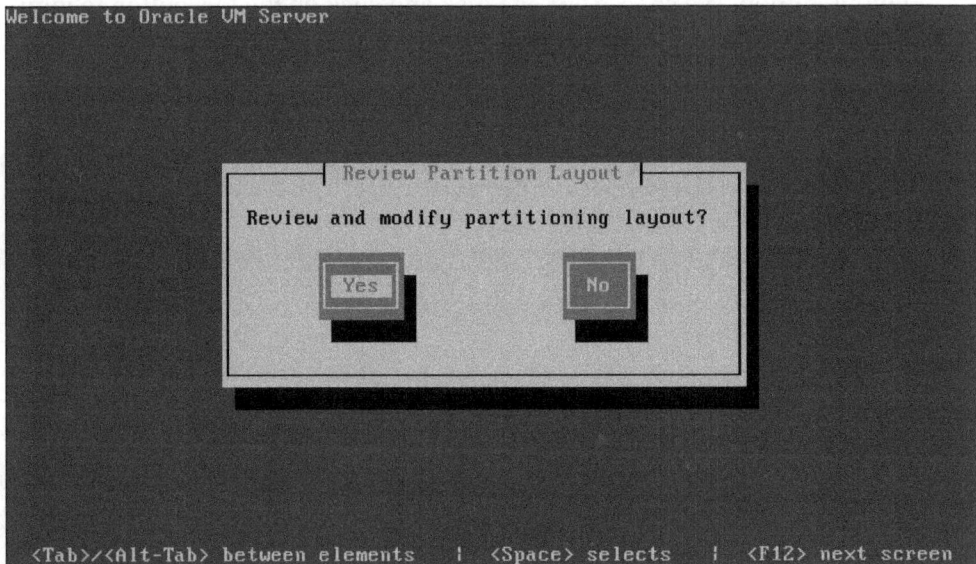

```
Welcome to Oracle VM Server


                 ┤ Review Partition Layout ├
         Review and modify partitioning layout?

              ┌─────┐              ┌─────┐
              │ Yes │              │ No  │
              └─────┘              └─────┘



 <Tab>/<Alt-Tab> between elements   |   <Space> selects   |   <F12> next screen
```

8. We will go ahead with the default installation. Make sure that you note the file system where the VMs will land; it is Oracle's famous **OCFS** (**Oracle Cluster File System**). Click on the **OK** button to move ahead:

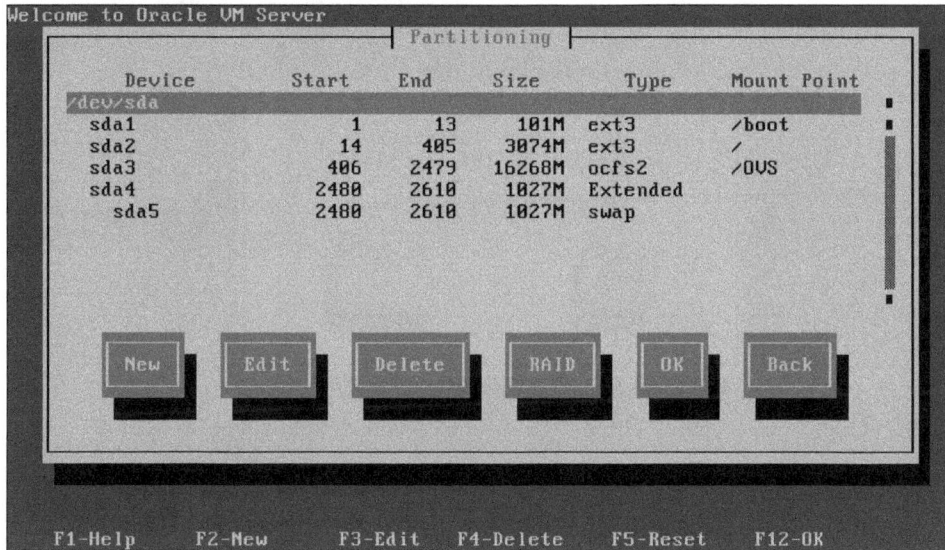

```
Welcome to Oracle VM Server
                      ┤ Partitioning ├
        Device        Start    End    Size     Type       Mount Point
    /dev/sda
      sda1              1       13     101M    ext3        /boot
      sda2             14      405    3074M    ext3        /
      sda3            406     2479   16268M    ocfs2       /OVS
      sda4           2480     2610    1027M    Extended
        sda5         2480     2610    1027M    swap


           New        Edit      Delete     RAID      OK        Back



   F1-Help     F2-New      F3-Edit    F4-Delete    F5-Reset    F12-OK
```

9. Choose **/dev/sda** to install the boot loader and click **OK**:

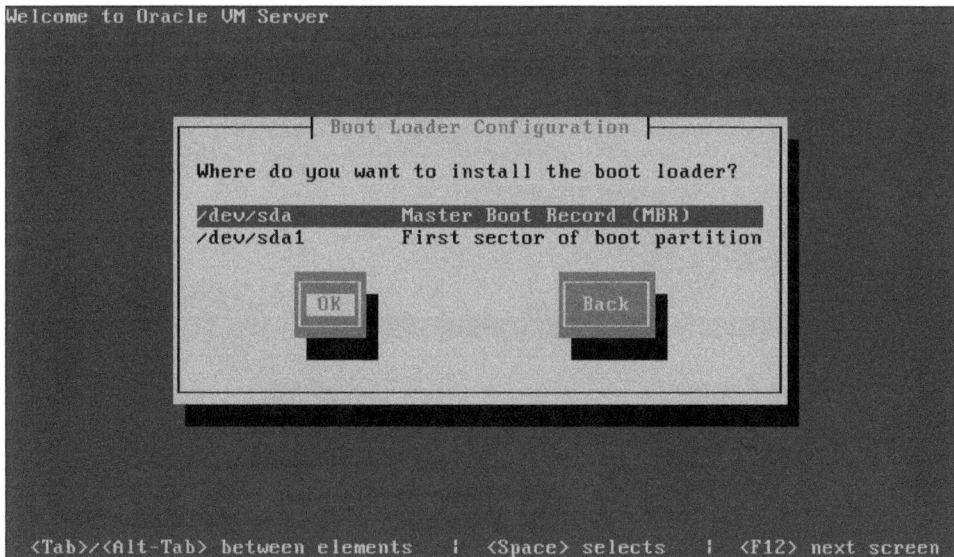

```
Welcome to Oracle VM Server

                  ┤ Boot Loader Configuration ├
        Where do you want to install the boot loader?

        /dev/sda         Master Boot Record (MBR)
        /dev/sda1        First sector of boot partition


                 OK                    Back




   <Tab>/<Alt-Tab> between elements  ¦  <Space> selects  ¦  <F12> next screen
```

10. Choose **eth0** as the **NIC** (**Network Interface Card**) for management purposes and click on the **OK** button:

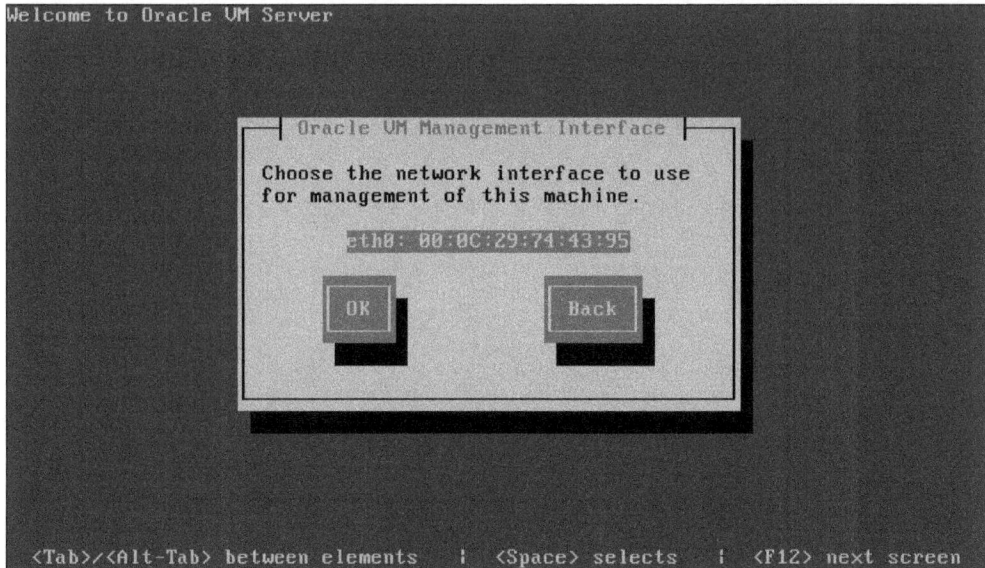

11. For Network configurations, check the following options — **Enable IP v4 support** and **Activate on boot**. Choose the IP address and Netmask that is suitable for your environment and click **OK** to move ahead:

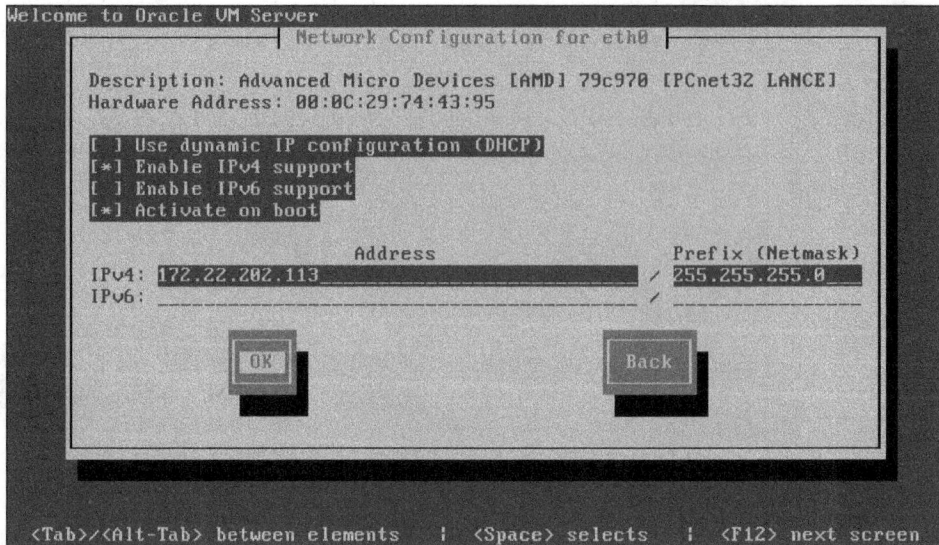

12. Type in the **Gateway**, **Primary DNS**, and **Secondary DNS** and click **OK**:

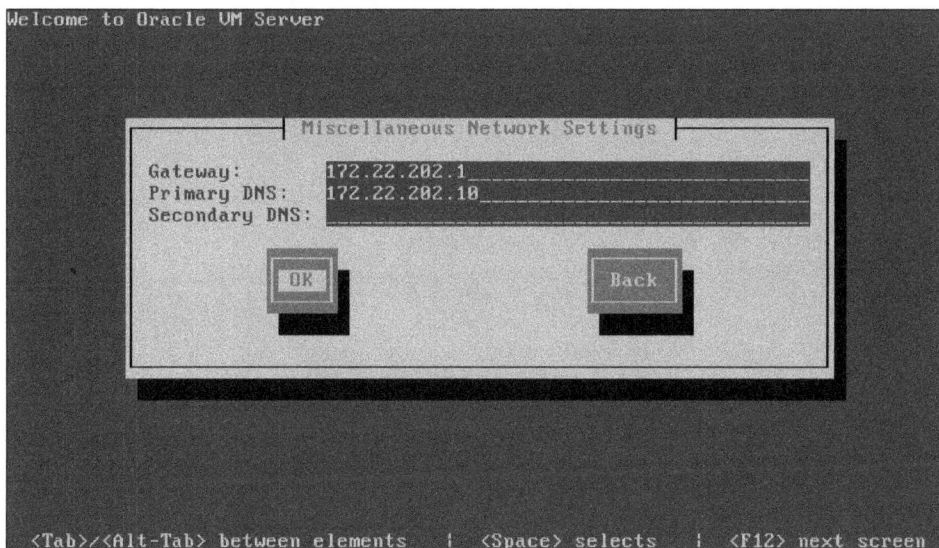

13. Always have a static IP address and names for your Oracle VM Servers, go ahead and check **manually** and assign the name to your Oracle VM Server. Click **OK**:

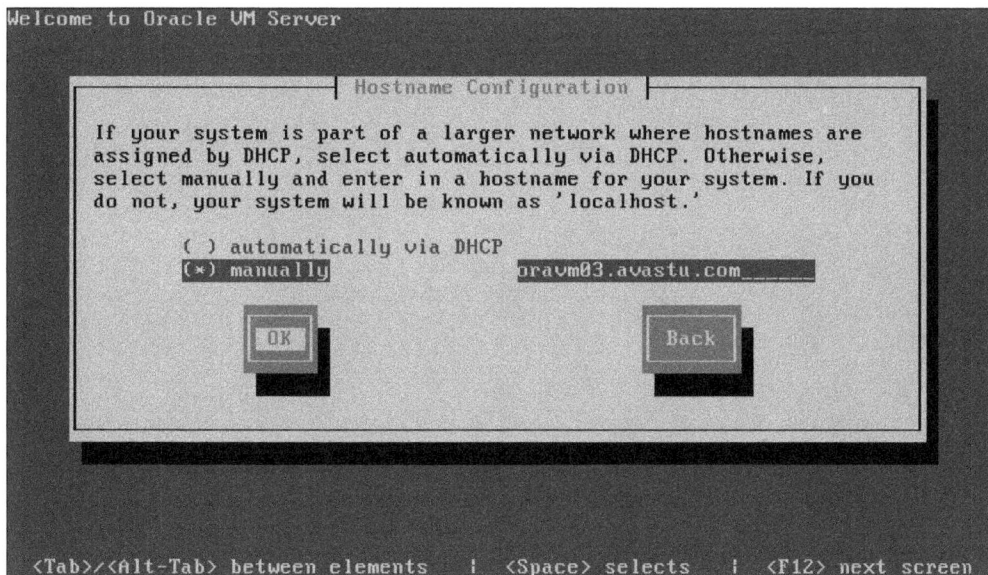

14. For **Time Zone Selection**, we can chose our time zone, (in this case it is **Amsterdam**), fill in the Time Zone where the Oracle VM Server will be provisioned, and click **OK** to move ahead:

```
Welcome to Oracle VM Server

                        ┤ Time Zone Selection ├

            What time zone are you located in?

            [*] System clock uses UTC

            Europe/Amsterdam
            Europe/Andorra
            Europe/Athens
            Europe/Belgrade
            Europe/Berlin

                   OK              Back


  <Tab>/<Alt-Tab> between elements  ┊  <Space> selects  ┊  <F12> next screen
```

15. Next, enter a tough-to-break password for `ovs-agent`, the Oracle VM Agent. This account is used to monitor and manage this VM Server and VMs running on top of the VM Servers:

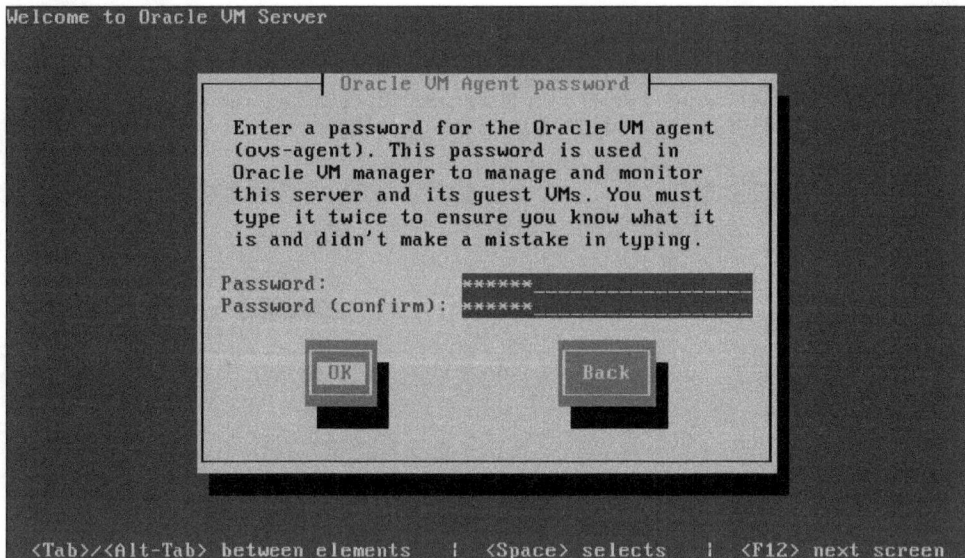

```
Welcome to Oracle VM Server

                    ┤ Oracle VM Agent password ├

          Enter a password for the Oracle VM agent
          (ovs-agent). This password is used in
          Oracle VM manager to manage and monitor
          this server and its guest VMs. You must
          type it twice to ensure you know what it
          is and didn't make a mistake in typing.

          Password:          ******
          Password (confirm): ******

                   OK              Back


  <Tab>/<Alt-Tab> between elements  ┊  <Space> selects  ┊  <F12> next screen
```

16. Choose an unbreakable password for the user `root`:

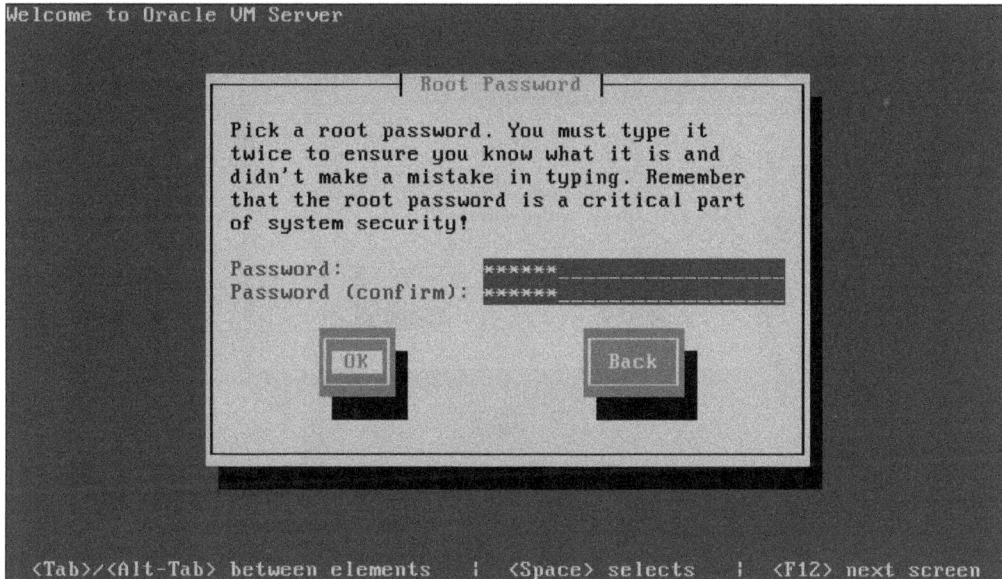

17. Once we click **OK**, the dependencies in packages are tested:

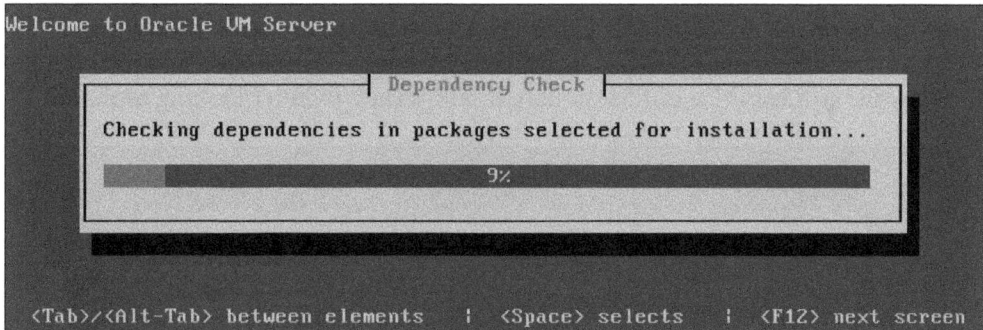

18. Click on the **OK** button to continue with the installation.

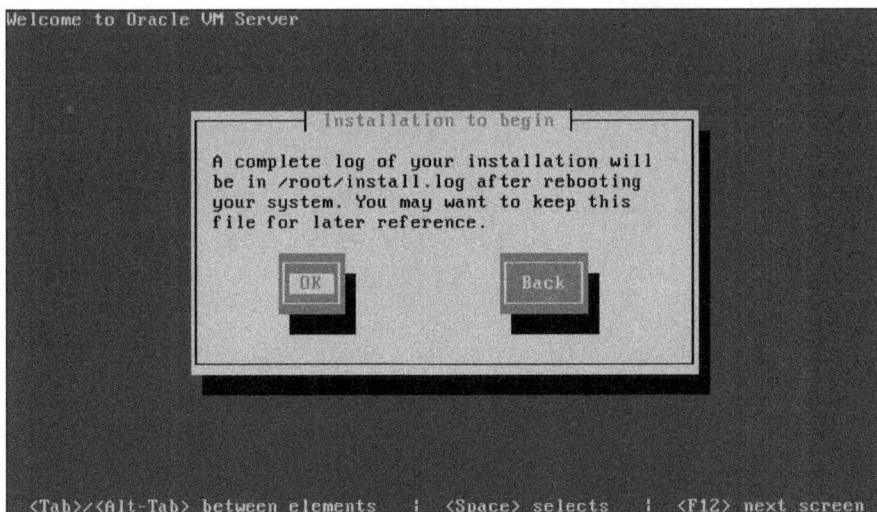

```
Welcome to Oracle VM Server


                          ┤ Installation to begin ├

                    A complete log of your installation will
                    be in /root/install.log after rebooting
                    your system. You may want to keep this
                    file for later reference.


                         ┌──────┐          ┌──────┐
                         │  OK  │          │ Back │
                         └──────┘          └──────┘




 <Tab>/<Alt-Tab> between elements  │  <Space> selects  │  <F12> next screen
```

19. The best thing about provisioning VM Servers is that they are installed very fast. This thin hypervisor layer installs within **1.5 minutes**! And this is just a typical On-Premise Cloud activity, where you need the physical presence of an administrator. You can imagine how Oracle VMs and appliances must be firing up in Amazon's EC2 Cloud.

    And is Oracle not planning its own data centers with its own source of OS, Apps, and Iron? I would seriously doubt if they weren't looking at that.

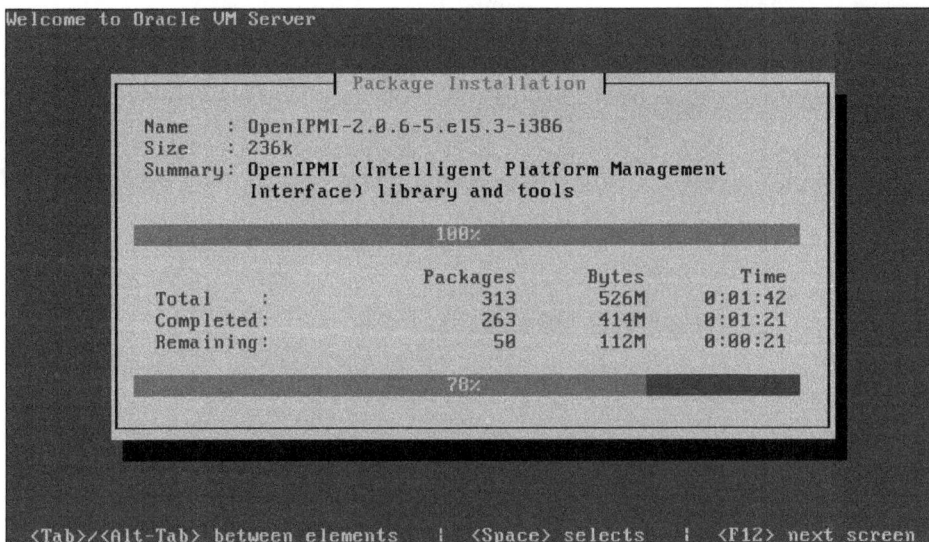

```
Welcome to Oracle VM Server


                         ┤ Package Installation ├

         Name    : OpenIPMI-2.0.6-5.el5.3-i386
         Size    : 236k
         Summary: OpenIPMI (Intelligent Platform Management
                  Interface) library and tools

         ├──────────────────── 100% ────────────────────┤

                         Packages      Bytes        Time
         Total    :           313       526M     0:01:42
         Completed:           263       414M     0:01:21
         Remaining:            50       112M     0:00:21

         ├───────────────── 78% ─────────────────────────┤



 <Tab>/<Alt-Tab> between elements  │  <Space> selects  │  <F12> next screen
```

20. Click **Reboot** to restart the server:

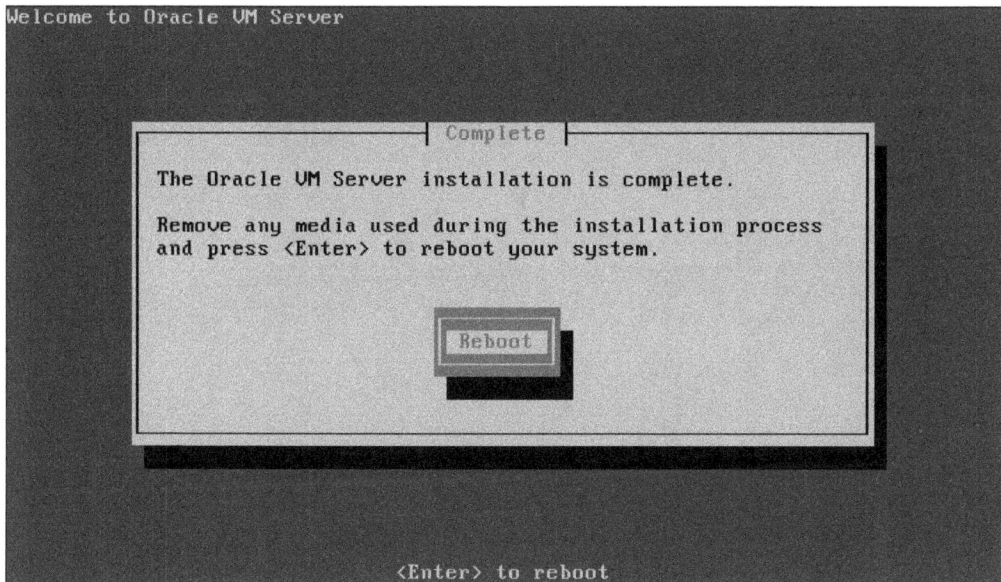

```
Welcome to Oracle VM Server




                        ┤ Complete ├

         The Oracle VM Server installation is complete.

         Remove any media used during the installation process
         and press <Enter> to reboot your system.



                          ┌──────────┐
                          │  Reboot  │
                          └──────────┘







                        <Enter> to reboot
```

21. Upon rebooting you get to sign the **EULA** (**End User License Agreement**), click on the **Agree** button to continue:

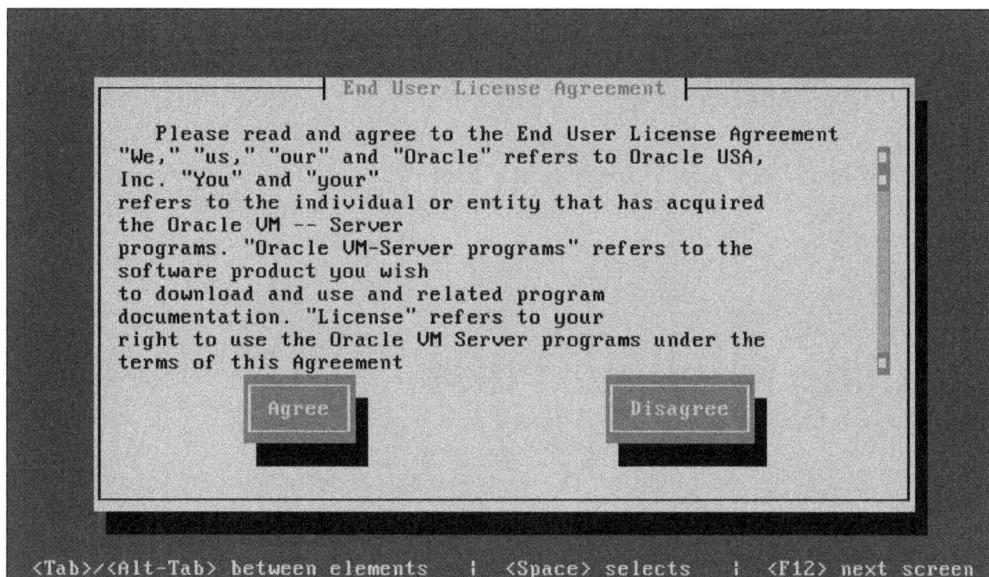

```
                      ┤ End User License Agreement ├

            Please read and agree to the End User License Agreement
      "We," "us," "our" and "Oracle" refers to Oracle USA,
      Inc. "You" and "your"
      refers to the individual or entity that has acquired
      the Oracle VM -- Server
      programs. "Oracle VM-Server programs" refers to the
      software product you wish
      to download and use and related program
      documentation. "License" refers to your
      right to use the Oracle VM Server programs under the
      terms of this Agreement
                 ┌───────┐                  ┌──────────┐
                 │ Agree │                  │ Disagree │
                 └───────┘                  └──────────┘



    <Tab>/<Alt-Tab> between elements  |  <Space> selects  |  <F12> next screen
```

And Voila!, you're done with the installation. As you can see this is a 64 bit installation with no hardware virtualization support. As of now it doesn't matter but we will occasionsally shift our tests to the machines that are Intel VT or AMD-V driven boxes to see the differences in performance and scalability.

```
Oracle VM server release 2.1.2
Hypervisor running in 64 bit mode with NO Hardware Virtualization support.

Network :
Management Interface   :
If : eth0(Up)  Mac : 00:0C:29:74:43:95 IP address : 172.22.202.113

Configured Networks and Bridges :
If : eth0       Mac : 00:0C:29:74:43:95
If : xenbr0     Mac : FE:FF:FF:FF:FF:FF

CPU :
cpu family    : 6
model         : 23
model name    : Intel(R) Core(TM)2 Duo CPU    T9300  @ 2.50GHz


oravm03 login: _
```

Off-premise Cloud installation: Installing Oracle VM Server from other sources

As more hardware is added modularly to the data centers and a more uniform approach is being adopted to build machines in racks, it is getting easier to quickly fire up Oracle VM Server remotely. All you need is a **LOM (Lights Out Management)** technology such as HP's iLO, Dell's DRAC, and so on and you can fire up the installation from anywhere in the world. That is what Cloud Computing offers—flexibility. We need to carry out some final checks during the installation process.

Installing from hard disk

Carry out the following steps to install from a hard disk:

1. Start the server and wait for the screen. Upon prompt type the following command:

    ```
    # linux askmethod
    ```

2. We can choose the keyboard type of our choice. In this case we choose the **us** option and click **OK**.

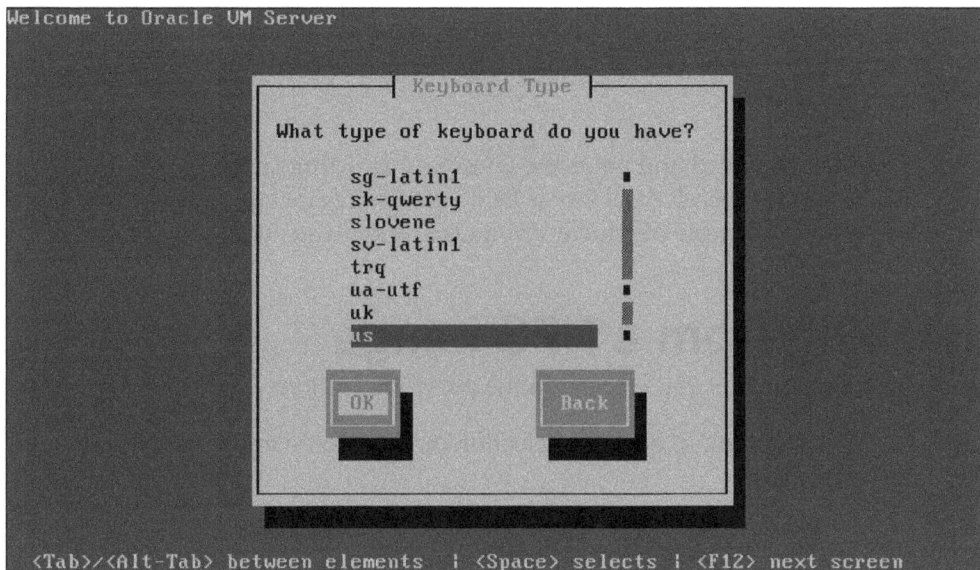

3. Select **Hard drive** in the screen that follows:

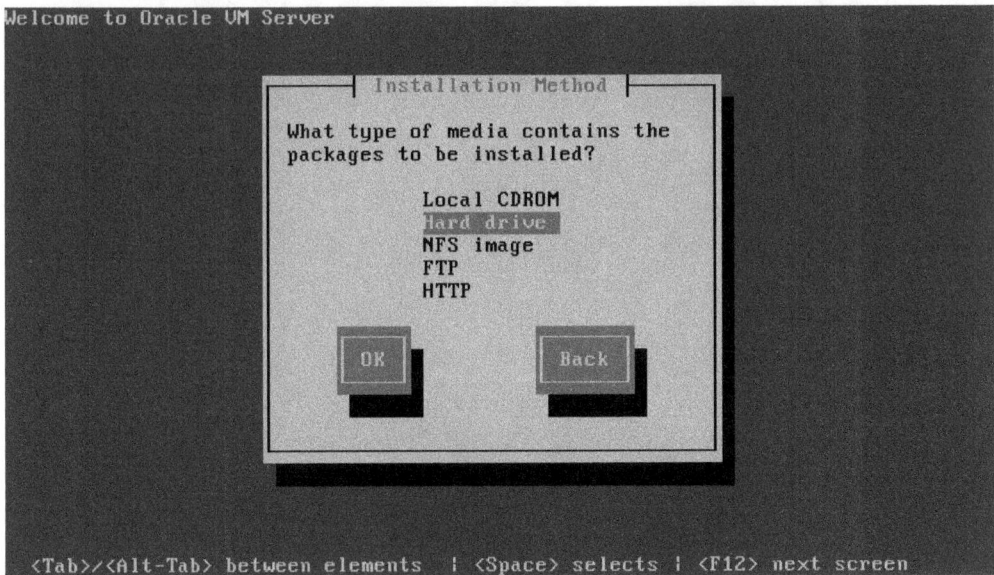

```
Welcome to Oracle VM Server

              ┤ Installation Method ├

         What type of media contains the
         packages to be installed?

                   Local CDROM
                   Hard drive
                   NFS image
                   FTP
                   HTTP


              OK              Back




 <Tab>/<Alt-Tab> between elements  │ <Space> selects │ <F12> next screen
```

4. Then we can go ahead and start selecting the partitions that we need to get our Oracle VM Server image from.

   For instance:

   ```
   dev/sda1
   dev/sda2
   ```

5. And then go ahead and enter the **Directory Holding Images** with the location to the Oracle VM Server ISO. For instance /rep/img/ will be a typical example of Oracle VM ISOs in a sub-directory.

Installing from a NFS image

Repeat the first two steps that we saw in the previous section.

1. For NFS installation, once the selection options come up, select **NFS image** and click **OK**:

```
Welcome to Oracle VM Server
                  ┤ Installation Method ├
          What type of media contains the
          packages to be installed?

                     Local CDROM
                     Hard drive
                     NFS image
                     FTP
                     HTTP

                  OK                Back

  <Tab>/<Alt-Tab> between elements  | <Space> selects | <F12> next screen
```

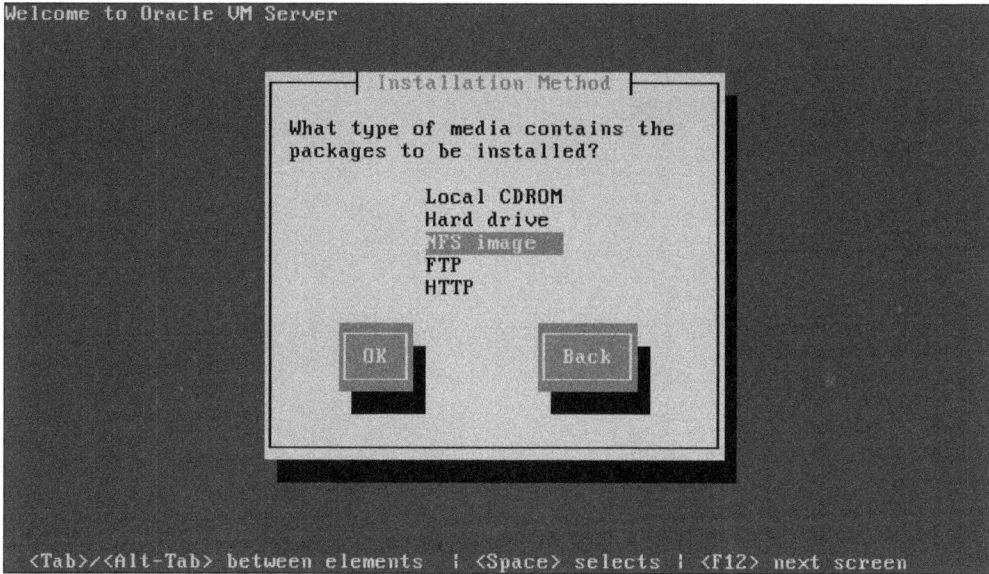

2. Next, we need to configure the IP address. We choose IPv4 and assign the IP address and hostname manually:

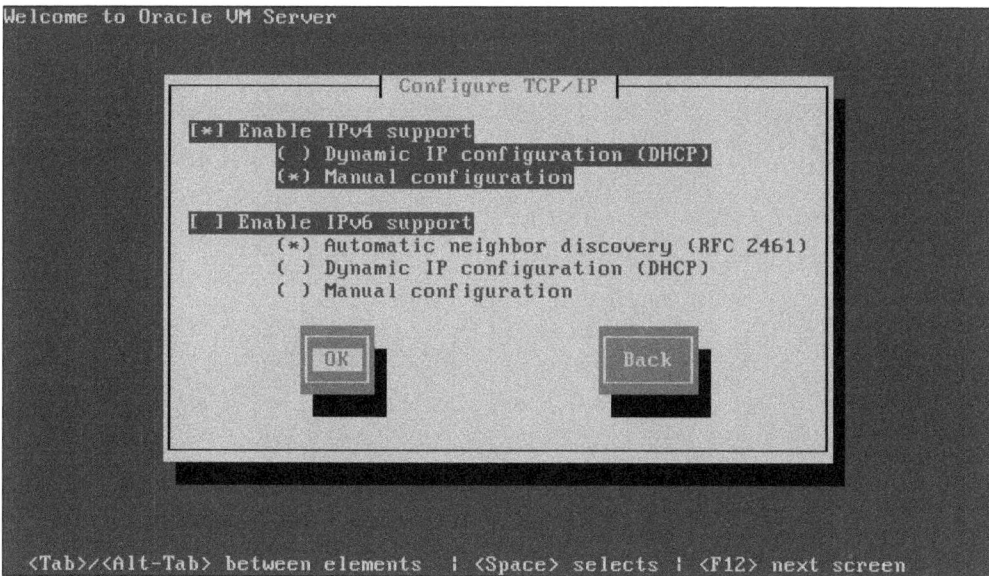

```
Welcome to Oracle VM Server
                     ┤ Configure TCP/IP ├
          [*] Enable IPv4 support
              ( ) Dynamic IP configuration (DHCP)
              (*) Manual configuration

          [ ] Enable IPv6 support
              (*) Automatic neighbor discovery (RFC 2461)
              ( ) Dynamic IP configuration (DHCP)
              ( ) Manual configuration

                  OK                Back

  <Tab>/<Alt-Tab> between elements  | <Space> selects | <F12> next screen
```

3. Click **OK** to move forward and type in the **IPv4 address**, **Gateway**, and the **Name Server** respectively:

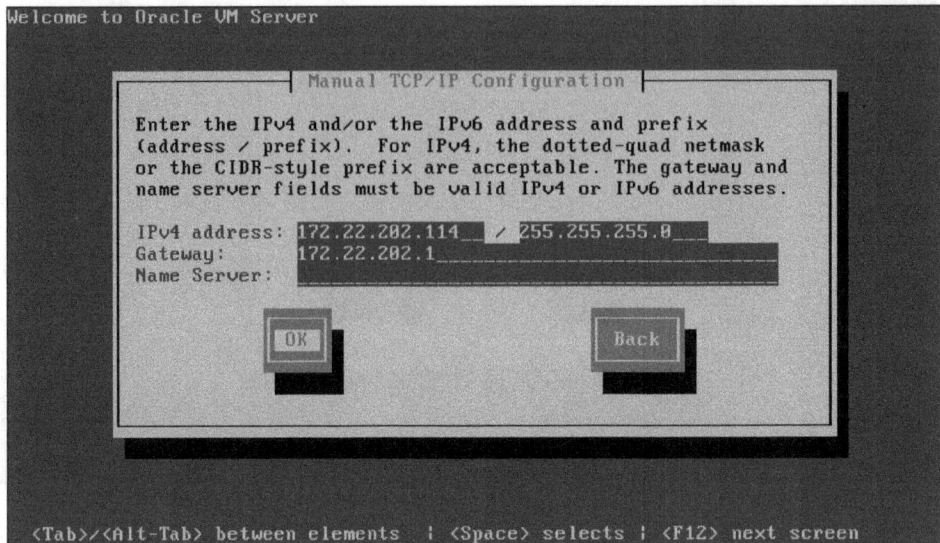

```
Welcome to Oracle VM Server

                ┤ Manual TCP/IP Configuration ├

      Enter the IPv4 and/or the IPv6 address and prefix
      (address / prefix).  For IPv4, the dotted-quad netmask
      or the CIDR-style prefix are acceptable. The gateway and
      name server fields must be valid IPv4 or IPv6 addresses.

      IPv4 address: 172.22.202.114__ / 255.255.255.0___
      Gateway:      172.22.202.1_____
      Name Server:  _____


                ┌──────┐                  ┌──────┐
                │  OK  │                  │ Back │
                └──────┘                  └──────┘



   <Tab>/<Alt-Tab> between elements  ¦ <Space> selects ¦ <F12> next screen
```

4. We will call our NFS server **NFSCloudStorage.com**. Obviously for your installation you will reference your own NFS server and Oracle VM Repository:

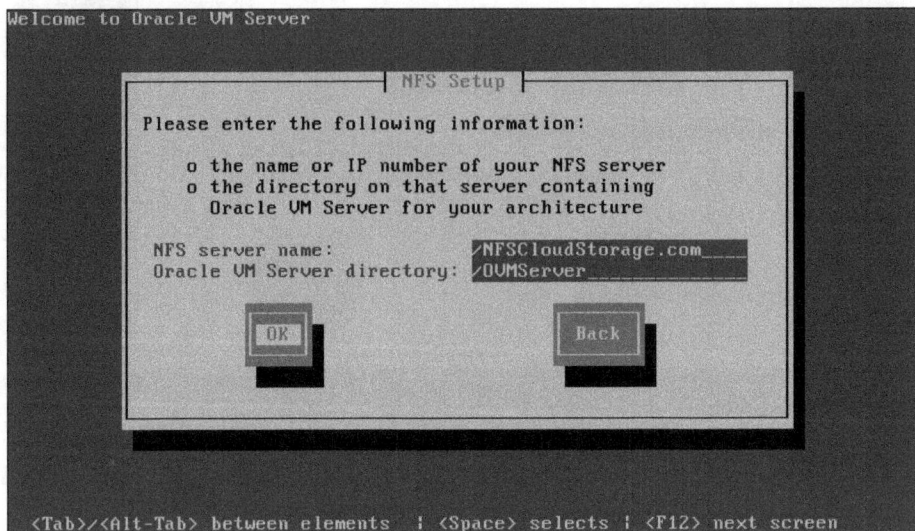

```
Welcome to Oracle VM Server

                       ┤ NFS Setup ├

      Please enter the following information:

            o the name or IP number of your NFS server
            o the directory on that server containing
              Oracle VM Server for your architecture

      NFS server name:           /NFSCloudStorage.com____
      Oracle VM Server directory: /OVMServer_____


                ┌──────┐                  ┌──────┐
                │  OK  │                  │ Back │
                └──────┘                  └──────┘



   <Tab>/<Alt-Tab> between elements  ¦ <Space> selects ¦ <F12> next screen
```

After this screen we will be presented with the partitioning screen and then we can continue the installation of the Oracle VM Server.

Installing from an FTP server

This is not much different than the ones that we just saw. Let's quickly try it out as well.

1. Carry out the same steps util you are presented with the following options screen. Choose **FTP** and click **OK**:

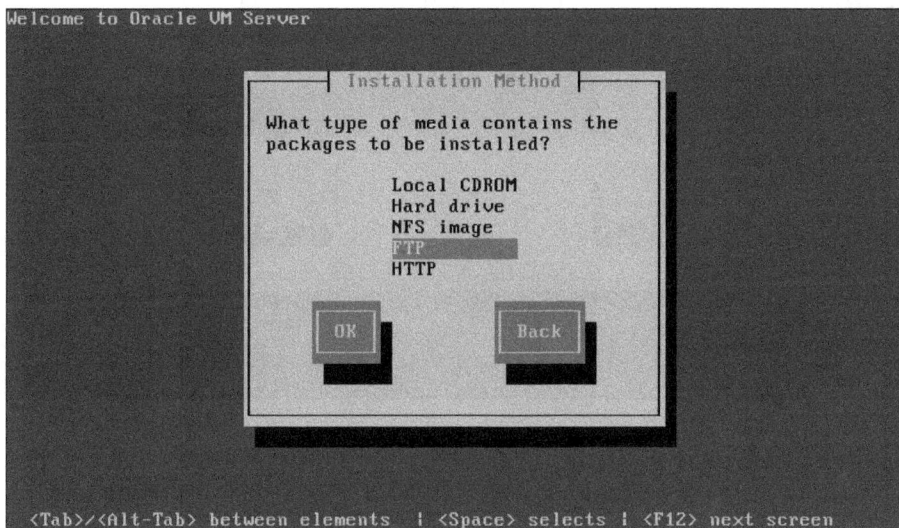

2. Next, we need to configure the IP Address. We choose IPv4 and assign the IP address and hostname manually:

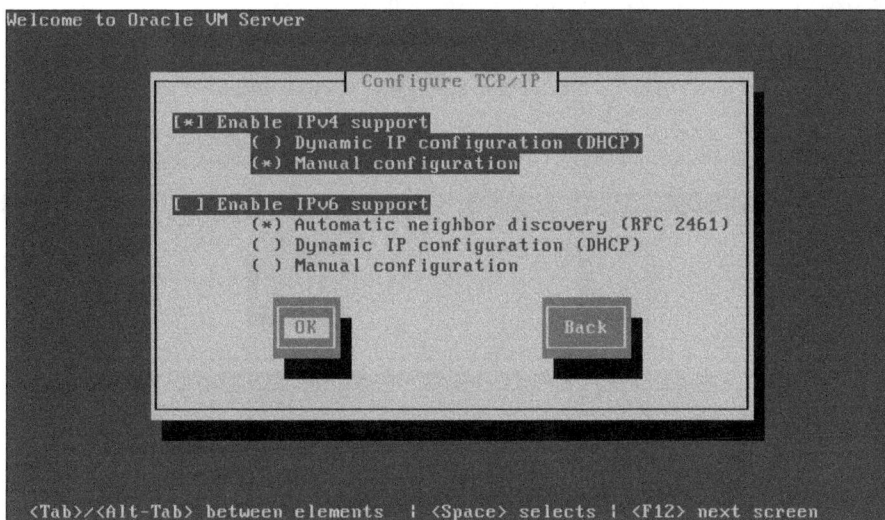

3. Click **OK** to move forward and type in the **IPv4 address**, **Gateway**, and the **Name Server** respectively:

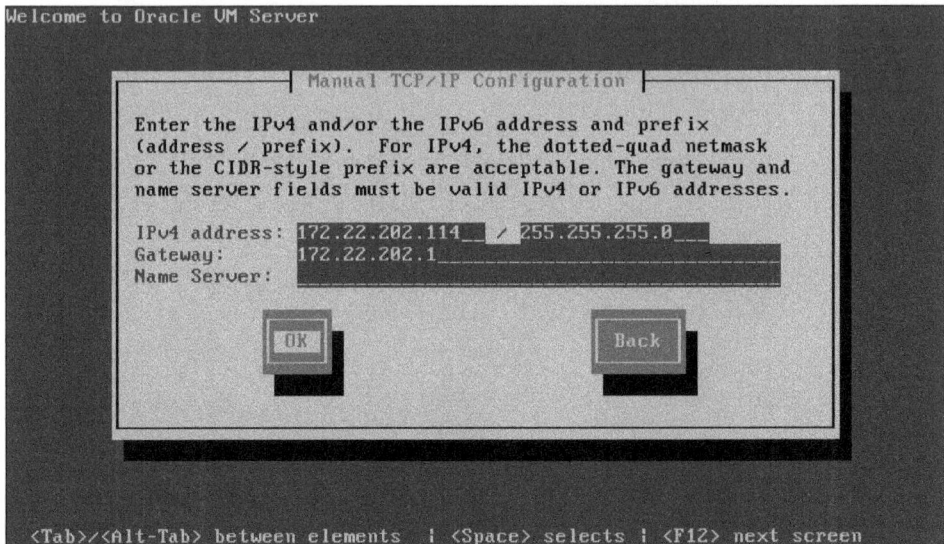

```
Welcome to Oracle VM Server

        ┤ Manual TCP/IP Configuration ├

      Enter the IPv4 and/or the IPv6 address and prefix
      (address / prefix).  For IPv4, the dotted-quad netmask
      or the CIDR-style prefix are acceptable. The gateway and
      name server fields must be valid IPv4 or IPv6 addresses.

      IPv4 address: 172.22.202.114__ / 255.255.255.0___
      Gateway:      172.22.202.1_____
      Name Server:  _____


              OK                      Back



    <Tab>/<Alt-Tab> between elements | <Space> selects | <F12> next screen
```

4. The FTP site that we are using is called **CloudStorage.com**. Hence, add the name in the next screen and continue to carry out the installation:

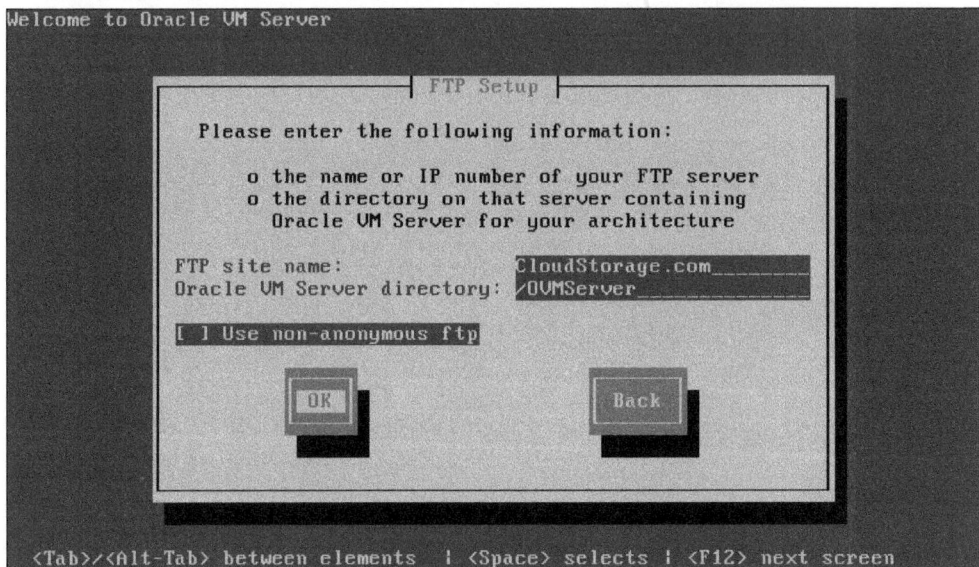

```
Welcome to Oracle VM Server

              ┤ FTP Setup ├

      Please enter the following information:

          o the name or IP number of your FTP server
          o the directory on that server containing
            Oracle VM Server for your architecture

      FTP site name:              CloudStorage.com_____
      Oracle VM Server directory: /OVMServer_____

      [ ] Use non-anonymous ftp


              OK                      Back



    <Tab>/<Alt-Tab> between elements | <Space> selects | <F12> next screen
```

5. Also fill in the **Account name** and **Password**:

```
Welcome to Oracle VM Server

                    ┤ Further FTP Setup ├
        If you are using non anonymous ftp, enter the
        account name and password you wish to use below.

            Account name: tarry.singh@avastu.com
            Password:     *********

                 OK                    Back


   <Tab>/<Alt-Tab> between elements | <Space> selects | <F12> next screen
```

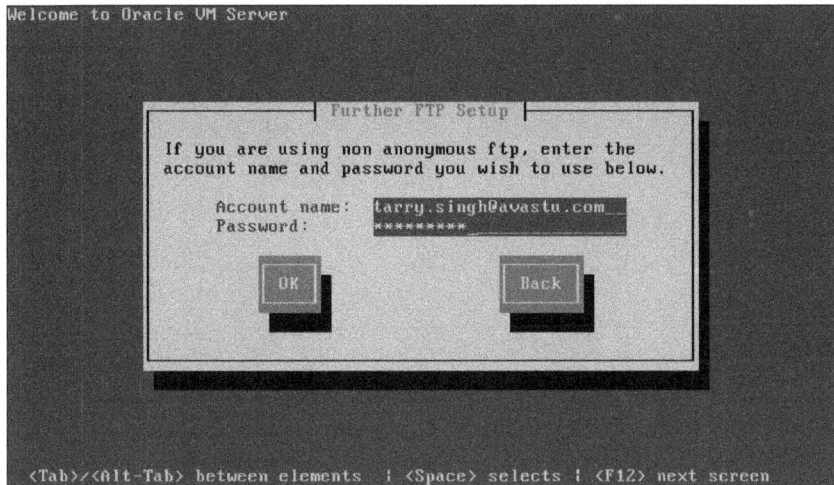

6. After this carry out the installation of the Oracle VM Server in the same fashion as the typical On-premise installation.

7. And finally our last step, is to fire the installation via the HTTP.

Installing from HTTP

This method is similar to the previous methods that we saw. Just follow these simple steps:

1. Carry out the same steps util you are presented with the following options screen. Choose **HTTP**:

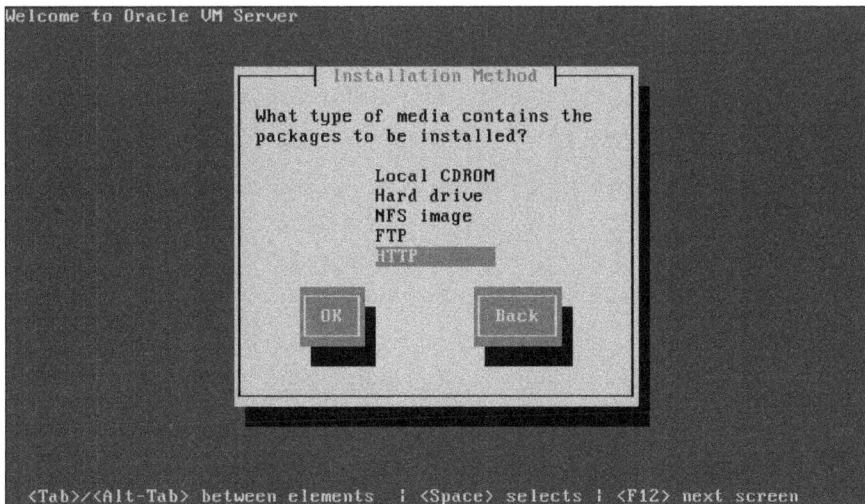

```
Welcome to Oracle VM Server

                    ┤ Installation Method ├
          What type of media contains the
          packages to be installed?

                    Local CDROM
                    Hard drive
                    NFS image
                    FTP
                    HTTP

                 OK                 Back


   <Tab>/<Alt-Tab> between elements | <Space> selects | <F12> next screen
```

2. Click **OK** to move forward and type in the **IPv4 address**, **Gateway**, and the **Name Server** respectively. Next, we are presented with the following screen.

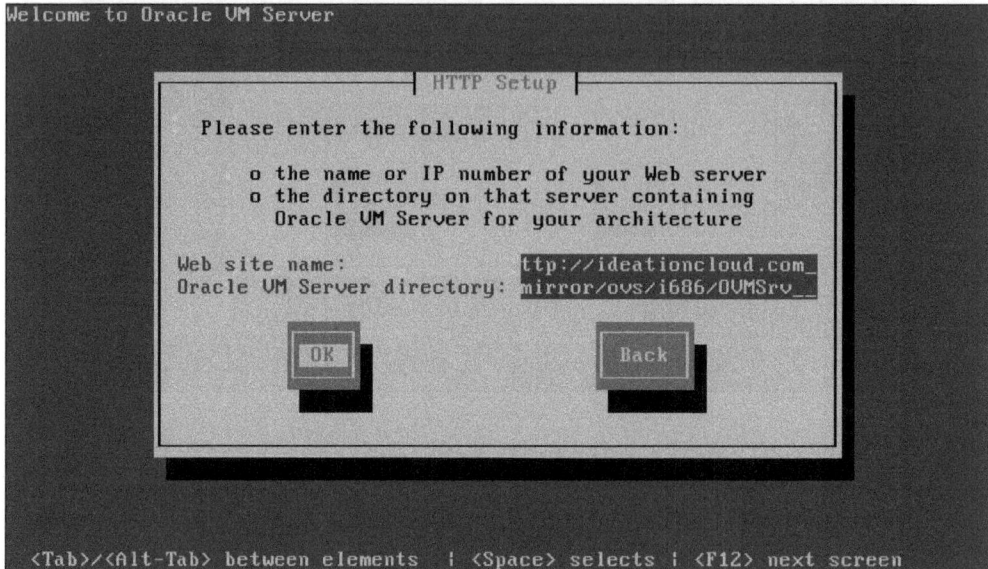

```
Welcome to Oracle VM Server



                    ┤ HTTP Setup ├

         Please enter the following information:

             o the name or IP number of your Web server
             o the directory on that server containing
               Oracle VM Server for your architecture

         Web site name:               ttp://ideationcloud.com_
         Oracle VM Server directory:  mirror/ovs/i686/OVMSrv__


                  OK                        Back




 <Tab>/<Alt-Tab> between elements  ¦ <Space> selects ¦ <F12> next screen
```

3. Type in the URL of the HTTP server and the location of the Oracle VM Server ISO.

4. Continue with the rest of the installation as described in the previous installation.

Upgrading Oracle VM Server

Upgrading Oracle VM is also a pretty straight forward process. Just insert the CD ROM and if you already have a previous installation, you will be confronted with the following screen, **System to Upgrade**.

1. Select **Oracle VM server 2.1 (hda2)** on the hard disk and click **OK.**

```
Welcome to Oracle VM Server

                    ┤ System to Upgrade ├

        One or more existing Linux installations have been
        found on your system.

        Please choose one to upgrade, or select 'Reinstall
        System' to freshly install your system.

                    Reinstall System
                    Oracle VM server 2.1 (hda2)

                 ┌──────┐              ┌──────┐
                 │  OK  │              │ Back │
                 └──────┘              └──────┘



  <Tab>/<Alt-Tab> between elements  │  <Space> selects  │  <F12> next screen
```

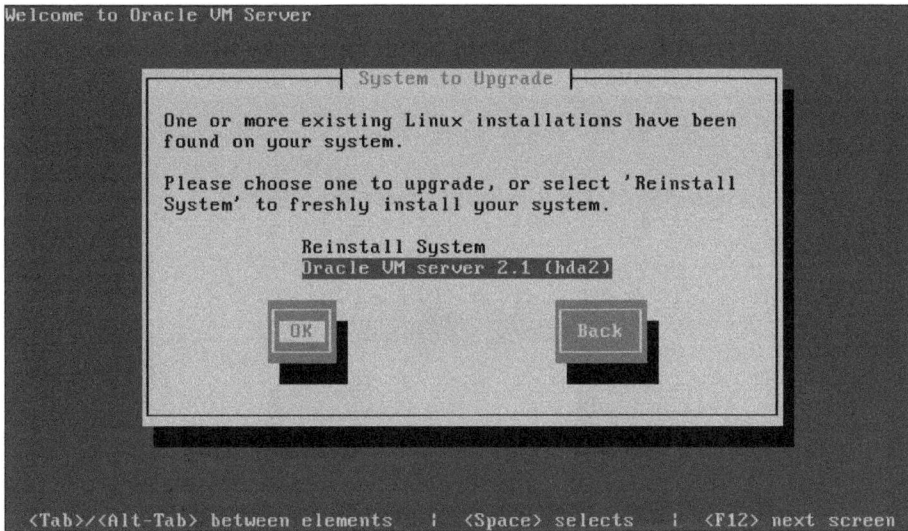

2. Next we will get the **Update Boot Loader Configuration** screen. Here we
    select the **Update boot loader configuration** or the other options as per your
    requirements and click **OK**:

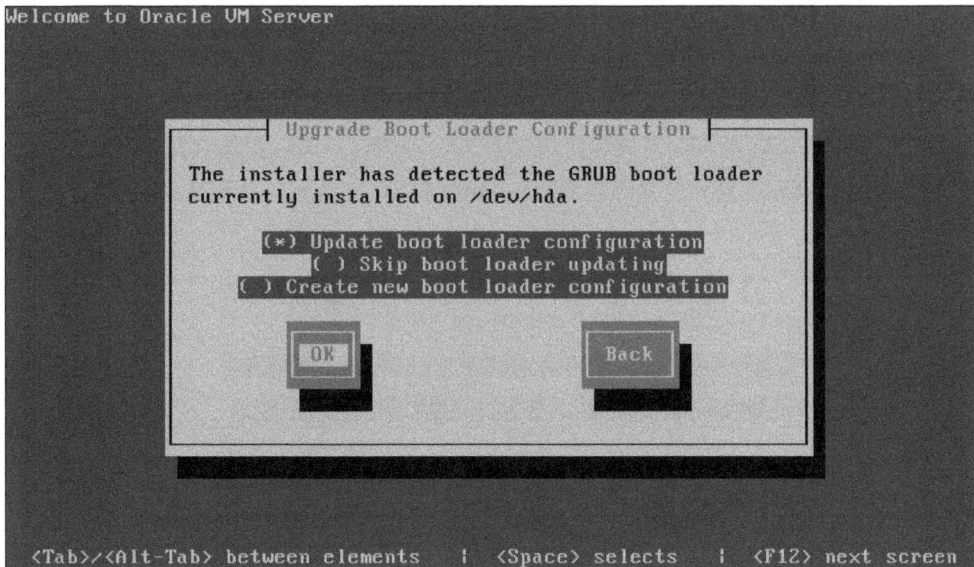

```
Welcome to Oracle VM Server


                    ┤ Upgrade Boot Loader Configuration ├

        The installer has detected the GRUB boot loader
        currently installed on /dev/hda.

                 (*) Update boot loader configuration
                 ( ) Skip boot loader updating
                 ( ) Create new boot loader configuration

                 ┌──────┐              ┌──────┐
                 │  OK  │              │ Back │
                 └──────┘              └──────┘



  <Tab>/<Alt-Tab> between elements  │  <Space> selects  │  <F12> next screen
```

3. If we happen to create a new boot loader then the following screen will appear. We select **Use GRUB Boot Loader** and click **OK**:

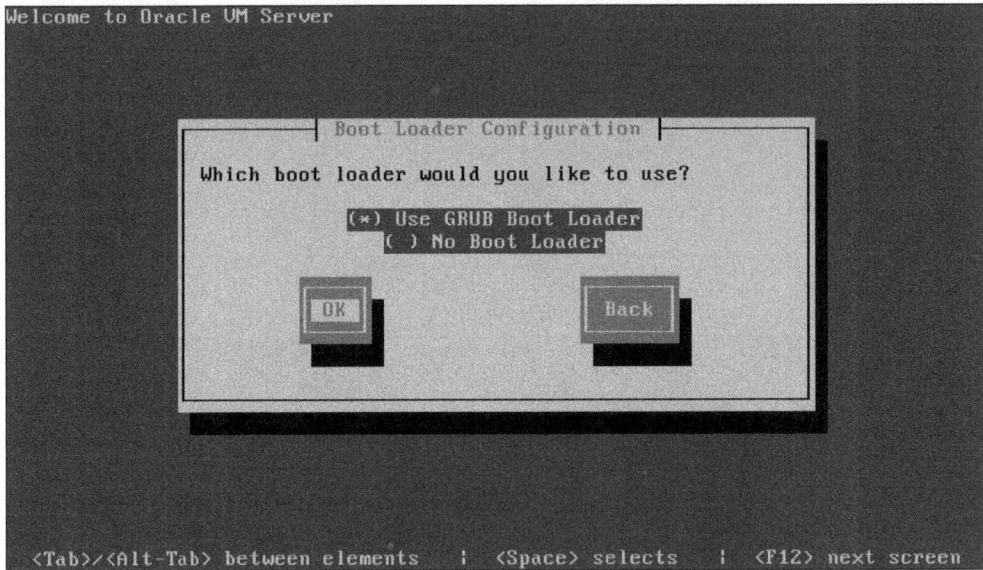

```
Welcome to Oracle VM Server

                  ┤ Boot Loader Configuration ├

          Which boot loader would you like to use?

                    (*) Use GRUB Boot Loader
                    ( ) No Boot Loader

               ┌────────┐              ┌────────┐
               │   OK   │              │  Back  │
               └────────┘              └────────┘

 <Tab>/<Alt-Tab> between elements  │  <Space> selects  │  <F12> next screen
```

4. Then we are presented with the GRUB configuration screen. If we wish to pass any extra booting options to the kernel then type them here, otherwise select **OK** to go to the next screen:

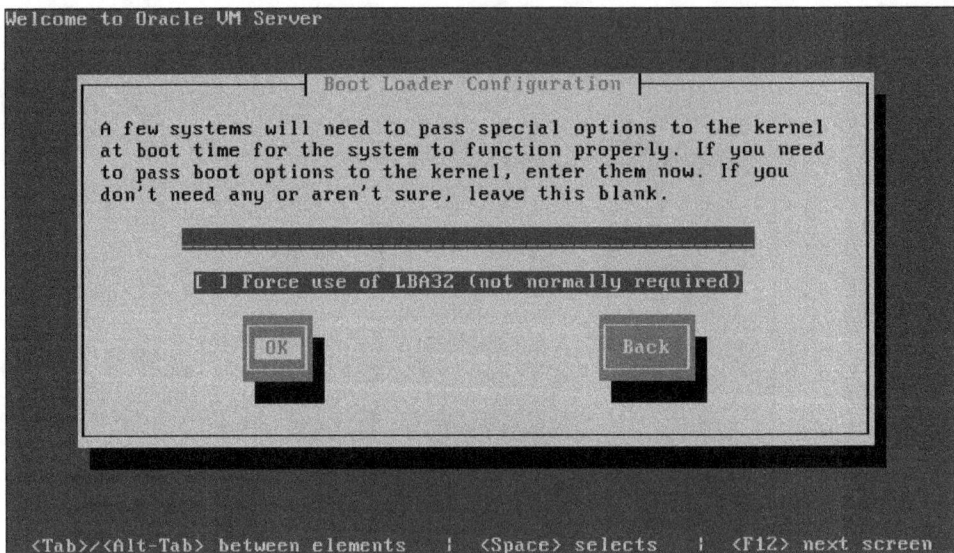

```
Welcome to Oracle VM Server

                  ┤ Boot Loader Configuration ├

      A few systems will need to pass special options to the kernel
      at boot time for the system to function properly. If you need
      to pass boot options to the kernel, enter them now. If you
      don't need any or aren't sure, leave this blank.

      ┌──────────────────────────────────────────────────────┐
      └──────────────────────────────────────────────────────┘

        [ ] Force use of LBA32 (not normally required)

               ┌────────┐              ┌────────┐
               │   OK   │              │  Back  │
               └────────┘              └────────┘

 <Tab>/<Alt-Tab> between elements  │  <Space> selects  │  <F12> next screen
```

5. For extra security it is prudent to have a strong **Boot Loader Password**:

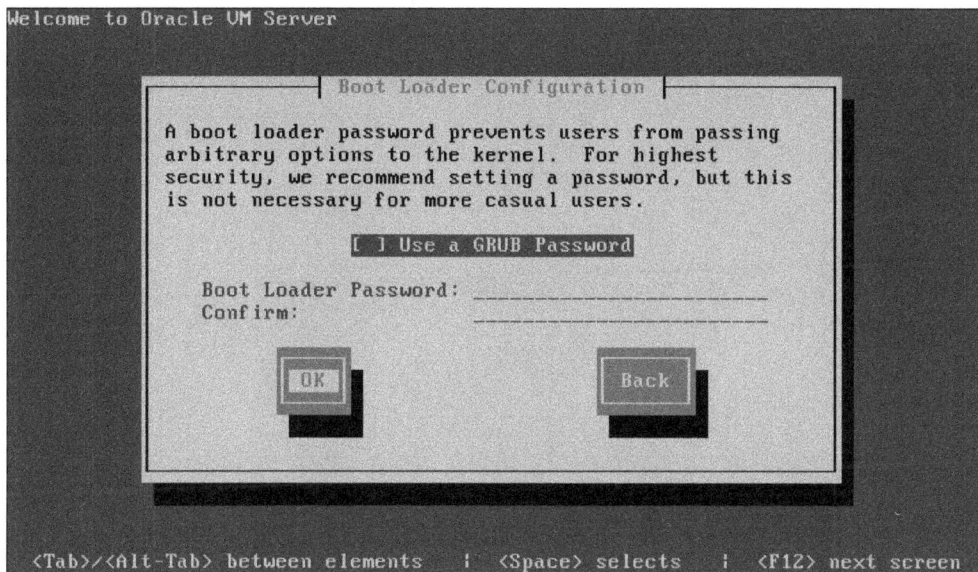

6. And we are finally presented with the following screen. Click **OK** to start the upgrade:

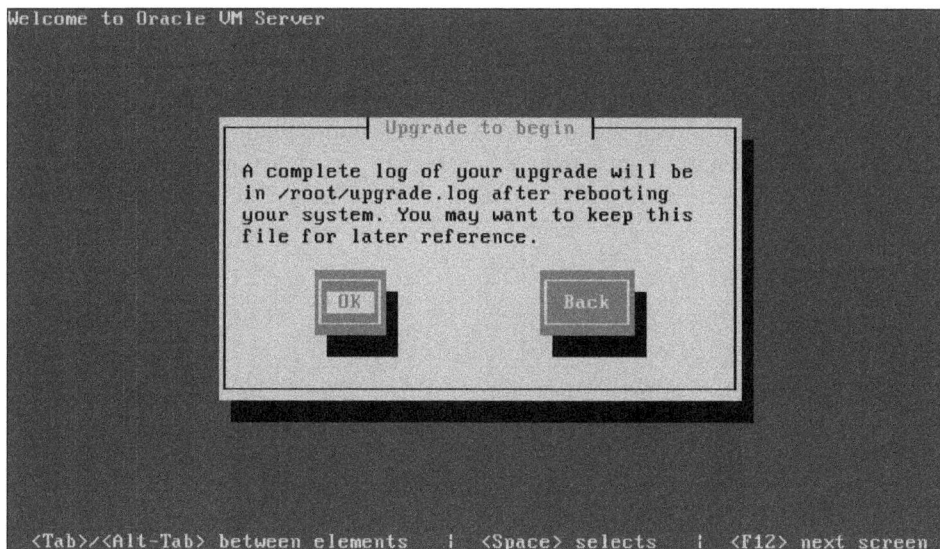

7. After completion of the upgrade remove any media and press *Enter* to reboot the system:

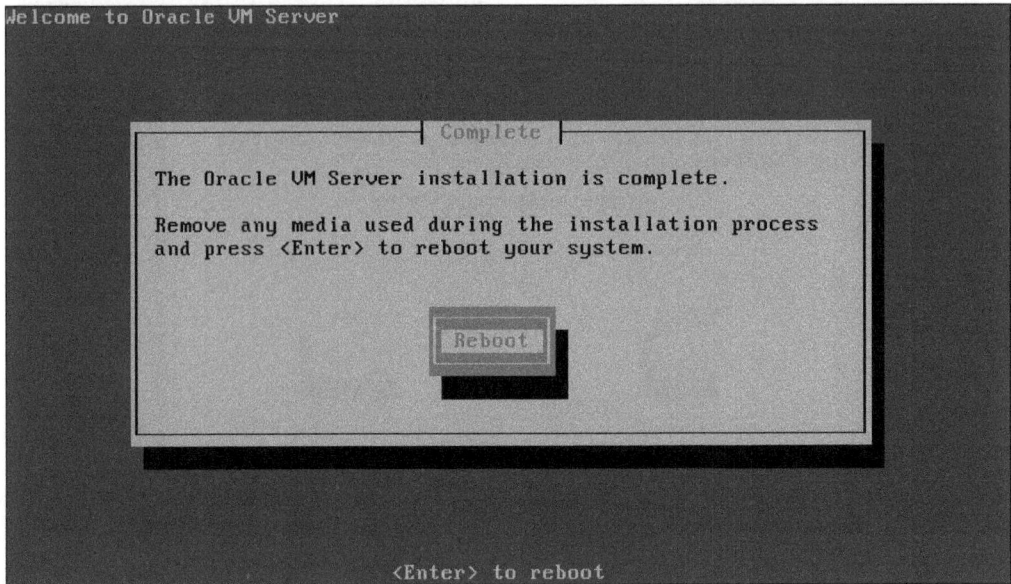

```
Welcome to Oracle VM Server




                          ┤ Complete ├

          The Oracle VM Server installation is complete.

          Remove any media used during the installation process
          and press <Enter> to reboot your system.




                            Reboot





                        <Enter> to reboot
```

Summary

Clearly the installation of Oracle VM Server is as simple as our Oracle VM Manager that we saw in the previous chapter. In the next chapter, we will start managing the environment. "Managing" is a big word and there are many directions that we can go with it. However, we will stick to a structured approach in order to make this journey a pleasurable and informative experience.

Part 2

Looking into the Architecture and Management

Oracle VM Management

Managing VMs with Oracle VM Manager – Part I

Managing VMs with Oracle VM Manager – Part II

Managing VMs with Oracle VM Manager – Part III

Troubleshooting & Gotchas

4
Oracle VM Management

In the previous chapter, we saw the Oracle VM Server installation. We'll begin this chapter by looking at the meaty aspects of the Oracle VM Manager and will explore it's management aspects.

The following topics will be covered in this chapter:

- Getting started with the Oracle VM Manager
- Managing Servers and Server Pools
- Managing Oracle VM Server repository
- Users and Groups management
- Backing up or Restoring Oracle VM Manager
- Enabling security

Before we get to manage the VMs in the Oracle VM Manager, let's take a quick look at the Oracle VM Manager by logging into it.

Getting started with Oracle VM Manager

In this chapter, we will perform the following actions while exploring the Oracle VM Manager:

- Registering an account
- Logging in to Oracle VM Manager
- Create a Server Pool

After we are done with the Oracle VM Manager installation, we will use one of the following links to log on to the Oracle VM Manager:

- Within the local machine: `http://127.0.0.1:8888/OVS`

- Logging in remotely: `http://vmmgr:8888/OVS`

Here, `vmmgr` refers to the host name or IP address of your Oracle VM Manager host.

How to register an account

Registering of an account can be done in several ways. If, during the installation of Oracle VM Manager, we have chosen to configure the default admin account "admin", then we can use this account directly to log on to Oracle's IntraCloud portal we call Oracle VM Manager. We will explain later in detail about the user accounts and why we would need separate accounts for separate roles for fine-grained access control; something that is crucial for security purposes. So let's have a quick look at the three available options:

- **Default installation**: This option applies if we have performed the default installation ourselves and have gone ahead to create the account ourselves. Here we have the default **administrator** role.

- **Request for account creation**: Contacting the administrator of Oracle VM Manager is another way to attain an account with the privileges, such as **administrator**, **manager**, and **user**.

- **Create yourself**: If we need to conduct basic functions of a common user with operator's role such as creating and using virtual machines, or importing resources, we can create a new account ourselves. However, we will need the administrator to assign us the server pools and groups to our account before we can get started. Here by default we are granted a **user** role. We will talk more about roles later in this chapter.

Now let's go about registering a new account with Oracle VM Manager.

1. Once on the **Oracle VM Manager Login** page click on the **Register** link.

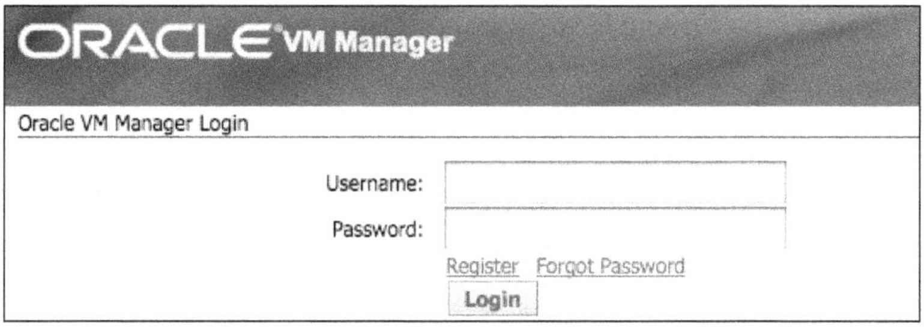

2. We are presented with the following screen. We must enter a **Username** of our choice and a hard-to-crack password twice. Also, we have to fill in our **First Name** and **Last Name** and complete the registration with a valid email address. Click **Next**:

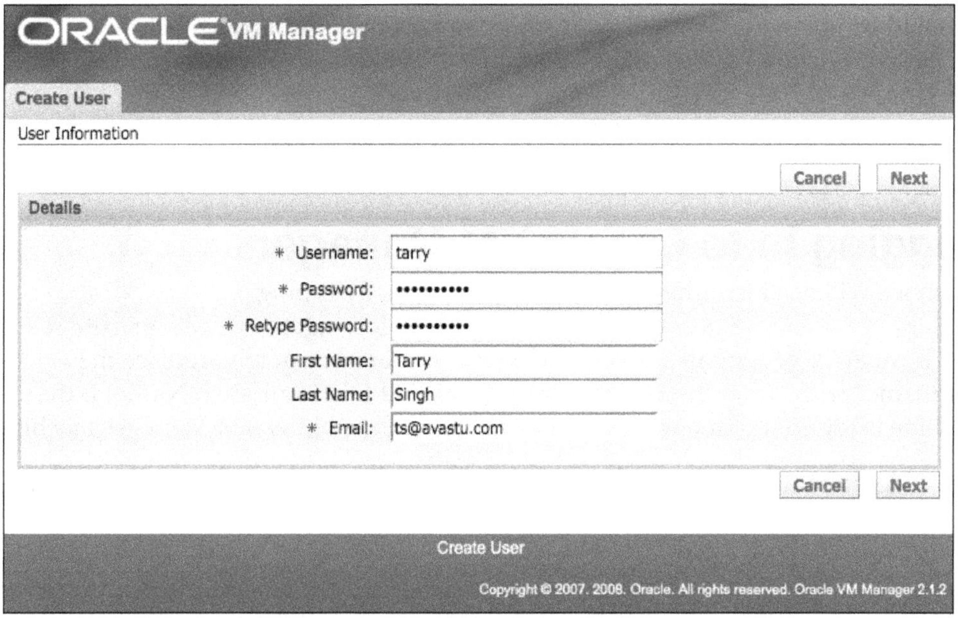

3. Next, we need to confirm our account details by clicking on the **Confirm** button. Now our account will be created and a confirmation message is displayed on the **Oracle VM Manager Login** screen.

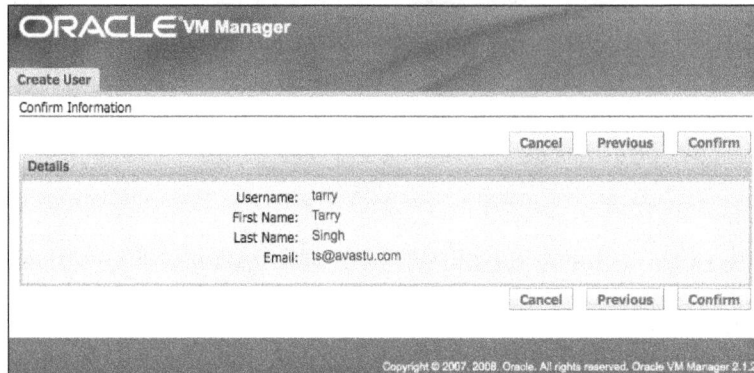

It should be noted that we will need some Server Pools and groups before we can get started. We will have to ask the administrator to assign us access to those pools and groups.

It's time now to login to our newly created account.

Logging in to Oracle VM Manager

Again we will need to either access the URL locally by typing `http://127.0.0.1:8888/OVS` or by typing the following: `http://hostname:8888/OVS`. If we are accessing the Oracle VM Manager Portal remotely, replace the "hostname" with either the **FQDN (Fully Qualified Distinguished Name)** if the machine is registered in our DNS or just the hostname of the VM Manager machine.

We can login to the portal by simply typing in our **Username** and **Password** that we just created.

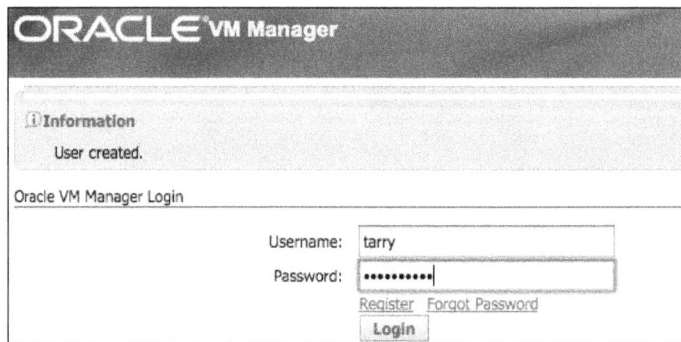

Depending on the role and the server pools that we have been assigned, we will be displayed with the tabs upon the screen as shown in the following table. To change the role, we will need to contact our enterprise domain administrator. Only administrators are allowed to change the roles of accounts.

If we forget our password, we can click on **Forgot Password** and on submitting our account name, the password will be sent to the registered email address that we had provided when we registered the account.

The following table discusses the assigned tabs that are displayed for each Oracle VM Manager roles:

Role	Grants
User	Virtual Machines and Resources
Administrator	Virtual Machines, Resources, Servers, Server Pools, and Administration
Manager	Virtual Machines, Resources, Servers, and Server Pools

We can obviously change the roles by editing the **Profile** (on the upper-right section of the portal).

As it can be seen in the following screenshot, we have access to the **Virtual Machines** pane and the **Resources** pane. We will continue to add Servers to the pool when logged in as **admin**.

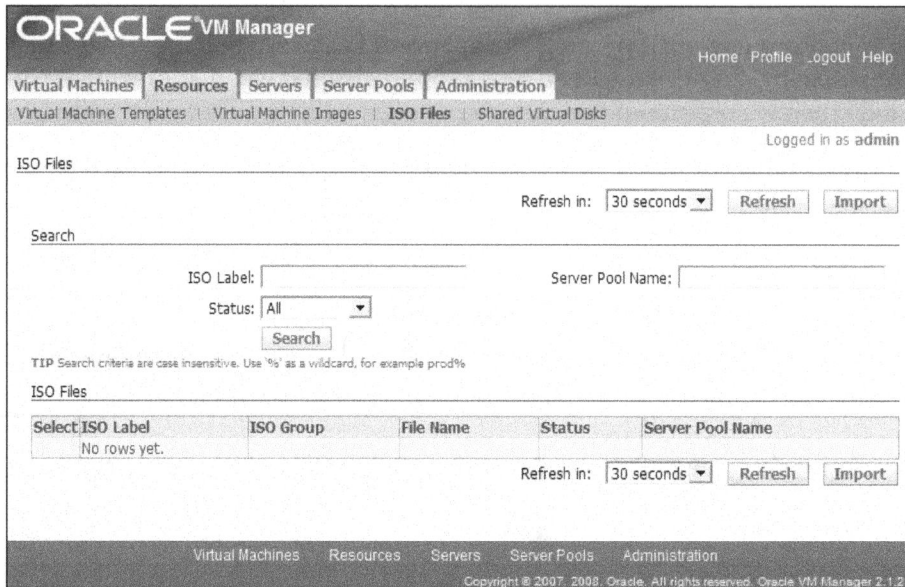

Oracle VM management: Managing Server Pool

A Server Pool is logically an autonomous region that contains one or more physical servers and the dynamic nature of such pool and pools of pools makes what we call an infinite Cloud infrastructure. Currently Oracle has its Cloud portal with Amazon but it is very much viable to have an IntraCloud portal or private Cloud where we can run all sorts of Linux and Windows flavors on our Cloud backbone. It eventually rests on the array of SAN, NAS, or other next generation storage substrate on which the VMs reside.

We must ensure that we have the following prerequisites properly checked before creating the Virtual Machines on our IntraCloud Oracle VM.

- **Oracle VM Servers**: These are available to deploy as Utility Master, Server Master pool, and Virtual Machine Servers.

- **Repositories**: Used for Live Migration or Hot Migration of the VMs and for local storage on the Oracle VM Servers.

- **FQDN/IP address of Oracle VM Servers**: It is better to have the Oracle VM Servers known as OracleVM01.AVASTU.COM and OracleVM02.AVASTU. COM. This way you don't have to bother about the IP changes or infrastructural relocation of the IntraCloud to another location.

- **Oracle VM Agent passwords**: Needed to access the Oracle VM Servers.

Let's now go about exploring the designing process of the Oracle VM. Then we will do the following systematically:

- Creating the Server Pool

- Editing Server Pool information

- Search and retrieval within Server Pool

- Restoring Server Pool

- Enabling HA

- Deleting a Server Pool

However, we can carry out these actions only as a Manager or an Administrator. But first let's take a look at the decisions on what type of Server Pools will suit us the best and what the architectural considerations could be around building your Oracle VM farm.

Architectural decisions around designing Server Pools

This section will not only guide us but also help us make the right architectural decisions around choosing the type of Server Pool for our Data Center. Designing a Data Center brings several challenges. Knowing how to not only architecturally design but also to orchestrate their roles within the substrate with embedded Oracle VM virtualization, helps us get closer to our goal of designing the Data Center or as we call it fondly Oracle VM farm. We will be using the term IntraCloud, which is nothing but the Private Cloud within the confines of your data center.

We obviously need to know how many servers we have and what role they will be playing within the Oracle VM environment. More capacity and more VMs will demand for more Oracle VM Servers in the Server Pool and therefore more hardware will be needed for that specific Server Pool. It is almost like adding more stateless servers to the Server Pool and thus creating an infinite array of servers in the Data Center. Simply said, these Server Pools are scalable and applications that are able to leverage the scalability will benefit the most out of such a scaled out Server Pool.

All that we need is extra or sufficient hardware capacity and we are ready to serve up more on-demand kind of workloads adaptively.

Now, let's take a look at the three kinds of Server Pools that we had mentioned previously in brief.

- **Separate configuration**: Here we will have servers performing a single task, one or more physical host(s) will function as Oracle VM Server, one or more physical servers can act as Utility Servers, and one single hardware box can function as Server Pool Master.

  This is a typical configuration when a large number of servers are required in a large Data Center. We could be looking at Data Centers with several thousands of physical servers. In this way, large capacity can be addressed and the consumption of the 4-core resources such as CPU, Network, RAM, and Storage can be evenly spread across the large substrate of stateless Oracle VM Servers.

  As we can see in the following diagram, the array of stateless Oracle VM Servers and the Utility Servers can be very elastic by adding or pausing capacity on-demand.

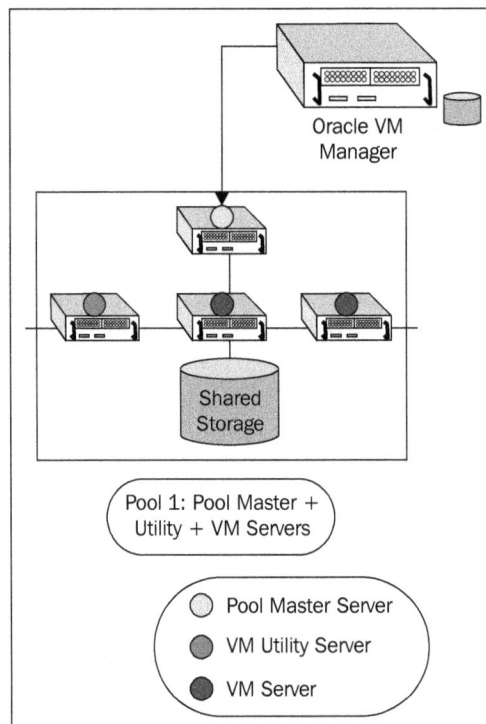

- **All-in-one SMB box**: This is a typical shop with few employees and a handful of servers that is looking to consolidate the current infrastructure with Oracle VM environment. It is a perfect case of building an IntraCloud environment where we can appoint one single server to conduct the following actions. It could be a Server Pool Master and a Utility Server, and also play the role of an Oracle VM Server to host the VMs.

  The ease of management and provisioning can be combined by smaller organizations to effectively optimize their already reduced staff members or **Full Time Employees (FTEs)**.

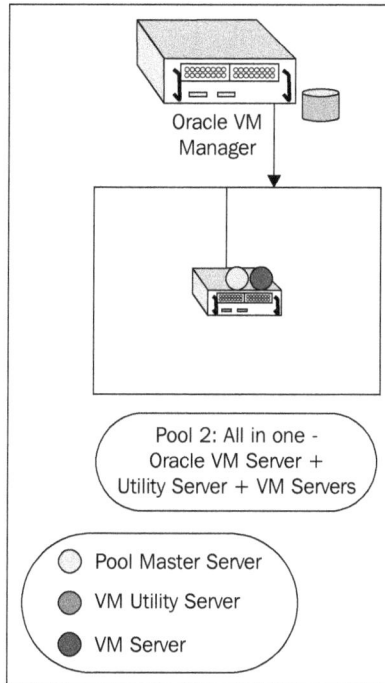

- **Two-in-one SMB+ configuration**: This is a typical configuration where a typical SMB shop, with approximately 20-50 Servers and about 5-8 FTEs, can deploy a single physical host to function as a Server Pool Master and as a Utility Server. The rest of the Servers can be consolidated to much fewer physical hosts, say 4-5 high-end servers, that can function as highly scalable Oracle VM Servers.

This scenario, as mentioned, is a typical IT shop that has moderate workloads and consumption peaks occasionally and can be handled effectively by the scalable Oracle VM Servers. However, note that the Oracle Utility and Server Pool Master Servers are not simply single servers per se. They should be duly backed up and IT shops should consider looking to migrate applications or workloads towards the Cloud infrastructures, whether in-house, internal clouds, or private clouds (external, but yet within the private domains of the outsourcing parties).

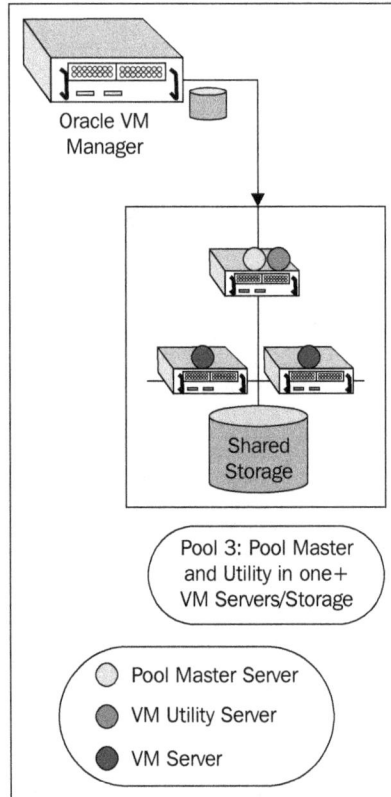

Server pool creation

We have had a quick look at the servers that we can add to the Server Pool but we haven't seen how to create one. So let's go ahead and do that.

To create a Server Pool, click on the **Create Pool** button on the Server Pool's page on the top-right corner of the page.

As mentioned, let's go ahead and login to the Oracle VM Manager portal as administrator, "Admin" and use the wizard to create a Server Pool by using our first Oracle VM Server as the Server Pool Master, the Virtual Machine Server, and the Utility Server.

Create a Server Pool by following the Wizard:

On the welcome page, click on **Next**:

On the **Server Information** page, we will enter the following information:

- **Server Host/IP**: We need to enter our first Oracle VM Server here. We simply fill in the IP address of the VM Server that will act as the Server pool Master, Oracle Utility Server, and also the Virtual Machine Server. We type in our first available IP address which is **172.22.202.112**. Alternatively we can also type in the hostname.domain.com, for instance **OracleVM01.AVASTU.COM**.

- **Server Name**: This name should be unique. We choose the IP address here as we haven't yet added these servers in our DNS.

- **Agent Password**: This password is used to access the Oracle VM Agent which in turn is used for accessing the Server Pool Master.

- **Server Username**: We simply type in user **root** for the Utility Server. However, note that in production systems **root** users are normally locked down. In such a case, we will type in the system admin user name provided to us by the administrator.

- **Server Password**: Type in the password for the Utility Server.

- **Server Location**: This will typically be the location of our server in our Data Center. We have conveniently chosen the **Avastu HQ** as the location.

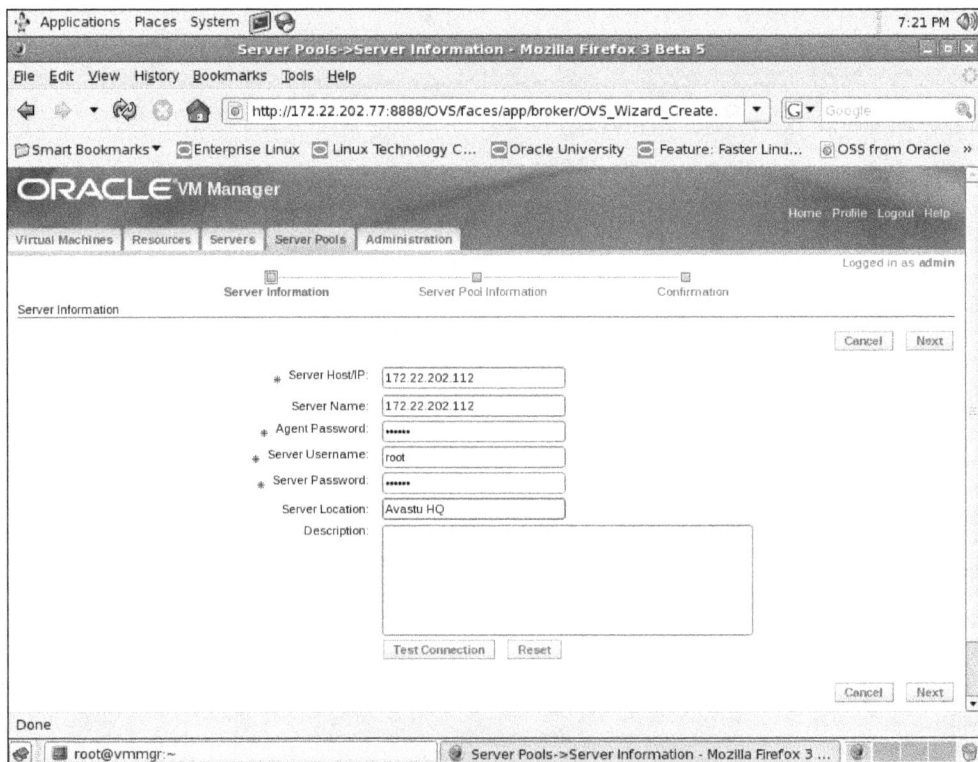

After entering the required values, click on the **Test Connection** button to connect to the specified Oracle VM Server. If you can connect to the server successfully, click **Next** to go to the next page. Confirm the **Server Pool Name**, or we can enter a new name. In this case, we choose **Avastu Pool**. We click on the **Next** button once we are done entering the name of the Server Pool.

In the next window, we confirm the information.

We can check for any incorrect information here. After we click on the **Confirm** button, we will get a confirmation stating the creation of the Server Pool as shown in the following screenshot:

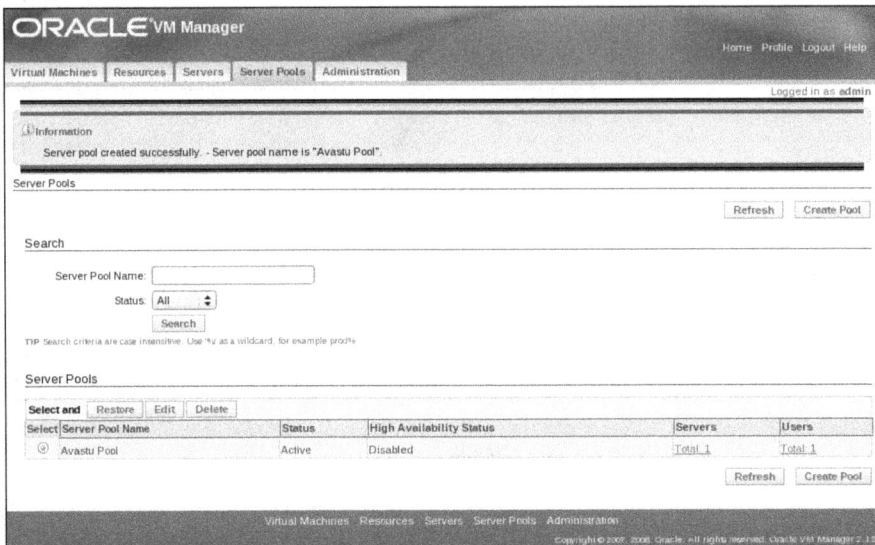

We have thus successfully created a Server Pool. We can further continue to add more servers if we feel the necessity. We go ahead and do that right away. We add another server and we will use it primarily as the Oracle VM Server. Let's do that in a few quick steps right away. After carrying out the typical steps following the wizard, we end up adding another server and our **Servers** pane looks like the following screenshot:

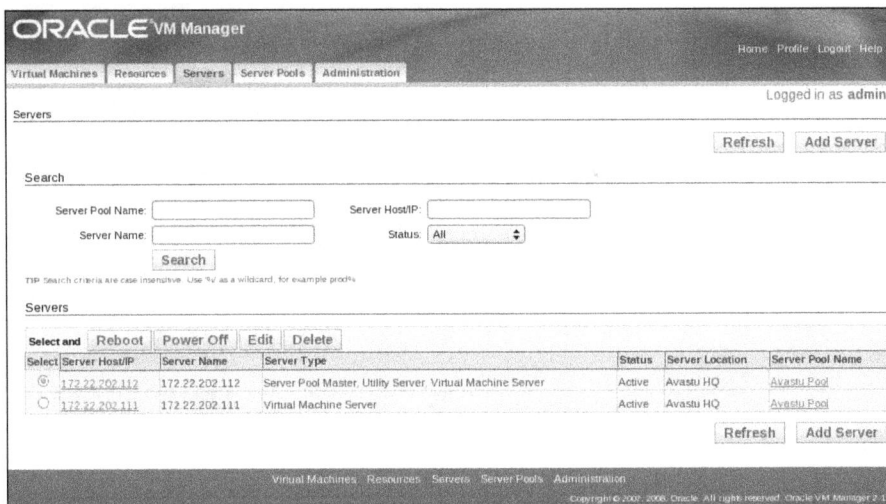

If we haven't assigned any users to this Server Pool, we can click on the **Administration** tab and allow users to this Server Pool. We had already created the user **tarry,** so let's assign him the role to manage this pool:

Edit

Cancel   Apply

General Information

Username: tarry
First Name: Tarry
Last Name: Singh
* Email: ts@avastu.com
* Status: Unlocked
* Role: User

Server Pool

Available Server Pools | Selected Server Pools

Avastu Pool

Move
Move All
Remove
Remove All

Now if we click on the **Server Pools** tab, we can see that there are a total of two users managing this Server Pool.

Server Pools

Select and Restore Edit Delete

Select	Server Pool Name	Status	High Availability Status	Servers	Users
⦿	Avastu Pool	Active	Disabled	Total: 2	Total: 2

When we click on the **Total: 2** link, we can see all of the users and their information. We will see more on Users and Groups later, as we move ahead in this chapter:

Server Pools > Edit User Information for the Server Pool   Logged in as admin
Edit User Information for the Server Pool

Cancel   Apply   OK

Server Pool Name: Avastu Pool

Select and Delete | Add

Select All | Select None

Select	Username	Email	First Name	Last Name	Status
☐	admin	tarry.singh@gmail.com			Unlocked
☐	tarry	ts@avastu.com	Tarry	Singh	Unlocked

Cancel   Apply   OK

Virtual Machines   Resources   Servers   Server Pools   Administration

In general, a Server Pool is named after the Server Pool Master, by default. To enable HA on the Server Pool, we will need all of the Oracle VM Servers in the Server Pool to have the following prerequisites:

- All Oracle VM Servers must use the same shared storage.
- Must be in the same **OCFS (Oracle Cluster File System)** cluster.
- Must have version 2.1.2 or above.
- Must have the same "Cluster root" for heartbeat purposes.
- Cluster root should be mounted on /OVS while all other storage could be located on /OVS/uuid.
- Mount points on /OVS to /etc/ovs/repositories. All storage must be mounted at /OVS and must be maintained in etc/ovs/repositories.
- Cluster root at /OVS must be shared and not local using Oracle's cluster file system OCFS2 on SAN/iSCSI or NFS on NAS. Default local storage is OCFS2 but is not supported with HA.

If all of these pre-requisites are met then you can enable HA.

Click **Next** and we will, depending upon the pre-requisites, get a message if HA is ready or not.

Editing Server Pool information

We can make several changes to the Server Pool such as changing the Server Pool name, managing servers, and adding or removing users. Let's start by editing the Server Pool:

To select our Avastu Pool we can click on the **Servers and Users** link and edit the Servers and Users. Both of those will be tackled later in this chapter.

For instance, if we take a quick look at our Oracle Utility, Server Pool Master, and Oracle VM Server, then we can see all of the properties of the machine here:

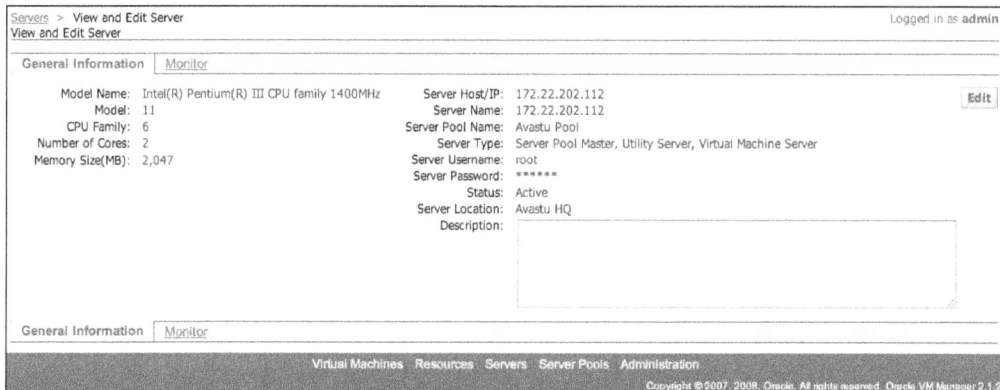

Searching and restoring Server Pools

This too isn't much of a trouble but still a very handy tool when we are in search for machines or other resources that would be available, or even Server Pools if we are in a large Data Center which is firing up Oracle VMs by the second (A sure dream for many Oracle VM enthusiasts, I guess). All we have to do is a wildcard entry appended with a % sign and we will have all of the machines displayed on the screen.

Restoring a Server Pool

If the Server Pool data on the Server Pool Master is damaged or corrupted, we can restore this data by synchronizing it with the data from the Oracle VM Manager database, an Oracle 11g Xpress Database.

To restore, we need to click on the **Restore** button and we are done.

> When you restore a Server Pool, all of the data stored in the Server Pool Master will be deleted, and will be synchronized with the latest information from the Oracle VM Manager database.

HA fundamentals and enabling HA

HA is a crucial part of our Data Center strategy and it is crucial because hardware failure is inevitable. It is important to prevent disruption of service and ensure business continuity. When an Oracle VM Server is restarted the VMs resting on it are either restarted or migrated to other available hosts.

The management of HA is done from the Oracle VM Manager and we must first create clusters of Oracle VM Servers Pools and let Oracle VM Manager manage them. It is not possible to implement HA on an Oracle VM Server alone. We need to enable HA before using it.

Note that HA must be enabled for both the Server Pool and the Virtual Machines. If HA is not enabled on both of these, then it will not work and is essentially disabled. When HA is enabled and when we restart, shutdown, or delete the Oracle VM Server, we will be prompted to migrate the VMs to other hosts. If we don't do it ourselves, the Oracle VM Agent attempts to find the next available Oracle VM Server.

The Oracle VM Server selection by the VM Agent is done by the settings that are available on the Oracle VM Manager. They are:

- **Auto**: As the name suggests, the available preferred server is selected automatically by the Agent.
- **Manual**: Here an available VM Server is selected manually.

Auto is generally the default when creating the pools in case of no preferred VM Server available or the next available server. The VMs are shutdown and restarted when the next Oracle VM Server is made available to the resources.

If the Server Pool Master fails, HA fails as well as for the VM Servers running in that Server Pool. Let's look at different HA scenarios here:

- **We shutdown the VM Server**: We will be prompted to do something with the VMs on that host. These VMs are required to be migrated to the other available hosts. If the VMs are not migrated, then they are restarted on the other hosts. So HA ensures that the VMs do not die with that VM Server.
- **Shutdown VM Server via Command line**: Oracle VM Agent restarts the VMs on the next available server.
- **Oracle VM Server fails**: If the VM Server fails then all of the VMs are restarted on the next available host.
- **VM Server fails and no VM Servers are available**: All running VMs are started the moment an Oracle VM Server is made available to the pool.

Any VMs that are not HA enabled will be cleanly shutdown in case of any of these scenarios. The following figure explains a bit about what happens when an Oracle VM Server fails or is interrupted inadvertently.

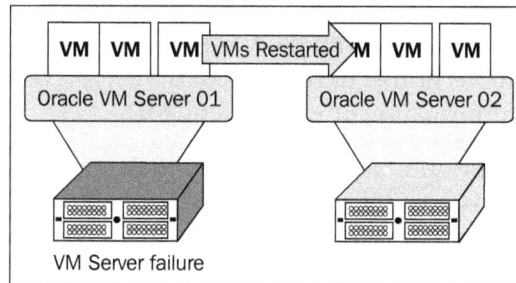

And in the following figure we can see the effect of rebooting or shutting down an Oracle VM Server in the pool. All of the HA-enabled VMs will be live migrated to the other available, preferred or plainly next available Oracle VM Servers.

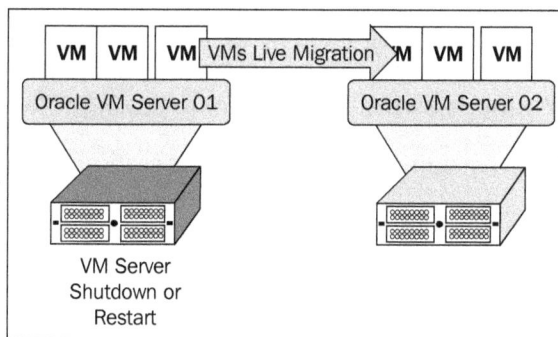

Deleting a Server Pool

Deleting a Server Pool is not that difficult either. All we have to do is go to the Server Pool page and click on the **Delete** button. Upon confirmation, we can select **Remove all the working directories from the server pool** if you have no intention of saving them. Not choosing this option means that the relevant directories and files are kept on the server.

> **Caution:**
> Do make sure that no VMs or any other production activity is being conducted on the Server Pool. Choosing to delete means that we will delete all of the VMs and Servers in that pool!

Oracle VM Management: Managing VM Servers and repositories

There must be at least one physical server in the Server Pool that we have created. There are many things you can do with the VM Servers in the Server Pool such as changing the configurations or role or function of the server, restarting it, shutting it down, monitoring its performance, or even deleting it.

The Server Pools are elastic and can adapt flexibly to the increase or decrease in the demand of workloads. It is possible to expand the pool with Oracle VM Servers and also possible to transfer the workloads or VMs to the VM Servers that are most capable of handling the workloads by throwing the available 4-core resources such as CPU, RAM, storage, and network capacity to the VMs. There is also a possibility of adding more Utility Servers to strengthen the capacity of the Server Pool and thus letting the Server Master handle the workload by assigning the server available to carry out the task. There can only be one Server Pool Master.

However, there are basic tasks to perform before we can add the extra servers to the resource pool such as identifying them by their IP address and see if they are available to fulfill tasks as Oracle VM Server or Server Pool Master. Also we will need the Oracle VM Agent password to add them to the IntraCloud farm.

Let's move on and start managing the servers. In this section, we will cover the following:

- How to add a Server
- Editing Server information
- Restart, shutdown, and deleting Servers

How to add a Server

In order to add Utility Servers or Oracle VM Servers to the array of the Oracle VM environment we will need to carry out the following actions:

1. Click on the **Add Server** link on the Server Page:

2. Search and select a Server Pool and then click **Next**.

3. Enter the necessary information for Oracle VM parameters:

Confirm the information, after testing the connection obviously, and you are done.

However, ensure that the Oracle VM Servers are unique while registering in order to avoid any duplication of IP accounts.

Editing Server information

In order to update information on an existing Oracle VM Server, click on **Edit**.

We can alternatively also click on the **General Information** tab.

General Information	Monitor	
Model Name:	Intel(R) Pentium(R) III CPU family 1400MHz	Server Host/IP: 172.22.202.112
Model:	11	Server Name: 172.22.202.112
CPU Family:	6	Server Pool Name: Avastu Pool
Number of Cores:	2	Server Type: Server Pool Master, Utility Server, Virtual Machine Server
Memory Size(MB):	2,047	Server Username: root
		Server Password: ******
		Status: Active
		Server Location: Avastu HQ
		Description:

To monitor the performance of the Oracle VM Server we can click on the **Monitor** tab, where we get real time access to CPU, memory, and storage usage:

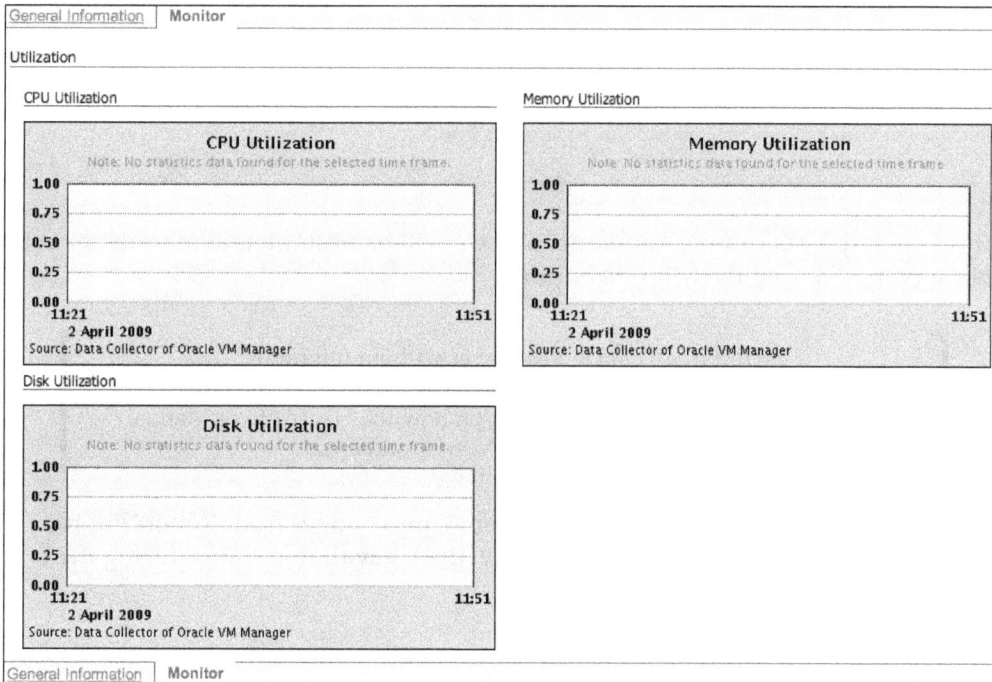

Restart, shutdown, and delete Servers

It is easy to remotely manage the Oracle VM Server. We could be anywhere in the world and we can carry out the restart, shutdown, and (unfortunately) delete the Server operations from a distance.

So, such an opportunity to manage large Oracle IntraCloud farms from a distance is a great deal, given that the ever-increasing need to be able to provide HA and continuous management, we could have teams that could geographically manage the Oracle Cloud Centers 24x7x7 — the last 7 for the continents that will help serve up the infinite demand.

To restart a server, click on the **Reboot** button on the **Servers** page:

⚠ Warning						
The selected server acts as a server pool master. Reboot will cause the related server pool to be temporarily inactive .						

Servers

Refresh in: 30 seconds ⬦ Refresh Cancel Reboot

General Information

Server Host/IP:	172.22.202.112		Server Name:	172.22.202.112
Server Pool Name:	Avastu Pool		Server Type:	Server Pool Master, Utility Server, Virtual Machine Server
Server Username:	root		Server Password:	******
Status:	Active		Server Location:	Avastu HQ

Running Virtual Machine Information

Select	Virtual Machine Name	Size(MB)	Status	High Availability Status	Destination Server
	No rows yet.				

TIP Virtual machines with High Availability enabled will take relevant actions according to High Availability policies.

Refresh in: 30 seconds ⬦ Refresh Cancel Reboot

If there are any VMs running on the servers we will be prompted to migrate them to other servers. Click on the **Migrate** button.

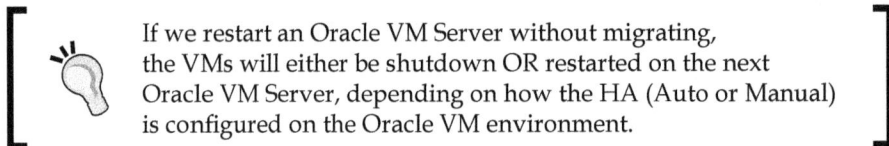

> If we restart an Oracle VM Server without migrating, the VMs will either be shutdown OR restarted on the next Oracle VM Server, depending on how the HA (Auto or Manual) is configured on the Oracle VM environment.

Click on the **Refresh** button so that the server status changes from **Rebooting** to **Active**. The server could temporarily display the **Unavailable** status during the reboot process.

Shutting down the server is also a simple operation. In order to shutdown, carry out the following operations:

Click on the **Power Off** button on the **Server** page:

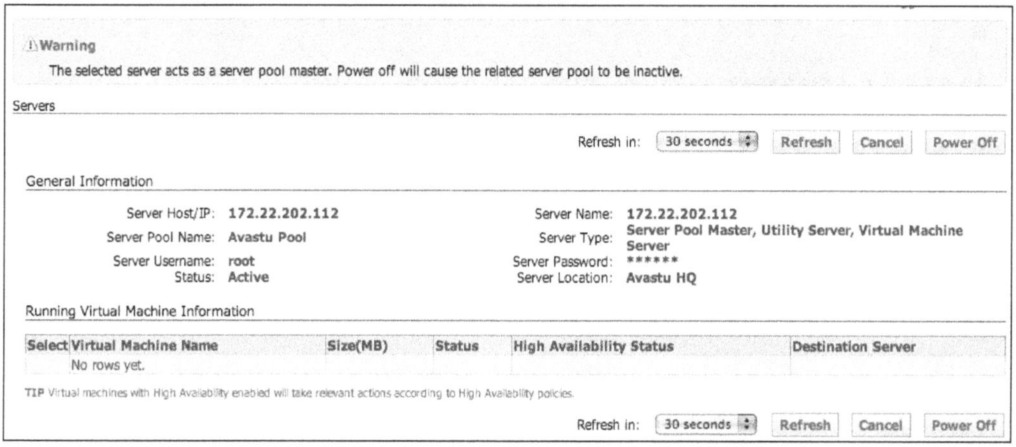

Again we will be prompted to migrate the VMs to other hosts and should we ignore and not carry out this function, the VMs will either be restarted OR shutdown again depending on how the HA is enabled. If it's Auto, then the VMs will look at the preferred VM Server. If it's Manual then it will look for the nearest available VM Server. Should there be no VM Server available, then the VMs will be shutdown and be fired up the moment a VM Server becomes available.

Once again, upon clicking on the **Refresh** button, the status of this server could be validated to **Unreachable** status from the **Shutting Down** status.

Deleting the VM Server can be easily done by just clicking the Server to delete on the **Servers** page and then click on the **Delete** button.

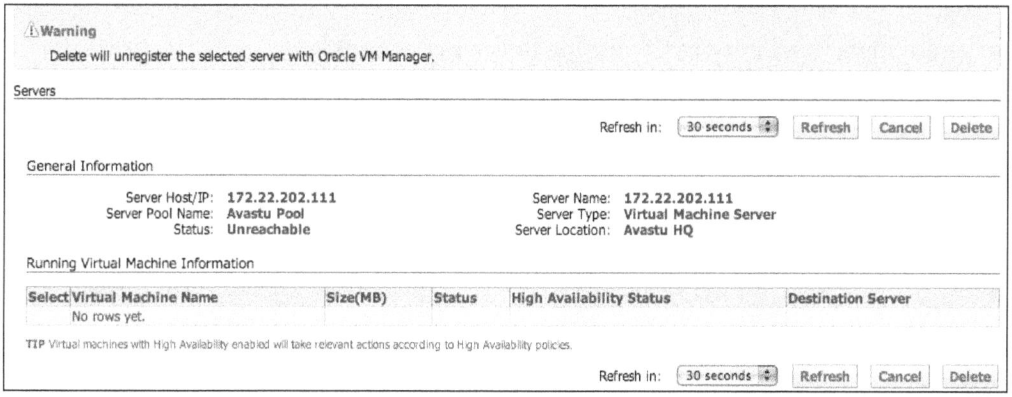

Running VMs on this server will obviously need to be migrated to other VM servers. Select the VMs to migrate and then click on the **Migrate** button.

If we ignore or forget to migrate these VMs to another server, then all of our VMs will be deleted! You have been warned!

About managing repositories

Here we will explore the possibilities of managing Oracle VM repositories.

What are exactly Oracle VM repositories

A repository is used for live migrations of VMs and local storage. They are normally found under:

```
/etc/ovs/repositories
```

Adding or removing the repository can be done by firing up the `ovs-makerepo` script and `ovs-offlinerepo` script respectively.

Oracle VM Agent does a fine job of managing these repositories but feel free to manually manage them with the following commands.

```
/etc/init.d/ovsrepositories [start|stop|restart|reload].
```

To understand more about the format click `--help` to get more information.

Adding and removing a repository

To add a repository use the following command:

```
/usr/lib/ovs/ovs-makerepo source shared description
```

See the upcoming screenshot for the commands and the descriptions of the flags.

For removing a repository carry out the following actions:

```
/usr/lib/ovs/ovs-offlinerepo [-d] uuid source
```

The `ovs-offlinerepo` script unmounts the repository and removes it from the configuration.

```
[root@oravm03 ~]# /usr/lib/ovs/ovs-makerepo --help
usage: /usr/lib/ovs/ovs-makerepo <source> <shared> <description>
        source: block device or nfs path to filesystem
        shared: filesystem shared between hosts?  1 or 0, or @ or C for cluster root (/OVS)
        description: descriptive text to be displayed in manager
[root@oravm03 ~]# /usr/lib/ovs/ovs-offlinerepo --help
usage: /usr/lib/ovs/ovs-offlinerepo [-d] <uuid> <source>
        -d: Remove the storage repo from the configuration
        uuid:   the unique ID of the storage repo source
        source: block device or nfs path to filesystem
[root@oravm03 ~]#
```

User and Group management

Here we will explore how to manage users and groups and will divide the section into the following two parts:

- Managing Users
- Managing Groups

> This function is only available to administrators, so use this role prudently. During the installation of the Oracle VM Manager, a default admin account is created. And with this admin's account we can go about managing the users and groups.

Managing Users

Here it is possible to create new users, delete older or unwanted ones, assign different roles to those users, reset user password, and so on. Let's break it up into a few topics and have a look at it.

- Creating a User
- Viewing or editing details
- Changing a role
- Deleting a User

Creating a User

To create a User, perform the following:

1. On the Administrator's page click **User** tab and then click on the **Create** button:

2. Enter the necessary information such as:
    ° **Username** (avoid using user, manager, and administrator as username)
    ° **Password**
    ° **Retype Password**
    ° **First Name**
    ° **Last Name**
    ° **Valid Email address**

3. We can select the account status, it could either be locked or unlocked and is only accessible when it's unlocked. We can lock an account for security reasons by using the status **Locked**. We can grant the following roles to this newly created user — **User**, **Manager**, or **Administrator**.

4. Then select the Server Pools for this user and also select the group to which this user should belong to.

5. Click on the **Confirm** button to confirm the information and we will get this information:

As we can see in the preceding screenshot this is a plain user and has no groups or servers assigned to it. However this was unlocked and was granted a User role.

Viewing or editing a User

Now let's view the User we just created.

1. Click on the **User** tab on the **Administrator** page:

TIP Search criteria are case insensitive. Use '%' as a wildcard, for example prod%					
User					

Select and	Edit	Delete			
Select	**Details**	**Username**	**Email**	**First Name**	**Last Name**
○	⊞ Show	tarry	ts@avastu.com	Tarry	Singh
⊙	⊞ Show	jack	jdoe@avastu.com	Jack	Doe
○	⊞ Show	admin	tarry.singh@gmail.com		

2. Click on the **Show** link to view the Server Pools that the user is allowed to use:

⊙	⊟ Hide jack	jdoe@avastu.com	Jack	Doe	Unlocked	User
Server Pool:			Group Name:			
• Not Available			• Not Available			

We can now edit account details such as change email address, change account status, and so on.

1. Let's change the User's email address:

General Information

Username:	jack
First Name:	Jack
Last Name:	Doe
* Email:	jdoe@gmail.com
* Status:	Unlocked
* Role:	User

2. Modifying the account status to either locked or unlocked:

General information

Username:	jack
First Name:	Jack
Last Name:	Doe
* Email:	
* Status:	Select Status
	✓ Unlocked
	Locked
* Role:	

3. Changing the role:

4. Next, add the User to the Server Pool:

5. Removing a User from groups or Server Pools:

Changing a User's role

Lets change regular Users' role to Administrator:

1. On the Administrator's page, select the newly created User and click on the **Edit** button.

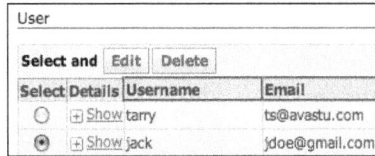

User			
Select and Edit Delete			
Select	**Details**	**Username**	**Email**
○	⊞ Show	tarry	ts@avastu.com
⦿	⊞ Show	jack	jdoe@gmail.com

2. Select the role and click **Apply** to effectively assign the role to the User:

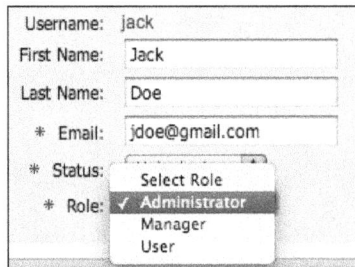

Username:	jack
First Name:	Jack
Last Name:	Doe
* Email:	jdoe@gmail.com
* Status:	Select Role
* Role:	✓ Administrator
	Manager
	User

3. Once applied, we will be presented with the following screen:

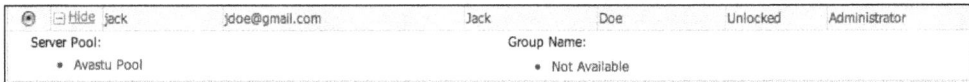

⦿	⊟ Hide jack	jdoe@gmail.com	Jack	Doe	Unlocked	Administrator
Server Pool:			Group Name:			
• Avastu Pool			• Not Available			

Deleting User

To delete a User, we need to do the following on the **Administrator's** page. We can carry out a search and then select the User that we want to delete.

Click on the **Delete** button and confirm the User you want to delete:

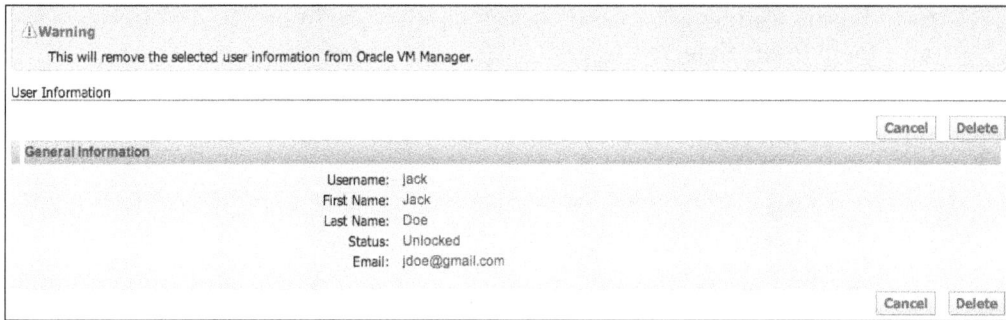

Managing Groups

Creating Groups in Oracle VM Manager is a convenient way to manage the endless number of users. It can be a very exhaustive task to assign privileges to the users and thus it is better to create groups for specific functions. That way we can copy users to those groups implying that all of the users can have the specific group functions that are designed for them.

Now let's go ahead with some Group Management tasks. By default, during installation, two groups are created namely, the "Public Group" and "My Workplace". The Public Group has all public virtual machines available to it and generally all users can deploy and view the VMs in this group. The My Workplace group contains private VMs and only the owners of the VMs can view VMs in this group.

Let's quickly check out some of the tasks within Group Management:

Creating a Group

Perform the following steps to create a Group:

1. On the **Administration** page, click on the **Group** tab.
2. Click on the **Create** button and enter the group name and description:

3. Select users for this group and click the user name in the **Available Users** to add them to the **Selected Users**:

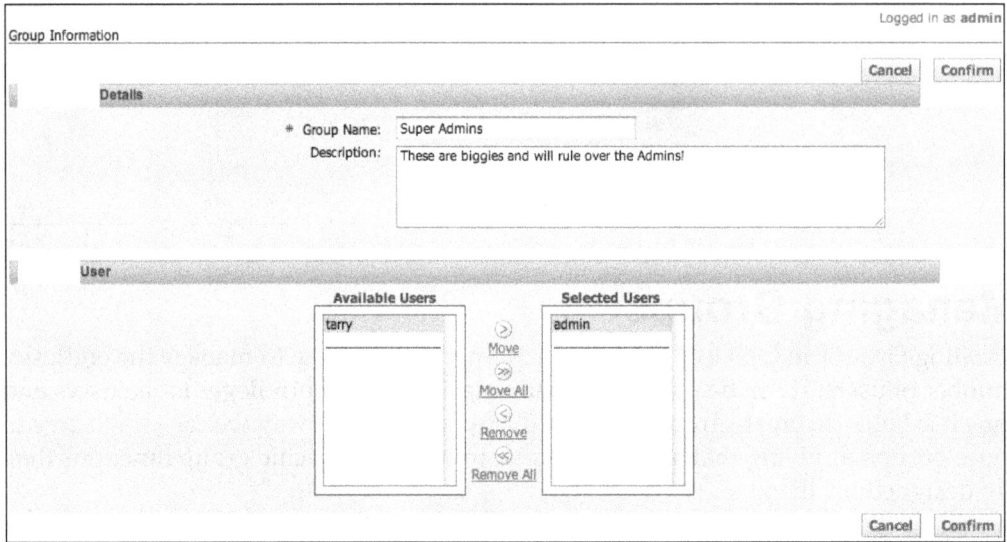

4. Click **Confirm** to see the creation of the groups filled with desired users.

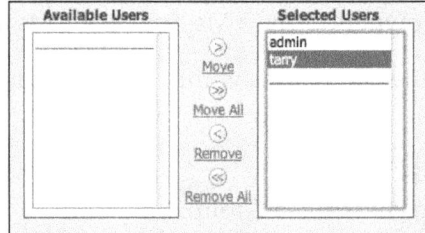

5. And Voila! Our Group has been created.

Adding Users to a Group

Perform the following steps to add users to the group:

1. On the **Administration** page, click on the **User** tab.

2. Select/search users that you want to add to this group and click **Edit**.

3. In the Group's section click the group under **Available Groups** column and move it to the **Selected Groups** column.

4. Click on the **Apply** button to see the changes.

Editing a Group

Carry out the following steps to edit a group:

1. Click on the group that you wish to modify or you can also search for it:

2. Next, click on the **Edit** button to update the information.

Deleting a Group

To delete a group, we need to do the following:

1. On the **Administration** page, select the group that you want to delete and click on the **Delete** button:

2. Confirm the group that you want to delete and the group will be deleted.

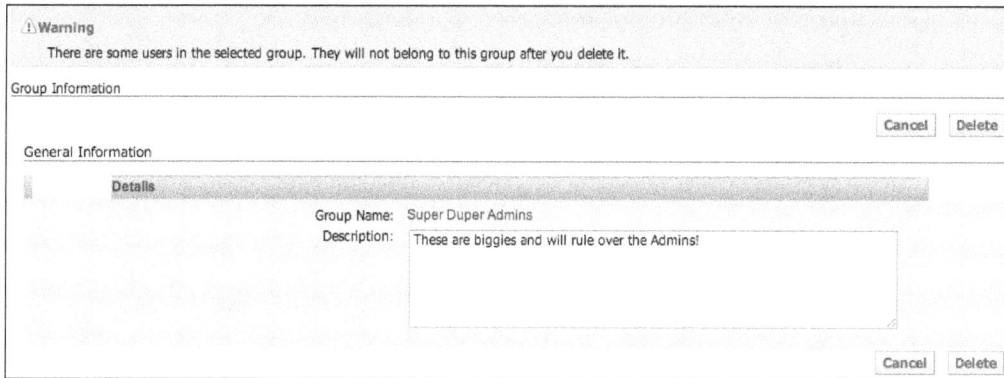

Backing up or restoring Oracle VM Manager

Before uninstalling, moving the VM Server from one location to another OR any other major change we would want to backup the Oracle VM Manager.

Let's learn how to back up and restore the Oracle VM Manager.

Backing up Oracle VM Manager

Ensure that all of our Oracle VM Servers are either running OR powered off. Any machine lost in space, such as VM Servers that are not reporting any state and could be rebooting or simply not communicating with the VM Agent, will not be taken in the backup.

Now to backup the Oracle VM Manager, perform the following steps:

- Log on to Oracle VM Manager as root.
- Back up Oracle VM Manager resources which reside on the VM Servers. They could be VM Images in the /OVS/running_pool, VM templates in /OVS/seed_pool, or ISO files in /OVS/iso_pool. You obviously don't have to do the following if you already have an enterprise backup solution in place in your Data Center.
- Backup Oracle VM Manager data by executing the following:

```
cd /opt/ovs-manager-2.1/bin
sh backup.sh
```

- Here upon the following prompt enter **1** to backup data:

  ```
  Please enter the choice: [1|2]
  1. Back up Oracle VM Manager,
  2. Restore Oracle VM Manager
  ```

- Enter the necessary information such as database account OVS, location of dump, and log file:

  ```
  Back up data now ...
  Please enter the password for database account 'OVS':
  Please specify the path for dump file?
  Please specify the path for log file?
  ```

And voila the Oracle VM Manager backup in created. A backup is worthless if it cannot be restored, so let's try restoring a recently created backup.

Restoring Oracle VM Manager

Execute the following steps to restore a backup of Oracle VM Manager:

- Log in to the VM Manager Server as root.

- Save or copy Oracle VM Manager resources into the following directories: VM images in /OVS/running_pool, VM templates in /OVS/seed_pool, and ISO files in /OVS/iso_pool.

- Restore backup by initiating the following commands:

  ```
  cd /opt/ovs-manager-2.1/bin
  sh backup.sh
  Please enter the choice: [1|2]
  1. Back up Oracle VM Manager,
  2. Restore Oracle VM Manager
  Enter [2] to restore data:
  ```

- Again, provide the database user OVS information and the location of the dump and log files:

  ```
  Please enter the password for database account 'SYS':
  Please enter the password for database account 'OVS':
  Please specify the path for dump file?
  Please specify the path for log file?
  ```

And we have just restored our Oracle VM Manager from its latest backup. Also we can login to the Oracle VM Manager and quickly scan the environment to check if it is the same as we would have expected.

Enabling secure access to Oracle VM Manager

When accessing the Oracle VM Manager remotely in the Cloud, we will have to ensure that we are providing a totally secure connection to our remote, geographically dispersed workforce.

To do so, we will have to provide a secure HTTP access to the Oracle VM Manager portal. We will be doing this by enabling the SSL with standalone OC4J. We need to ensure that we set the PATH to be included in the JDK bin directory.

Let's get going and create a certificate:

Carry out the following commands in the OC4J directory:

```
/opt/oc4j/java/jdk1.5.0_11/bin/keytool -genkey -keyalg "RSA"
-keystore keystore_file -storepass password -validity days
```

In this command, the **keystore** option sets the file name where the keys are stored, the **storepass** option sets the password for the keystore, and the **validity** option sets the number of days of the certificate's validity.

For example, enter:

```
  [root@vmmgr ~]# /opt/oc4j/java/jdk1.5.0_11/bin/keytool -genkey
  -keyalg "RSA" -keystore sslfile -storepass securep@ss -validity 365
What is your first and last name?
  [Unknown]:  Tarry Singh
What is the name of your organizational unit?
  [Unknown]:  Avastu
What is the name of your organization?
  [Unknown]:  Avastu
What is the name of your City or Locality?
  [Unknown]:  Your State
What is the name of your State or Province?
  [Unknown]:  Your Province
What is the two-letter country code for this unit?
  [Unknown]:  NL
```

```
Is CN=Tarry Singh, OU=Avastu, O=Avastu, L=Assen, ST=Drenthe, C=NL
correct?

  [no]:  yes

Enter key password for <mykey>
          (RETURN if same as keystore password):
[root@vmmgr ~]#
```

Answering these questions on prompt helps us in creating the new keystore file, which is an `sslfile`. It is stored in the current directory. We can go to that directory and check if the file is created there.

Our next step is to configure the OC4J. We can do this by first creating a `secure-web-site.xml` file. If we don't have one created in the OC4J config directory, we should make one by either copying the existing `http-web-site.xml` or `default-web-site.xml` and then renaming it to `secure-web-site.xml`.

Let's go ahead and edit the `secure-web-site.xml` file.

We can configure OC4J by performing the following steps:

1. Create `secure-web-site.xml`.

    If you do not have the `secure-web-site.xml` file in the OC4J configuration directory, create one by copying the existing `http-web-site.xml`, or `default-web-site.xml`. Rename the copy to `secure-web-site.xml`.

    This how what XML file looks like before editing:

```xml
<?xml version="1.0"?>

<web-site xmlns:xsi="http://www.w3.org/2001/XMLSchema-instance"
xsi:noNamespaceSchemaLocation="http://xmlns.oracle.com/oracleas/schema/web-site-10_0.xsd"
port="8888" display-name="OC4J 10g (10.1.3) Default Web Site" schema-major-version="10" schema-
minor-version="0" >
        <default-web-app application="default" name="defaultWebApp" />
        <web-app application="system" name="dms0" root="/dmsoc4j" />
        <web-app application="system" name="dms0" root="/dms0" />
        <web-app application="system" name="JMXSoapAdapter-web" root="/JMXSoapAdapter" />
        <web-app application="default" name="jmsrouter_web" load-on-startup="true" root="/
jmsrouter" />
        <web-app application="javasso" name="javasso-web" root="/jsso" />
        <web-app application="ascontrol" name="ascontrol" load-on-startup="true" root="/em" ohs-
routing="false" />
        <web-app application="datatags" name="webapp" load-on-startup="true" root="/webapp" />
        <web-app application="OVS" name="webapp1" load-on-startup="true" root="/OVS" />
        <web-app application="help" name="ohw-ovs-help" load-on-startup="true" root="/help" />
        <access-log path="../log/default-web-access.log" split="day" />
</web-site>
```

2. Edit the `secure-web-site.xml` file.

    Edit the web site element as follows:

    ```
    <web-site xmlns:xsi="http://www.w3.org/2001/XMLSchema-instance"
    ```

```
xsi:noNamespaceSchemaLocation="http://xmlns.example.com/example/
schema/web-site-10_0.xsd" port="4443" display-name="OC4J
10g (10.1.3) Default Web Site" schema-major-version="10"
schema-minor-version="0" secure="true"> <ssl-config
keystore="sslfile" keystore-password="securep@ss"/>
```

In the web site element we added `secure = "true"`. We added the keystore name (`sslfile`) and our password (`securep@ss`) to this file which we used when creating the `sslfile`. We use a different port here just for safety purposes.

Save the file with the changes.

3. Now go ahead and edit the `server.xml` file and uncomment the following:

    ```
    <web-site path="./secure-web-site.xml" />
    ```

Save the changes.

This is how it will look:

```
start="true" />
        <application name="javasso" path="../../home/applications/javasso.ear"
parent="default" start="false" />
        <application name="ascontrol" path="../../home/applications/ascontrol.ear"
parent="system" start="true" />
        <application name="OVS" path="../applications/OVS.ear" parent="default"
start="true" />
        <application name="help" path="../applications/help.ear" parent="default"
start="true" />
        <global-web-app-config path="global-web-application.xml" />
        <transaction-manager-config path="transaction-manager.xml" />
        <web-site default="true" path="../default-web-site.xml" />
        <web-site path="./secure-web-site.xml"/>
        <cluster  id="32462998320650" />
</application-server>
```

4. Restart the OC4J daemon by clicking on the **Restart** button in the following OC4Jadmin pane:

OC4J: home

Page Refreshed Apr 3, 2009 1:38:43 AM CEST • View Data | Manual Refresh |

| Home | Applications | Web Services | Performance | Administration |

General

Stop | Restart

Status **Up**
Start Time **Apr 2, 2009 9:33:27 PM CEST**
Version **10.1.3.2.0**
Oracle Home **/opt/oc4j**
Host **vmmgr.avastu.com**
Virtual Machines **1**
Notifications **0**

Response and Load

1.5
1.0
0.5
0.0
1
0

11:32 AM 12:00 12:40 01:20
2 April

■ Request Processing Time (seconds)
□ Requests per second

5. We need to click on the **Yes** button when prompted with the following warning and our `/opt/OC4J` would get restarted.

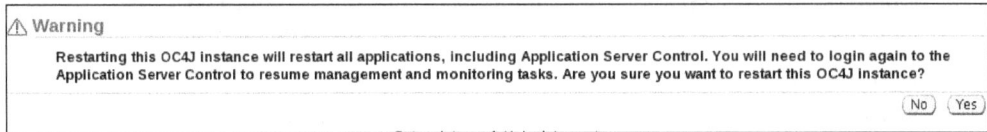

⚠ Warning

Restarting this OC4J instance will restart all applications, including Application Server Control. You will need to login again to the Application Server Control to resume management and monitoring tasks. Are you sure you want to restart this OC4J instance?

(No) (Yes)

Now it will also start listening to the SSL port that we assigned, namely 4443.

OC4J will listen for both SSL request (port 4443 in the example) and non-SSL requests (port 8888).

Now all we need is to go ahead and log on to the HTTPS site by typing `https:vmmgr:4443/OVS`. We can use the non-SSL site as well and always switch them on or off by editing them in the `server.xml` file.

Summary

As we can clearly see, the management of Oracle VM Servers and the VMs, which we will see in the upcoming chapters, is rather crucial to managing our Oracle cloud farm. Fortunately, the feature-rich portal of Oracle is well equipped to manage an Oracle VM farm with its VMs.

In the next two chapters, we will see more on Virtual Machines or Guests as they are also called. We have divided the chapters into two parts so we don't end up filling up all of the information in one chapter alone.

5
Managing Virtual Machines with Oracle VM Manager: Part 1

In our last chapter we saw the Oracle VM Manager management. Here we will do some detailed installation, importing and all Virtual Machine activities. This chapter is a part of the three chapters where we talk about virtual machines within the Oracle VM environment.

In this chapter, we will be discussing the following:

- Oracle VM management with VM Manager
- Overview of VMs and lifecycle management
- General VM management tasks such as starting, shutdown, delete, re-provision, and edit configuration of the VMs

We will explore through **suspending** and **resuming** the VM in this chapter and then continue with the rest in the upcoming chapters.

Clearly Oracle is slowly and gradually working towards the commoditization path of Virtual Infrastructure with Xen, where features such as HA, on-demand usage, and real-time Smart Metering make perfect sense for a Cloud computing model.

Managing and provisioning Virtual Machines or Workloads within an elastic data center will be the key to the Cloud environments.

We will cover several interesting and exciting parts of the VM creation using virt-install and manual creation in the Appendix, but assuming that we have setup our Oracle VM environment, we can move on with VM management from the Oracle VM Manager itself.

Oracle VM management with Oracle VM Manager

A **VM** (**Virtual Machine**) is a guest operating system or a guest appliance that contains an operating system, be it Linux or Windows. A VM can also come pre-packaged with applications which we normally call a **Virtual Appliance**. These appliances run on an array of Oracle VM Servers fully packaged with the applications.

Following are the pre-requisites for creating VMs on Oracle VM:

- Oracle VM Manager installed and running.
- Server Pool must be present.
- Minimum of one VM Server must be running.
- ISO files or Template images must be available for either creating VMs from scratch OR provisioning the VMs from those provided templates. We have downloaded a full Oracle VM Appliance package, which is packaged with Oracle 11g Version 1 Database Server and one template with Oracle EL 5.

Now, let's get started with the overview of what Virtual Machines are and also note that as a mere user one can only manage VMs created by him or her. If we want to manage VMs Server Pool-wide then we must have a Manager or Administrator role. For the sake of simplicity we will use the Administrator's role as we go about managing VMs in our Oracle IntraCloud VM farm.

General overview and lifecycle management of Virtual Machines

Here we will cover several sections such as the types and statuses of VMs, Lifecycle management of VMs and viewing the error information of the VMs.

Types of Virtual Machines

There are several types of VMs within the Oracle VM farm. The VMs are generally created from a security standpoint and are secure and private unless chosen otherwise. A VM by default is created as a Private VM. VMs can be shared among Administrators and such VMs are called Shared VMs. Finally VMs that are accessible to all users are called Public VMs. These VMs can be deployed by all users. These types of VMs are further elaborated:

Private VMs

VMs are created private by default and can be managed by only those who created them. Administrators and Managers are however authorized to manage VMs across the Server Pool. All Private VMs are created in a default group called **My Workspace.**

Shared VMs

Sharing the VMs with members of some specific groups is also possible. Once we create our shared **Super Admin** group, we can deploy the VMs while granting access to members of other groups who we can allow access the VMs as well. Such a VM can be called a **Shared VM**.

Public Virtual Machine

VMs that are shared among all users are called **Public Virtual Machines** or **Public VMs**. Anyone can view and deploy public VMs.

However, note that people with User and Manager Roles may have some restrictions for accessing VMs across a Server Pool. They are namely not allowed to carry out Administrative tasks on the VMs which are assigned to the Administrators only.

Let's see the Virtual Machine statuses.

Status of Virtual Machines

There are several statuses of Virtual Machines such as creating, initializing and running, pausing and unpausing, suspending and resuming, shutdown and powered off, saving, cloning, migrating, and error. We can easily identify where our Virtual Machines are and what status they currently have.

Let's have a closer look at these statuses:

- **Creating VMs**: Here is the clear indication that the VM is still being created. One must wait before using a VM with this status.

- **Running VMs**: When you start a VM, its status changes from powered off to initializing and also when periodically refreshing the pane by clicking on the **Refresh** button. Normally the pane is refreshed every 30 seconds — we can see that the VM achieves a running status. We can now log in and carry out all necessary actions on the VM.

- **Pausing and Unpausing VMs**: A running VM's status changes to pause when we want to stop the VM temporarily. Refreshing the status of the VM periodically, we can see that it is now paused. When we want to start re-using the VM, the machine is unpaused and upon refreshing the status, we can see that the VM is in running state again and is free to be accessed.

- **Suspending and Resuming VMs**: After choosing to suspend the VM we will see that its status changes from running to suspending. Again periodically refreshing the VM will give the suspended status. Similarly upon resuming the VM, the status changes from suspended to resuming. Periodically refreshing the page gives the status change from resuming to running.

- **Shutting down or Powering off a VM**: After we shutdown a VM, its status changes from shutting down to powered off. Now we can perform tasks such as cloning, cold migrating, and deploying on that VM.

- **Cloning or Migrating**: When a VM is being cloned, its status is changed to cloning. After the cloning is complete, we can see the status change back from cloning to powered off. When we need to perform a live migration, we will see the status change from running to migrating. Refreshing periodically the status changes back to running, once the live migration is completed.

- **Error status**: A VM will display an error status if there are some errors with the Virtual Machine and it cannot be used. There are several ways to resolve the errors in the VMs and we'll try to tackle them in later chapters.

Now let's take a look at the schematic view of the Lifecycle Management of Virtual Machines.

Lifecycle management of a Virtual Machine

Typically, the lifecycle of a VM could be seen as follows. I see this as a fundamental step towards the supply chain mechanism of the workloads. I have often called this process as **SCVMM (Supply Chain Virtual Machine Management)**, where the birth and the death of a VM are fully orchestrated. This orchestration will consist of:

- Creating the VM
- Starting the VM
- Using it optimally (shutting down, pausing, and so on)
- Decommissioning or deleting a VM

Obviously it may vary as there are different ways of giving birth to a VM or workloads. So if we have created a VM from a template, the lifecycle would look like this:

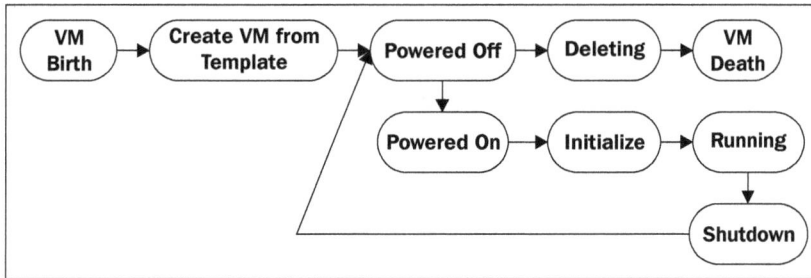

The lifecycle of a VM created from an installation media would look like this:

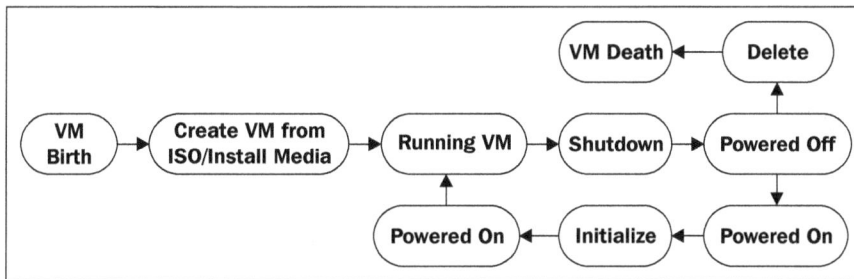

The following activities can be conducted during the life of a VM:

- **Error viewing**: General trouble-shooting and viewing.

- **Stopping, Pausing, or Unpausing a VM**: We can do this in order to stop a VM temporarily.

- **Suspending and Resuming a VM**: This way we can move the memory to disk or any other action that we may want to carry out.

- **Other VM Management functions**: Obviously there are many other actions you can carry out with the VM Manager console such as changing the configurations of the VM by adding extra memory, network cards, or storage. Deploying VMs and/or sharing can also take place by moving VM from one share pool to another. We can also create multiple copies of the VMs, a process we call cloning, thus creating a baseline provisioning practice for our VMs. We could also save VMs as a template and move the VMs around in our Oracle VM farm by either cold or hot migration capabilities within our data center. And naturally to decommission VMs, we will delete it from our active farm by maintaining its template on idle Cloud storage.

Viewing VM errors

All of the errors are logged in the Oracle VM Manager and the errors provide us with crucial information to eventually troubleshoot our VMs and/or applications associated within the VMs.

The error log contains the following information: operation, operation details, start time, and status. In a later chapter, we will take a look at troubleshooting, to do some basic investigation on the Oracle VM errors.

Error logs

We need to click on the **Log** link in the following screenshot:

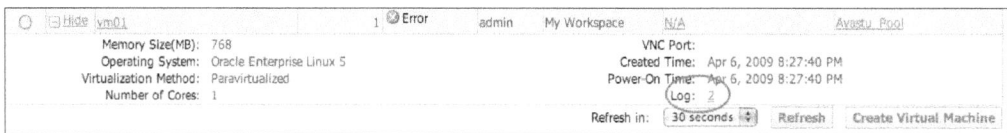

Upon clicking, we can clearly see the entire log as shown in the following screenshot:

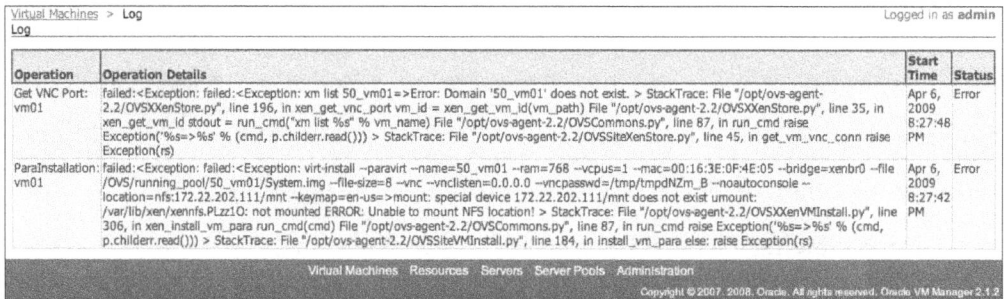

General overview of VM management

Here we will explore general activities in VM management such as creating VMs, starting and shutting down, and so on. Let's get started by creating the VMs.

Creating a Virtual Machine

We can create a VM in several ways. We can copy a VM, clone a VM, create a VM from a template, and install a VM from installation media such as ISO files and importing a VM from a Virtual Appliance market place. It is also possible to do VMcasting, a method where we can use RSS 2.0 technologies to stream VMs in order to export or import them to or from our data center locations. We can also convert a VM from several industry formats such as VMware template and VMware machines.

So we can create VMs quickly using any of the following methods:

- **From VM templates**: There are several conditions for importing the VMs but all we have to do is to fire up a new VM using the already imported templates in our OVS server.

- **Using installation media**: If we have the ISO files, we can create a VM using the installation media. We can then eventually load the ISO files to create Guest Operating Systems or VMs.

- **Using Preboot eXecution Environment (PXE boot)**: We can create a network bootable VM, if we wish to fire up a VM to boot from PXE over network.

- **Import VMs from marketplace**: We can either import VMs from an HTTP or FTP site or from public libraries. Here you can also convert VMware VMs to Oracle VMs.

- **P2V**: We can always use P2V to convert VMs from other formats such as Linux machines to Oracle VM format.

Obviously, we shouldn't forget to create a Server Pool that contains the Oracle VM Server. If we don't have it then we will not be able to provide VMs across the Oracle VM environment.

Let us also see a schematic view of creating VMs. This will give a better and visual understanding of creating VMs within an Oracle VM environment.

Schematic view of VM creation

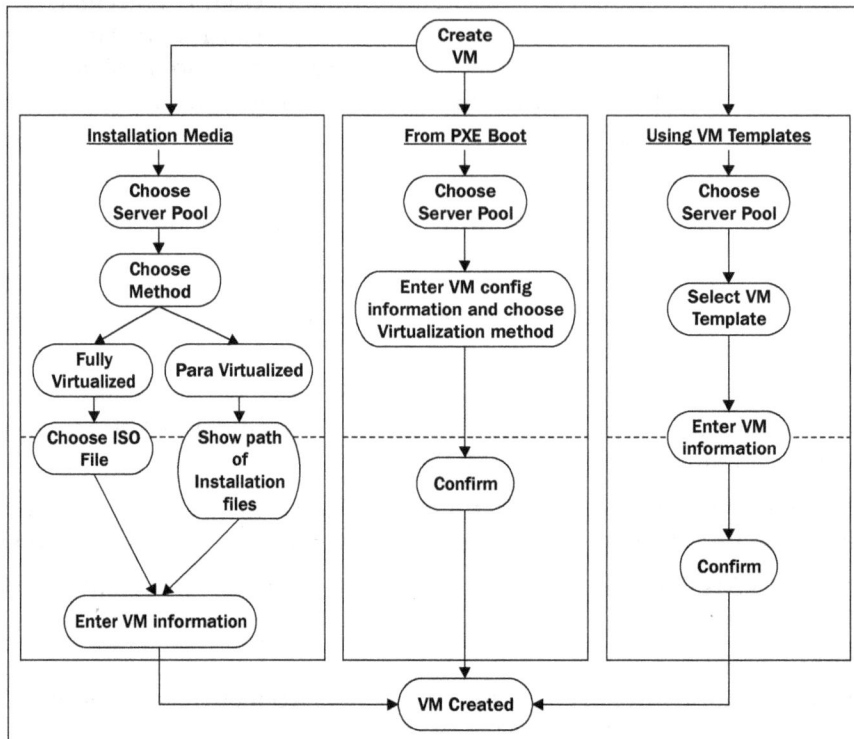

Now let's quickly try to demonstrate what we just visualized in the illustration here by creating the VM using a VM template

Creating a new Virtual Machine based on a Virtual Machine template

A VM template is actually a pre-packaged and hopefully a fully tested and working image of a VM. This will typically contain an OS, a basic configuration of a VM such as pre-configured memory, CPU and NICs, and finally also a fully packaged application stack. We have downloaded and stored two VM templates in our OVS root folder on one of our Oracle VM Servers. One of them is a OS (Oracle EL5U2, which we can use to eventually create templates of our own) while the other one is a OS+Apps (Oracle EL5U2+Oracle Enterprise DB 11GR1, which we can use to deploy our Oracle DB and even fire up our Oracle RAC on a typical Oracle IntraCloud environment). As we can see, we can go wild with our fantasies while playing with the application stack not needing to worry anymore about how and who will do the installation. It all comes pre-packaged with the Oracle VM templates. We need to carry out the following steps in order to create the new VM.

1. Let's import the Oracle VM template first:

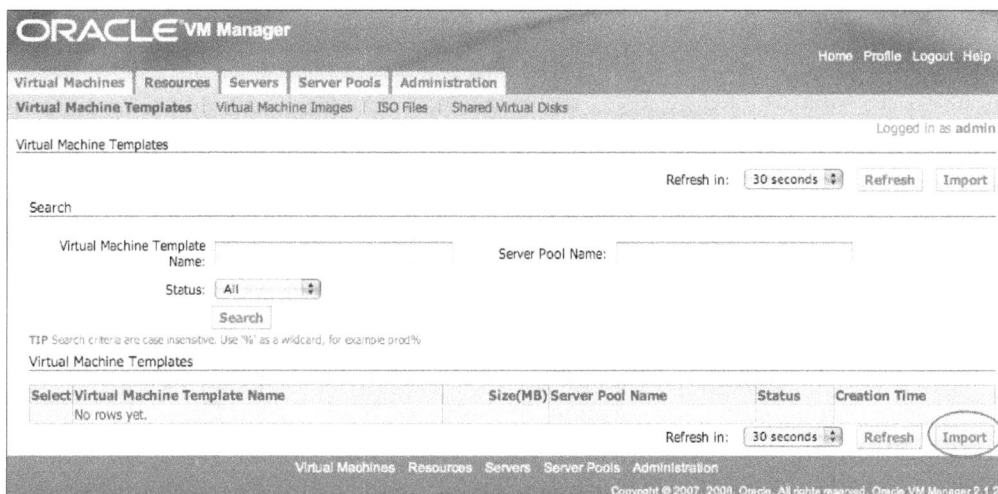

2. Choose the **Select from Server Pool (Discover and register)** option and click **Next**:

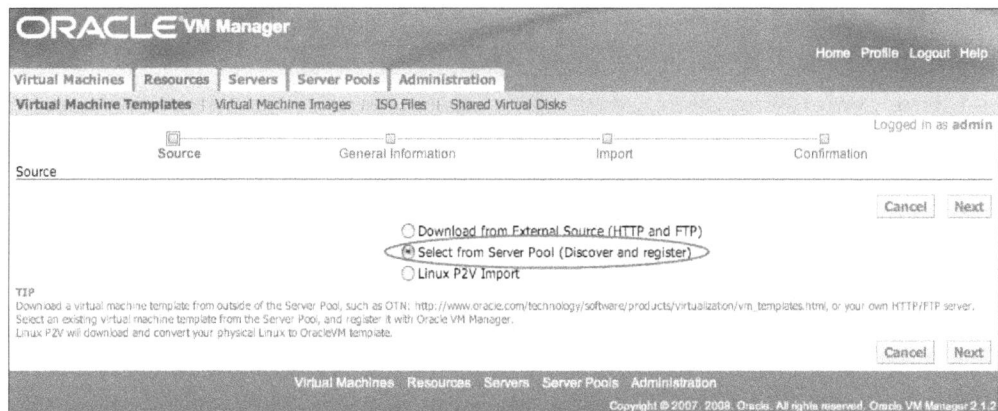

3. We go ahead and select **Pool2** as our Server Pool:

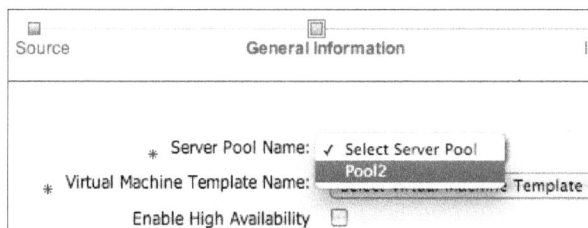

4. For the **Virtual Machine Template Name** option we choose the name for our VM template as **OVM_ELU2_X86_64_PVM_4G**:

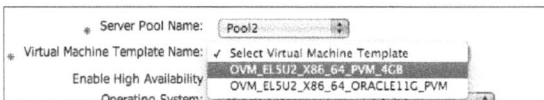

5. We also check the **Enable High Availability** option:

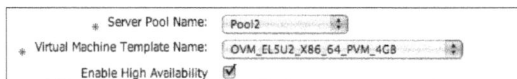

6. For the **Operating System** option, we choose the appropriate option, as per our system configuration. In this case I have chosen **Oracle Enterprise Linux 5 64-bit**:

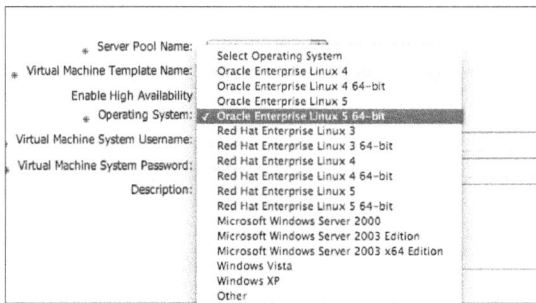

7. After choosing the Virtual Machine system username and password, we click on the **Next** button to go ahead:

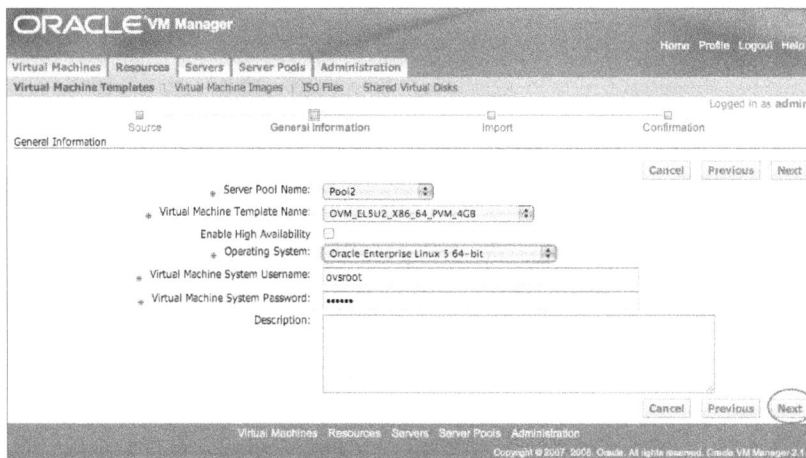

8. After checking the chosen information we click on the **Confirm** button:

9. As seen in the screenshot, the template appears under the Virtual Machine Template page under the **Resources** tab; it only needs to get approved:

10. Now all we have to do is to approve the VM template. We can do that by clicking on the **Approve** button:

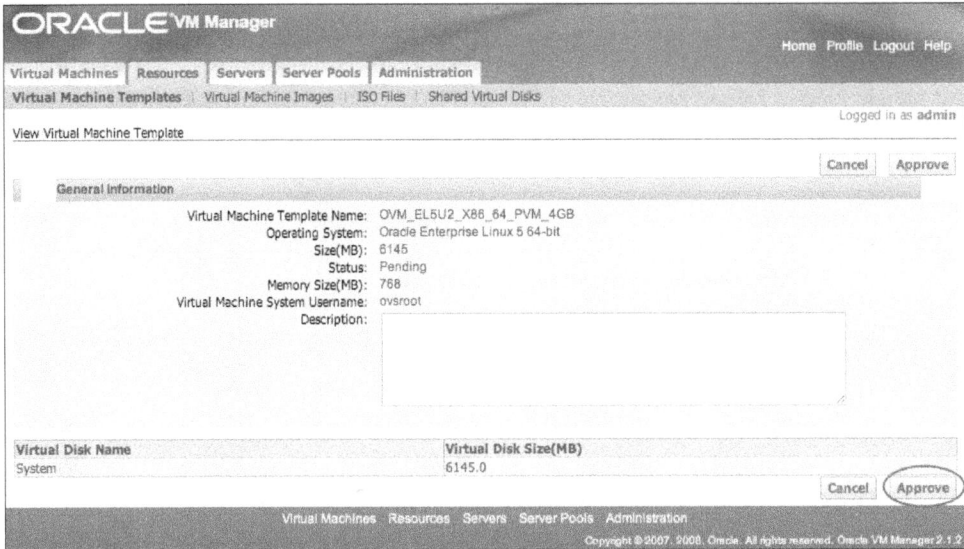

11. Now that the VM template is approved we can see the **Approve** button is now grayed out:

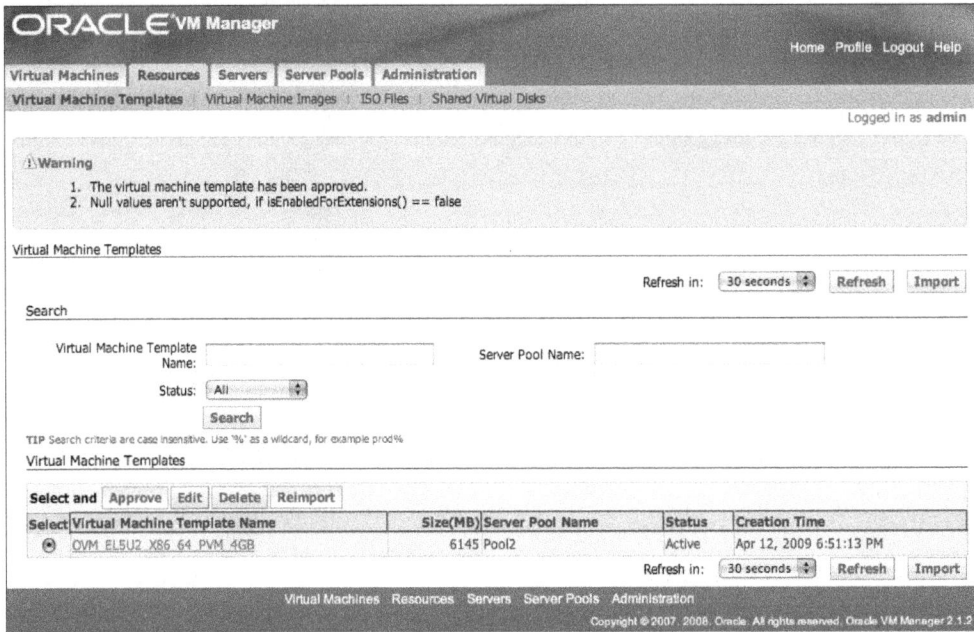

12. Our next step is to activate this template for immediate use. So we click on **Edit** and then change the status from **Inactive** to **Active**:

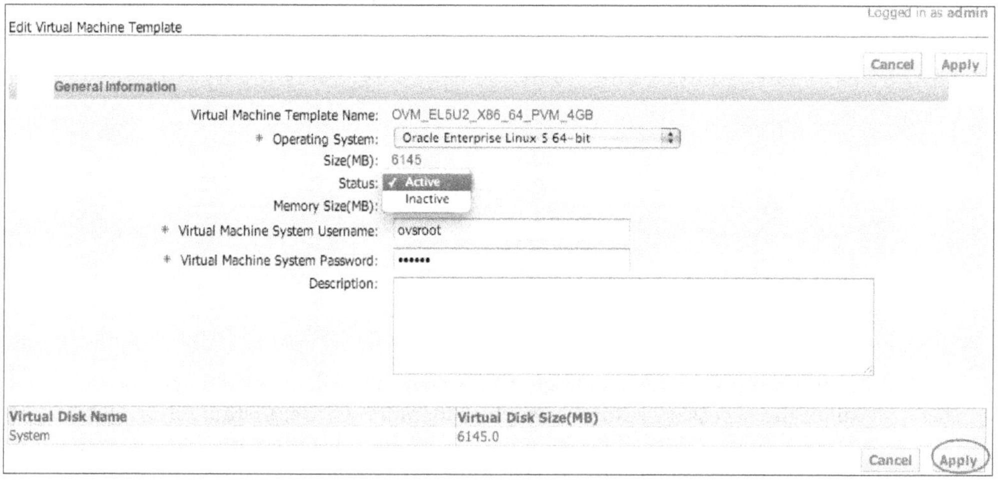

Importing a new Virtual Machine based on a Virtual Machine template

Now that we have imported our Oracle VM image, it's time to create a VM by cloning the template. The VM will then get all of the attributes and configurations of the VM template.

1. Select the **Create virtual machine based on virtual machine template** option and click on **Next** button:

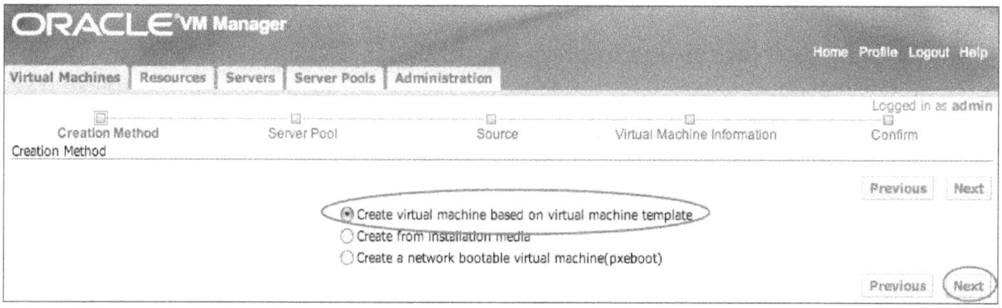

2. Choose the Server Pool where the VM is to be located and then select the preferred server:

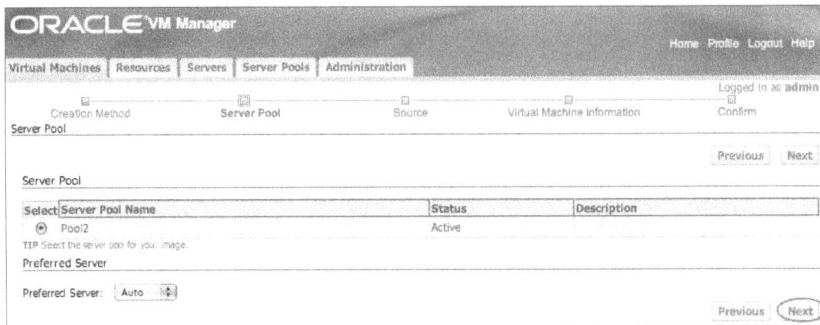

> A preferred server is an Oracle VM Server that will eventually provide all of the necessary resources such as memory, CPUs, Virtual NICs, and storage to the VMs. Choosing multiple preferred servers might be a better option since the VM starts it and looks at an Oracle VM Server that has the most available resources, while choosing one preferred server would imply that the VM will always start on that specific VM Server.
>
> There are two ways of selecting a Virtual Machine Server for the VM:
>
> **Auto**: Here we don't have to choose any preferred server(s) as the Oracle VM automatically assigns a VM with the maximum available resources such as memory, CPU, bandwidths, and so on; the VM runs on this VM Server.
>
> **Manual**: Here you select one or multiple VM servers as preferred server(s). The VM then starts based on the choices you have made. If it's a single server, it's stuck to it and if it was multiple servers then it gets to pick the one with most resources available.

3. Click on the **Next** button to proceed and then select a template on which the VM is based.

4. We can take a closer look at the template that we have imported by clicking on the **Show** tab:

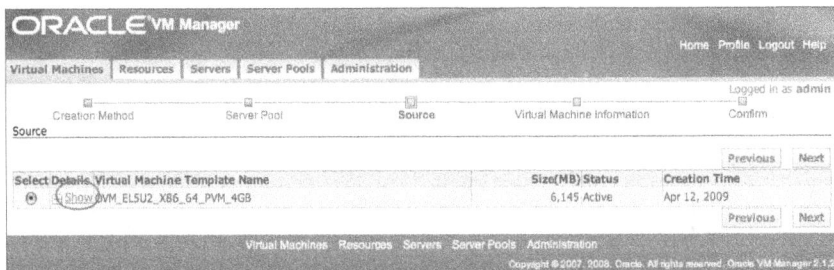

5. After clicking on the **Next** button, enter the VM's name and set a console password to it. The name will be used as the name of the directory under / OVS/running_pool where the files associated with the VMs will be located. Enabling HA is a possibility as well and for that we will have to select the **Enable HA** option. We need to check if our Oracle VM environment is HA ready as discussed in the previous chapter.

					Previous	Next
Select	Details	Virtual Machine Template Name		Size(MB) Status	Creation Time	
⦿	⊟ Hide	OVM_EL5U2_X86_64_PVM_4GB		6,145 Active	Apr 12, 2009	
		Memory Size(MB): 768		Virtualization Method: Paravirtualized		
		Operating System: Oracle Enterprise Linux 5 64-bit		Number of Cores: 1.0		
					Previous	Next

6. We can also click on the **Add row** option to add more virtual NICs (by default they are named VIF0, VIF1, VIF2). We can always rename them as per our uniform data center standards.

7. Select a bridge for Virtual NICs so that the VMs can interact with the external network. An Oracle VM automatically attaches a random MAC address to the virtual NIC.

> The number of bridges is same as the number of physical adapters on that Oracle VM Server. For instance, if you add three virtual NICs to a VM and all of them were to be bridged, then they would be called xenbr0, xenbr1, xenbr2 for the physical interfaces eth0, eth1, and eth2 respectively. Also, note that you can set a maximum of three virtual NICs to a VM during creation and after the VM is created you can increase that to eight interfaces.

8. Click on the **Next** button to get to the next page:

9. We can however choose up to eight NICs and not more:

10. We reset the NIC information back to one for the sake of simplicity:

11. Confirm the VM information:

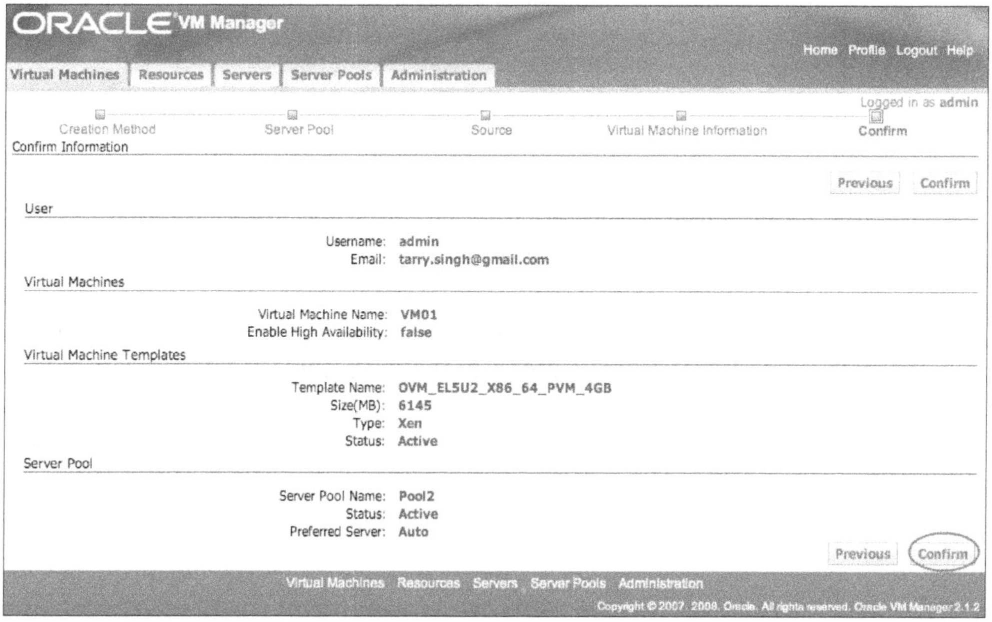

Upon confirming the information, we will be presented with the following screen:

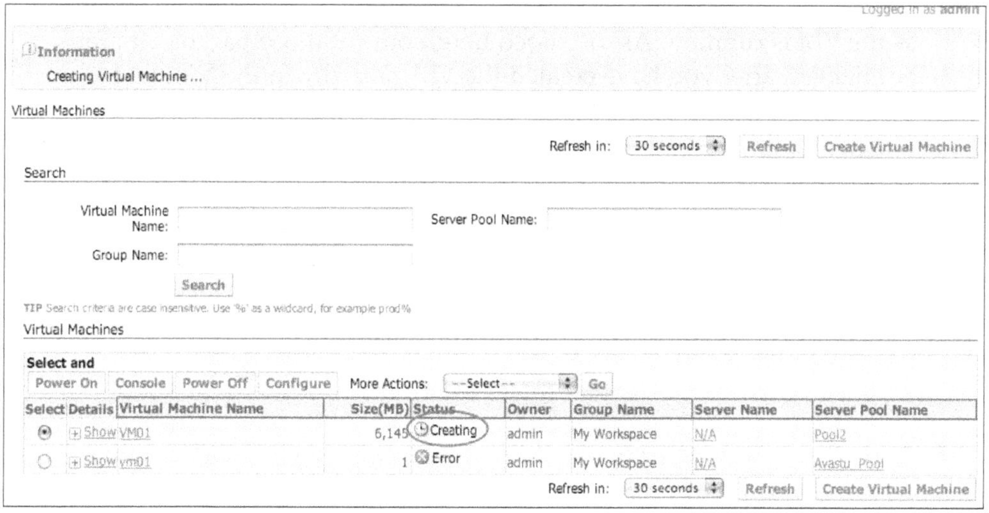

12. A closer look at the status:

	More Actions:	--Select--	⬍	Go
Size(MB)	**Status**	**Owner**	**Grou**	
6,145	⟳ Creating	admin	My W	
1	⊗ Error	admin	My W	

13. VM creation, depending on how big and complex the setup is, can take time. Do click on the **Refresh** button occasionally to set the status of your VM from being created to being **Powered Off**. In case of an error you can look into the error logs as described previously in this chapter.

14. Now you can power on the VM and log into the VM. By default this VM will be private and only you have access to this VM. You can always change this at a later stage as discussed previously.

15. Click on the **Show** button to check the status of the configuration of the VM:

Virtual Machines								
Select and								
Power On	Console	Power Off	Configure	More Actions:	--Select-- ⬍	Go		
Select	**Details**	**Virtual Machine Name**		**Size(MB)**	**Status**	**Owner**	**Group Name**	**Server Name**	**Server Pool Name**
⦿	⊟Hide	VM01		6,145	⬛ Powered Off	admin	My Workspace	N/A	Pool2

Memory Size(MB): 768   VNC Port:
Operating System: Oracle Enterprise Linux 5 64-bit   Created Time: Apr 12, 2009 6:57:05 PM
Virtualization Method: Paravirtualized   Power-On Time: Apr 12, 2009 6:57:05 PM
Number of Cores: 1   Log: 0

16. As you can see there are several things that you are not allowed to change as the VM is running. As discussed here, some of those parameters can be changed after you have created the VM, shut down the VM, and reconfigured the settings as required.

17. Power on the VM after you have done the necessary changes and you will see the status initializing:

Select and						
Power On	Console	Power Off	Configure	More Actions:	--Select-- ⬍	G
Select	**Details**	**Virtual Machine Name**		**Size(MB)**	**Status**	**Owner**	**Gr**
⦿	⊞Show	VM01		6,145	⟳ Initializing	admin	My
◯	⊞Show	vm01		1	⊗ Error	admin	My
						Refresh i

18. And after refreshing a couple of times, you can see your VM running:

Select and							
Power On	Console	Power Off	Configure	More Actions:	--Select--	⬥	Go
Select	Details	Virtual Machine Name		Size(MB)	Status	Owner	Group Nar
⦿	⊞ Show	VM01		6,145	▷ Running	admin	My Worksp:
○	⊞ Show	vm01		1	⊗ Error	admin	My Worksp:
							Refresh in:

VM creation using installation media such as ISO files

If you have ISO files, then you can create a VM from the installation media and configure the VM as per your requirements. So let's try to quickly create a VM from an ISO file.

1. Select **Create from installation media** and click **Next** on the Virtual Machine page:

2. Select the Server Pool. In this case, we select **Pool2** where the VM will be parked and also select the VM Server.

3. You can obviously choose **Auto** to assign the VM Server—in such a case the Oracle VM will choose for the VM to run on. Alternatively, you can also choose **Manual** to specify a server or servers that the VM can run on.

4. Click **Next** to proceed and select the **Virtualized Method** as per
   your requirement:

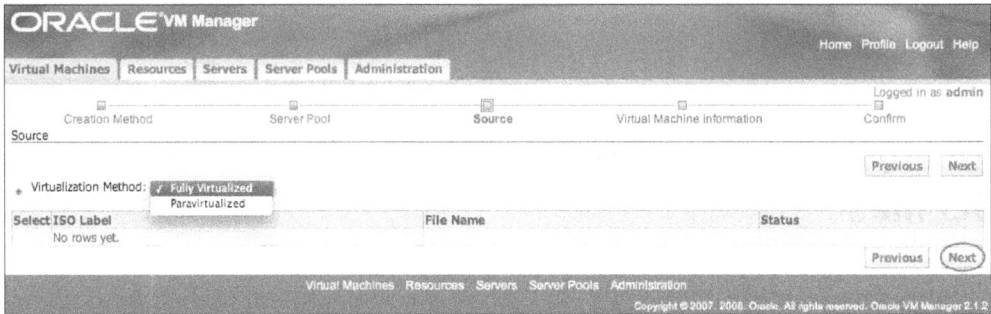

There is a clear and distinct difference between a Fully Virtualized and
Paravirtualized. Let's take a look at them both.

Fully virtualized or HVM

Here we can select the ISO file from the list. We can go about installing from multiple
ISO files as we would have done while physically installing an OS. In a fully
virtualized mode which is often known as **HVM (Hardware Virtualized Machine)**,
the unmodified guest OS runs on the VM. The fully virtualized VM traps and
emulates all instruction sets. Every single I/O and hardware instruction is passed to
the VM, thus isolating it totally from the hypervisor underneath.

To have a HVM or fully virtualized mode, you MUST have hardware that
either supports Intel-**VT (Virtualization Technology)**, previously known as
Vanderpool Technology, or an AMD processor with a **SVM (Secure Virtual Machine)**
extension, also called AMD-V on the hardware. For more information please refer to
`http://wiki.xensource.com/xenwiki/HVM_Compatible_Processors`. We need to
make sure that virtualization is enabled in the BIOS. If our hardware does not support
it then we can only create **PVMs** or (**ParaVirtualized Virtual Machines**), for which, all
HVM capabilities will be disallowed.

If we are to create a PVM then we must mount all of the ISO files to a single mount
point on the VM Server. We can achieve this by executing the following commands:

```
# mkdir mount-point
# mount -o loop,ro cd1.iso mount-point
```

In the **Resource Location** field, enter the full path of the mount point. HTTP, FTP, and NFS are supported. We can enter the NFS path as follows:

```
nfs:myhost:/mnt
```

Paravirtualized

In a Paravirtualized method, the Guest OS or the VM's Operating System is modified before it is installed on a VM. A typical PVM performs better than the HVM machine or a fully virtualized machine because it does not need to trap privileged instructions and all of the encapsulation is time consuming and can have a negative performance impact. The full IA32 instruction set capturing or trapping inhibits performance and a VM running in a PVM mode can run at near native speeds.

Continuing with our installation process:

5.   Enter the following information for the VM:

- **Virtual Machine Name**: This VM name must be unique within the server pool. This name will also be seen in the Oracle VM Server's directory /OVS/running_pool. This is where all of the VM files will be located.

- **Number of Cores**: The amount of cores that we will need for our VM, the Guest OS, and the applications that rest on the VM. Maximum number of cores that are allowed for VMs are 32. Choose the number of cores carefully by first checking if the added capacity will help the VM's performance or not.

> Note that if the sum of all the cores on all of the VMs exceeds the physical CPU then the VMs will get a fraction of that CPU time. So if we have 8 physical CPUs on the Oracle VM Server and sum of cores on all of the VMs is, say 16, then each VM gets 8/16 or 50% of the CPU time, if all of the cores are being fully utilized at the same time.

- **Keyboard Layout**: Choose an appropriate keyboard, for instance U.S. English, and so on.

- **Memory Size(MB)**: Select the memory size in MBs. It is advisable to allocate a minimum of 256 MB of memory to the VMs. Do take into consideration the following factors:
    - Applications that may be required to run on the VMs—check the requirements of these applications and what amount of memory they may need
    - Memory already allocated within the pool to other VMs—we cannot just go ahead and allocate memory that compromises the performance of the VMs in the pool
    - Applications that may be required to be installed at a later stage

- **Virtual Disk Size(MB) or Storage Requirements**: Allocate at least 1024 MB or 1 GB of disk size to the VMs. We need to take into account the following factors:
    - Allocate enough disk space and create enough disks per VM based on the consumption that we expect the VMs to use.
    - Allocate enough disk space for VMs that might be needed for existing applications. For instance, if we have an Oracle DB which is 11G then we will be allocating storage based on current and future storage demand.
    - Also, we need to take into account the total shared storage that may be available within the server pool.

- **Console Password**: Enter the console password for the VM. This password will be the one that we will need to connect to the VM by using VNC. Enter the password twice correctly.

- **Enable High Availability**: We can enable HA if that is a requirement. We need to always check with our server pool if it is HA aware.

6. Now you can click on the **Next** button and you will be presented with the following screenshot:

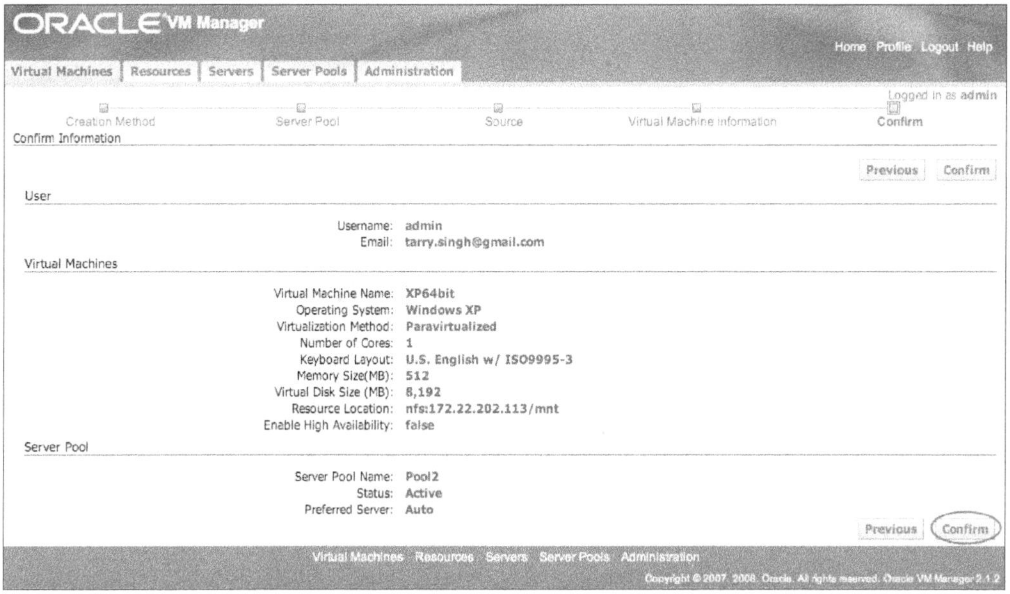

7. Here, you need to confirm all of the details. After you are done checking these, click on the **Confirm** button to proceed further. Next, you can click on the **Add Row** button to add two or more virtual NICs. A maximum of three virtual NICs is possible during creation and a max of eight virtual NICs is possible when you have created the VM.

8. Click on the **Next** button to move on to next page and create the VM. It will be stopped after a successful creation:

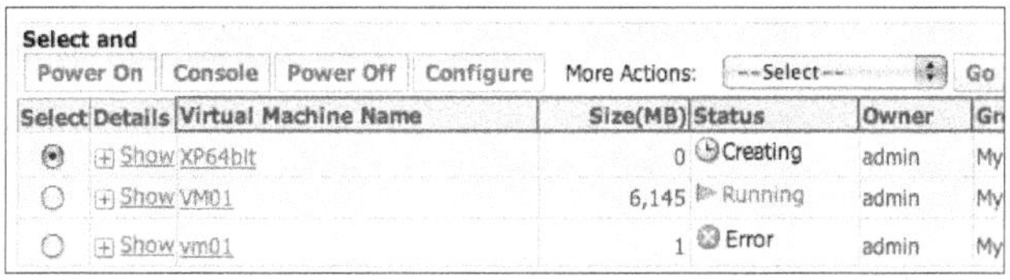

9. As the VMs are being created, you will have to click on the **Refresh** button to see the real status of your VM. As mentioned earlier, your VM will be private and you are the only one who may have access to it.

10. Click on the **Show** button to edit the details of your VM:

Creating a network bootable (PXE boot) Virtual Machine

If we don't have VM templates or ISO files, then we can create a network bootable VM (PXE boot) with minimum configuration and alter our settings as per requirements. We can always start the VM through PXE over the network to install the Guest OS at a later stage.

Let's get started by creating the PXE bootable VM:

1. Select the **Create a network bootable virtual machine (pxeboot)** option:

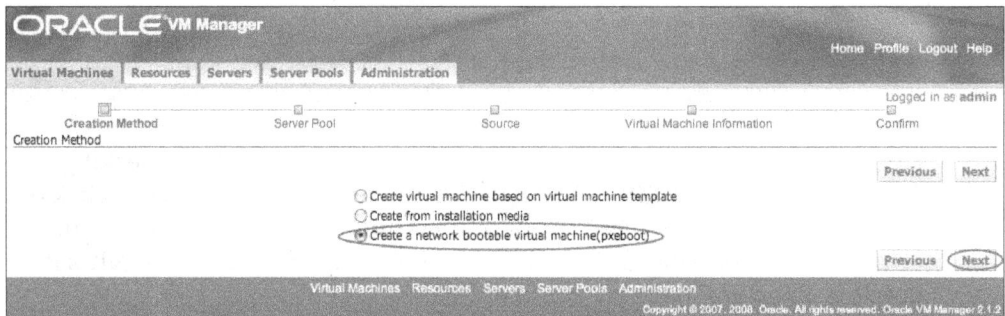

2. Click **Next** and select a Server Pool. We select by default our **Pool2** and you can select the VM Server that you want the VM to run on:

3. Select **Auto** if you wish Oracle VM to arrange the **Preferred Server** for you automatically.

4. Next, enter the **Virtualization Method**, for instance **Paravirtualized**. In this case we choose **HVM** or **Fully Virtualized**:

5. As you can see in the preceding screenshot, we picked up three VIFs or Virtual NICs and customized our OS to be Red Hat Enterprise Linux 5, as our Centos 5.2 is based on RHEL 5 source, 1 Virtual CPU, 512 MB RAM, and 8 GB disk.

> Choose the VM name and Virtualization Method (PVM or HVM) as mentioned above. Choose your NIV cards, Disk size, and other options carefully. Make sure there are no spaces between the VM names otherwise you will get an exception.
>
> Also, before you start the VM, you will need to configure the DHCP and TFTP server first and then start the VM remotely over the network to install the Guest OS. By default the network bootable VM starts through PXE.

6. Creating your VM will take a few seconds:

7. Click **Show** to check the details of the VM. Some parameters such as Virtual NICs cannot be changed during the VM creation but at a later stage they can be reconfigured.

Powering on and powering off a VM

On the Virtual Machines page, click on the **Power On** tab to start a VM:

Click **Refresh** a couple of times to have the VM change its status from **Starting** to **Running**:

Powering Off works in the same way. Once again go to the Virtual Machines page and click **Power Off**.

Click **Refresh** periodically to change the status from **Powering Off** to **Powered Off**.

For VMs that are HA-enabled, powering off a VM will trigger the VM to be restarted elsewhere in the Server Pool, so you will have to turn it off to eventually shut it down as per requirement.

Pausing and unpausing a Virtual Machine

When we pause a virtual machine, it allows us to save the virtual machine at a certain processing point, and resume it again quickly.

A typical example of what I most commonly come across is large banking organizations that have a typical **ROBO (Remote Office Branch Office)** environment. At branch offices a typical operation may require pausing—customers are registering and the bank employee needs to go ahead with another machine, which they typically do and then come back to their machine to resume the operation. I have implemented Citrix and VMware **VDI (Virtual Desktop Infrastructure)** there and the demand for pausing an operation to resume it at a later stage was one of the important requirements.

What actually happens is that the VM's state is saved and the operations will not be restarted as long as they do not have any sort of persistent communications with other VMs or computers. The resources allocated to the VM such as the CPU, VIFs, memory, and so on remain the same. The only difference is that the VM processes are not scheduled by the Oracle VM Server to run on any CPU. If this VM was in front of the DMZ such as a web server, then it will appear to be shutdown.

You can only pause and unpause a running VM.

Now let's pause a running VM.

1. Click on the **Virtual Machines** tab and then on the Virtual Machines page, select the VM that you want to pause. Use the drop-down menu and click on the **Pause** button and next click on **Go**:

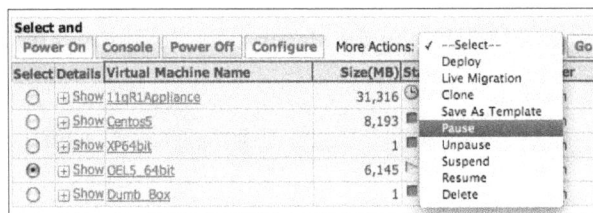

2. You will be asked to confirm the message:

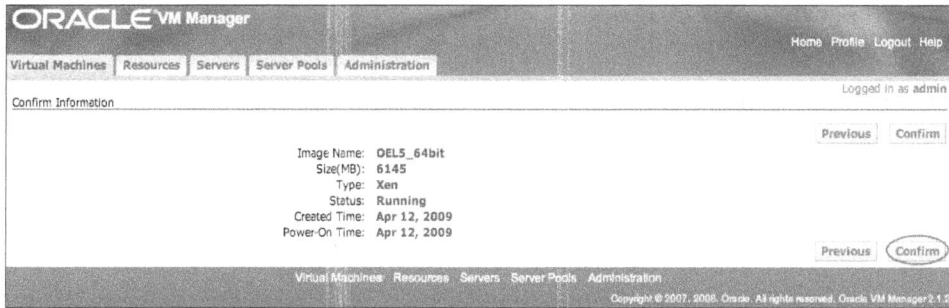

3. And the machine begins to pause:

4. By clicking on the **Refresh** button or waiting for a couple of seconds we can now see that our VM is paused:

5. To unpause the machine, do the same action. Go to the dropdown menu, click **Resume**, and then **Go**:

6. You get to **Confirm** again:

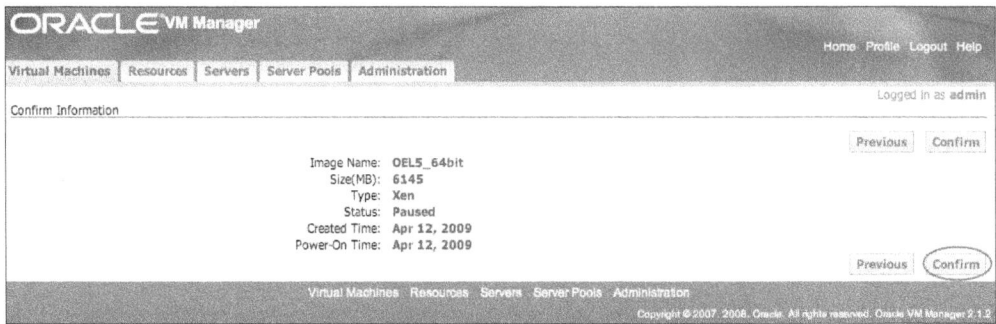

ORACLE VM Manager

Home Profile Logout Help

| Virtual Machines | Resources | Servers | Server Pools | Administration |

Logged in as **admin**

Confirm Information

Previous   Confirm

Image Name: OEL5_64bit
Size(MB): 6145
Type: Xen
Status: Paused
Created Time: Apr 12, 2009
Power-On Time: Apr 12, 2009

Previous   Confirm

Virtual Machines Resources Servers Server Pools Administration

Copyright © 2007, 2008, Oracle. All rights reserved. Oracle VM Manager 2.1.2

7. And the VM begins to **Resume**:

Select	Details	Virtual Machine Name	Size(MB)	Status	Owner
⦿	⊞ Show	11gR1Appliance	31,316	■ Powered Off	admin
○	⊞ Show	Centos5	8,193	■ Powered Off	admin
○	⊞ Show	XP64bit	1	■ Powered Off	admin
○	⊞ Show	OEL5_64bit	6,145	↻ Unpausing	admin
○	⊞ Show	Dumb_Box	1	■ Powered Off	admin

8. You can click **Refresh** to see the status or wait for a few seconds and your VM is up and available for transactions as usual.

Select and

| Power On | Console | Power Off | Configure | More Actions: | --Select-- |

Select	Details	Virtual Machine Name	Size(MB)	Status	O
⦿	⊞ Show	11gR1Appliance	31,316	■ Powered Off	ad
○	⊞ Show	Centos5	8,193	■ Powered Off	ad
○	⊞ Show	XP64bit	1	■ Powered Off	ad
○	⊞ Show	OEL5_64bit	6,145	▶ Running	ad
○	⊞ Show	Dumb_Box	1	■ Powered Off	ad

Suspending and resuming a Virtual Machine

You can use the **Suspend** function to perform tasks such as backing up the VM's contents and restoring them immediately. This is done by saving the information of the VM on the disk so that you can restore the information quickly to the similar state elsewhere.

Since the VM is no longer running and all of the memory allocated to this VM can be released and be used for other Virtual Machines. When a VM is suspended all other resources such as NICs won't be available either. And again you can only suspend a running machine.

So let's start suspending our VM by clicking on **Suspend** that you can see on the Virtual Machines' page. Click **Go** immediately after doing so:

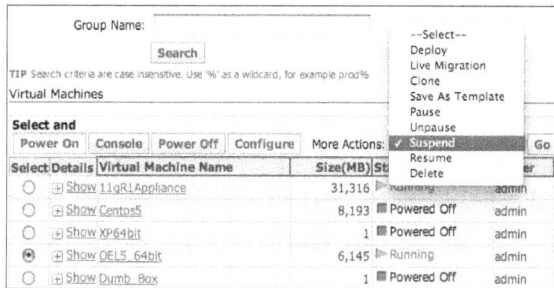

Click **Confirm** to proceed:

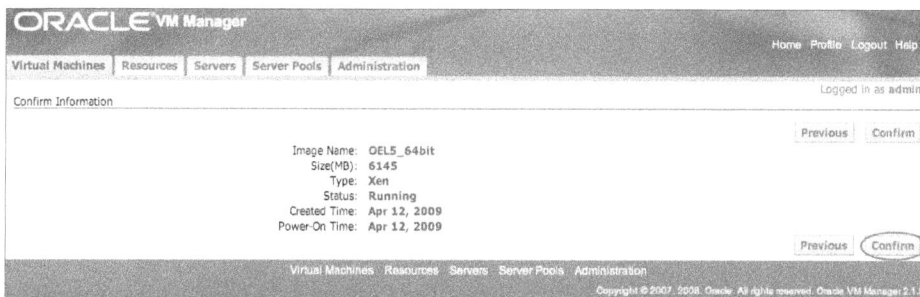

The VM starts suspending:

If you quickly go to the Oracle VM Server and browse to the /OVS/running_pool, you will notice that the information is being saved in the form of vm.save:

```
[root@oravm03 running_pool]# cd 72_OEL5_64bit/
[root@oravm03 72_OEL5_64bit]# ls
README  System.img  vm.cfg  vm.cfg.orig
[root@oravm03 72_OEL5_64bit]# ls
README  System.img  vm.cfg  vm.cfg.orig  vm.save
[root@oravm03 72_OEL5_64bit]#
```

In the meanwhile the machine is completely **Suspended**.

Select	Details	Virtual Machine Name	Size(MB)	Status	Owner	G
⦿	⊞ Show	11gR1Appliance	31,316	▶ Running	admin	M
○	⊞ Show	Centos5	8,193	■ Powered Off	admin	M
○	⊞ Show	XP64bit	1	■ Powered Off	admin	M
○	⊞ Show	OEL5_64bit	6,145	⏾ Suspended	admin	M
○	⊞ Show	Dumb_Box	1	■ Powered Off	admin	M

Unsuspending goes just about that easily as well. Click **Resume** on the Virtual Machines page from the drop-down menu **More Actions**:

	Name:		Server Pool Name:	
Group Name:			--Select--	
			Deploy	
	Search		Live Migration	
			Clone	
TIP Search criteria are case insensitive. Use '%' as a wildcard, for example prod%			Save As Template	
Virtual Machines			Pause	
			Unpause	
Select and			Suspend	
Power On	Console	Power Off	Configure	More Actions: ✓ Resume	Go
				Delete	

Select	Details	Virtual Machine Name	Size(MB)	St...	...
○	⊞ Show	11gR1Appliance	31,316	▶ Running	admin
○	⊞ Show	Centos5	8,193	■ Powered Off	admin
○	⊞ Show	XP64bit	1	■ Powered Off	admin
⦿	⊞ Show	OEL5_64bit	6,145	⏾ Suspended	admin
○	⊞ Show	Dumb_Box	1	■ Powered Off	admin

Click **Confirm** to proceed:

ORACLE VM Manager

Home   Profile   Logout   Help

Virtual Machines | Resources | Servers | Server Pools | Administration

Logged in as **admin**

Confirm Information

Previous   Confirm

Image Name: OEL5_64bit
Size(MB): 6145
Type: Xen
Status: Suspended
Created Time: Apr 12, 2009
Power-On Time: Apr 12, 2009

Previous   Confirm

Virtual Machines   Resources   Servers   Server Pools   Administration

Copyright © 2007, 2008, Oracle. All rights reserved. Oracle VM Manager 2.1.2

The VM starts **Resuming**:

Select	Details	Virtual Machine Name	Size(MB)	Status	Owner
⦿	⊞ Show	11gR1Appliance	31,316	▶ Running	admin
○	⊞ Show	Centos5	8,193	■ Powered Off	admin
○	⊞ Show	XP64bit	1	■ Powered Off	admin
○	⊞ Show	OEL5_64bit	6,145	⏾ Resuming	admin
○	⊞ Show	Dumb_Box	1	■ Powered Off	admin

A quick look at the file system shows that the information of the vm.save file is used to resume the operations and then vm.save file is deleted:

```
[root@oravm03 running_pool]# cd 72_OEL5_64bit/
[root@oravm03 72_OEL5_64bit]# ls
README  System.img  vm.cfg  vm.cfg.orig  vm.save
[root@oravm03 72_OEL5_64bit]# ls
README  System.img  vm.cfg  vm.cfg.orig  vm.save
[root@oravm03 72_OEL5_64bit]# ls
README  System.img  vm.cfg  vm.cfg.orig  vm.save
[root@oravm03 72_OEL5_64bit]# ls
README  System.img  vm.cfg  vm.cfg.orig
[root@oravm03 72_OEL5_64bit]#
```

And Voila! The VM is running again:

Select	Details	Virtual Machine Name	Size(MB)	Status	Owner
●	⊕ Show	11gR1Appliance	31,316	▶ Running	admin
○	⊕ Show	Centos5	8,193	■ Powered Off	admin
○	⊕ Show	XP64bit	1	■ Powered Off	admin
○	⊕ Show	OEL5_64bit	6,145	▶ Running	admin
○	⊕ Show	Dumb_Box	1	■ Powered Off	admin

Summary

This chapter covered managing Virtual Machines and continues through to the next chapter. Here we saw the overall VM management within the Oracle VM farm. Now let's move on to the next chapter where we continue managing our VMs within Oracle VM environment.

6
Managing Virtual Machines with Oracle VM Manager: Part 2

Let's pick up from the trails of the last chapter—where we focused on several VM management tasks such as VM suspend and pause and play, we also saw how convenient it is to manage the VMs and their lifecycle management within an elastic data center with Oracle VM as its core.

This chapter will be a continuation of the management of VMs as we scale out our data center and make slices of virtual data centers from it. We will explore the compute substrate of the Oracle VM infrastructure and also use the web-based portal to change the configurations on the fly.

In this chapter, we will cover the following topics:

- Installing VNC and connecting remotely
- Editing VM settings such as Network, Storage, CPU and more
- VM storage: Using shared and non-shared disks
- A few more VM management actions—such as copying, deploying, live migration, and so on

Connecting remotely to a VM Console

You need to access your VM to set all the parameters as required, such as changing the **Network Interface Card** (**NIC**) or **Internet Protocol** (**IP**) address and configuring your VM to your choice. This you do by enabling the console and installing the plugin to the Oracle VM Manager. After you have installed the VM plugin, you can go ahead and log into the VM.

Let's start with installing the Console plugin.

Installing the Console plugin

The plugins you need could vary depending upon the browser you may be using and the OS you are using to access the Oracle VM Manager. In our case, I have a MacBook and will simply use the Oracle VM Manager VM which is an Oracle Enterprise Linux 5 U2 with a Mozilla browser, so that shouldn't be much of a problem for us to carry out the following tasks:

1. Download the Console plugin from the following link and install it on the computer, accessing the Oracle VM:

    http://oss.oracle.com/oraclevm/manager/RPMS/

2. The files on the boss site are shown in the following screenshot:

    ## Index of /oraclevm/manager/RPMS

Name	Last modified	Size	Description
Parent Directory		-	
README-console	20-Nov-2007 14:09	1.0K	
ovm-console-1.0.0-2.i386.rpm	13-Nov-2007 20:46	42K	
ovm-console-1.0.0-2.x86_64.rpm	14-Nov-2007 12:03	44K	
tightvnc-java-1.3.9-3.noarch.rpm	20-Nov-2007 12:55	311K	

3. Now, install the plugin, as shown in the following screenshot:

    ```
    [root@vmmgr ~]# cd Desktop/
    [root@vmmgr Desktop]# ls
    ovm-console-1.0.0-2.i386.rpm  tightvnc-java-1.3.9-3.noarch.rpm
    [root@vmmgr Desktop]# rpm -ivh ovm-console-1.0.0-2.i386.rpm
    Preparing...                ########################################### [100%]
       1:ovm-console            ########################################### [100%]
    [root@vmmgr Desktop]#
    ```

In case you do not have any standard installation of Mozilla Firefox, copy the following files:

- ° `# cp /opt/ovm-console/etc/mozpluggerrc /etc/`

- ° `# cp /opt/ovm-console/bin/* /usr/bin`

- ° `# cp /opt/ovm-console/lib/mozilla/plugins/ovm-console-mozplugger.so /opt/firefox/plugins`

Here, `/opt/firefox/plugins` refers to the Firefox's plugin folder. If you are using Microsoft Internet Explorer, you might have to download the Tight-VNC-Java applet on the Oracle VM Manager host.

4. Restart Firefox and you should be able to load the VNC Viewer by clicking on **Console.**

5. Now, we need get the jar file:

   ```
   Get VNCViewer.jar (It should be in the /opt/oc4j/j2ee/home/
   applications/OVS/webapp1/Class directory)
   ```

6. Sign the jar file like this:

   ```
   /opt/oc4j/java/jdk1.5.0_11/bin/keytool

       -genkey -alias vncviewer -validity 365

   /opt/oc4j/java/jdk1.5.0_11/bin/jarsigner vncviewer.jar vncviewer
   ```

7. Now let's try logging into the VM console:

   On my Mac, I get the following message, which I agree to **Trust**:

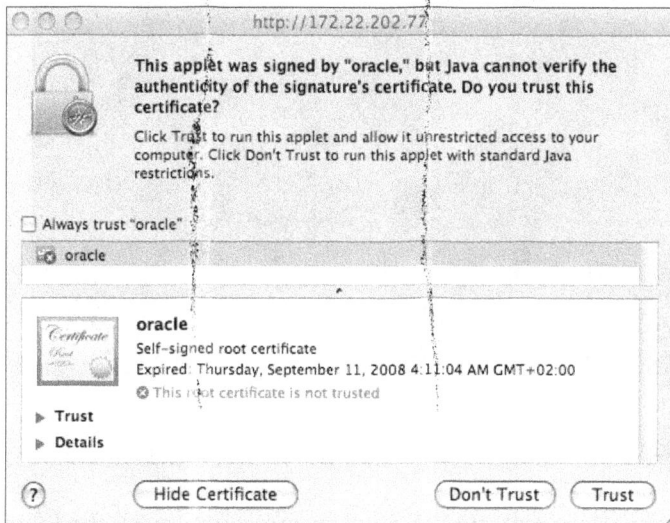

8. Then we go ahead and log on to the VNC, where we type in the VNC or the Console password, which we choose while creating the VM:

9. And then, we are asked to pass on the necessary information to the pre-baked VM. Obviously, the first one happens to be the IP address. We choose to fill in the following details:

Static IP: 172.22.202.120

Netmask: 255.255.255.0

Gateway: 172.22.202.1

DNS: 172.22.202.10

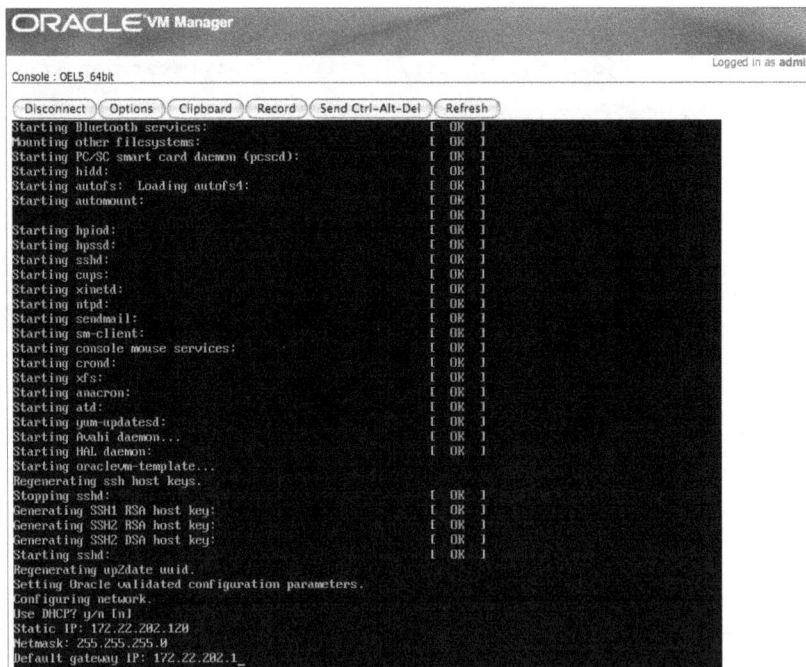

The Network settings are restarted and we are presented with the login details of the VM once again. Alternatively, you can also ping and SSH the machine from any console of your choice.

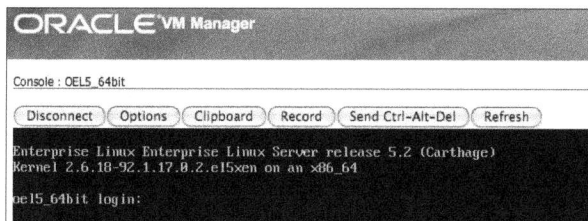

There may be other tasks you may have to perform depending on the mode which you have used to create this VM. If you had used a template, like in our case, then you can go ahead and reconfigure the IP address—if you didn't want a DHCP address—and you are ready to go.

If you have created this VM using a HVM or a fully virtualized method, the installation of the **GOS** (**Guest Operating System**) is fired after your first login. Follow the installation wizard to install the GOS.

More ISO files may be needed. For instance, we just imported some Windows Server 2003 ISO files for Release 2 and they came in two CDs. This you can do by clicking on **Change CD** to use the files on the second CD.

You can repeat this step until all the ISO files have been installed.

Viewing Virtual Machine details

To see more about a VM, go to the **Virtual Machines** tab and click on the **Details** column on the **Show** link. Here, you get to see all sorts of information such as the VNC port, time created, powered on, virtualization method, and so on:

You can also click on the sublink **Log,** to view the errors, if any, that may have occurred.

Editing and reconfiguring the Virtual Machines

During the creation of a VM, you can configure some parameters but not all parameters are fully configurable during the time of installation. This is where the default settings of Oracle VM Manager come into force, for instance assigning the **VIFs** (**Virtual Network Interfaces**), number of cores, and so on.

In order to modify the VM, you will click on the **Virtual Machines** page and in the VM table go ahead and click on **Configure** button. Alternatively, you can click on the VM itself to open the edit page of the VM:

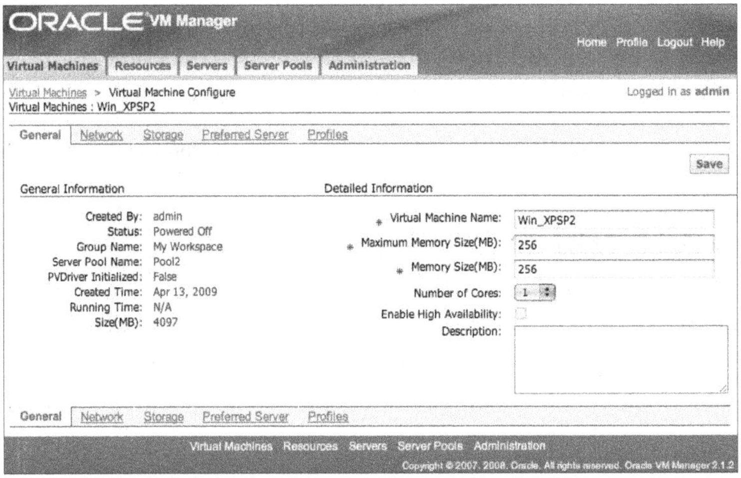

On the edit page, you will be able to see the following tabs:

- General
- Network
- Storage
- Preferred Server
- Profiles

Some of the settings like increasing the memory, modifying NIC information, modifying the storage information, and so on, can take place immediately. For other settings you will need to bring the VM down and restart it for the changes to take effect.

The General tab

The landing page is the **General** tab, and here you can modify the general parameters of the VM, including **Virtual Machine Name**. It is here you can rename a VM.

- **Maximum Memory Size (MB)**: You can enter the maximum memory size that a VM can consume. This is where you can play around with the memory parameters. You can change the memory size only when the VM is turned off. Memory is noted in MBs.

- **Memory Size (MB)**: You can increase or decrease the memory size; it is advisable to allocate a minimum of 256MB memory. Increasing memory can take place online, whereas, in order to decrease memory you will have to restart the VM.

- **Number of cores**: A maximum of 32 cores can be selected for the VMs. Changes will only take effect after the VM has rebooted.

- **Enabling HA**: You can enable **HA** (**High Availability**). This ensures that the VMs will always migrate or restart on another host, if one or more VM Servers on the Oracle VM farm fail.

Furthermore, you have information regarding the following:

Created by	The creator of this VM. In our case, we used admin to create this VM.
Status	This could be **Running**, **Paused**, **Shutdown**, and so on.
Group Name	We have chosen to keep the VMs private, as of now, and our default group is **My Workspace**.
Server Pool Name	The **Server Pool**, where the VM resides, will be displayed here.
Created Time	The date and time when the VM was created.
Running Time	This is the uptime of the VM created.
Size (MB)	Disk size of the VM.
PVDriver Initialized	Paravirtualized VMs do not have this setting. This setting explains whether the PVDriver is initialized on the HVM or not.
	If the setting is **True** then the PVDriver is installed on this HVM.
	If the setting is **False** could mean that it is not initialized on the HVM and is only installed on it.
	The **Unknown** parameter could mean several things, the VM may be shutdown, the Oracle VM Manager Agent may need to be upgraded to support this feature. Oracle VM Manager cannot detect this status of the PVDriver.

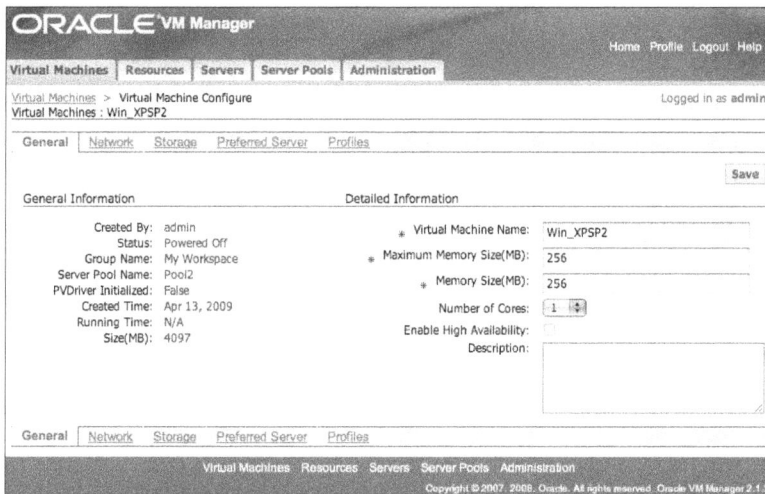

The Network tab

Here you can add, edit, or delete Virtual NICs. You can set a maximum of eight Virtual NICs.

Selecting Virtual Machine type

If the VM is Fully Virtualized (HVM), you can configure the VIFs type to be either of the following:

- Fully virtualized
- Paravirtualized

The Paravirtualized driver, also called a netfront driver, can be used with either a paravirtualized or fully virtualized VM, whereas the HVM driver, also known as ioemu driver, can only be used with an HVM or a fully virtualized VM.

In the **Network Type** option, you change from **Fully Virtualized** to **Paravirtualized**, as shown in the following screenshot:

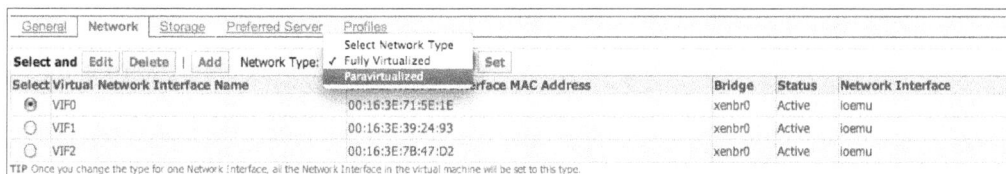

And now it is changed to PVM driver or a **netfront** driver:

Select	Virtual Network Interface Name	Virtual Network Interface MAC Address	Bridge	Status	Network Interface
⦿	VIF0	00:16:3E:71:5E:1E	xenbr0	Active	netfront
○	VIF1	00:16:3E:39:24:93	xenbr0	Active	netfront
○	VIF2	00:16:3E:7B:47:D2	xenbr0	Active	netfront

TIP Once you change the type for one Network Interface, all the Network Interface in the virtual machine will be set to this type.

Both the drivers contain the BIOS and device emulation code that support the HVM or Fully Virtualized VMs.

For HVM, the type of driver is Fully Virtualized (ioemu), by default, or PVM (netfront). For PVM machines the default driver is Paravirtualized (netfront) and this cannot be changed.

Once you change the network type of one VIF, all the VIFs change to the same type.

Adding a VIF (Virtual Network Interface)

Let's carry out the following steps to add a Virtual Network Interface (VIF)

1. Click on the **Add** button, in the **Network** tab:

Network Interface Card Information

Logged in as admin

Previous   Next

Virtual Network Interface Name: private
Bridge: xenbr0
Enable Rate Limit: ☑
Rate Limit (Mbit): 100
Status: Active

Previous   Next

2. Click on the **Next** button. Here we want to create a private NIC that will be used for measuring traffic only between VMs and want to limit the traffic, therefore, we shall choose **Enable Rate Limit** and the traffic will not exceed the desired limit—provided by us in the **Rate Limit (Mbit)** option.

Confirm Information

Logged in as admin

Previous   Confirm

Virtual Machines

Virtual Machine Name: Centos5
Size(MB): 8193
Type: Xen
Status: Powered Off
Created Time: Apr 12, 2009

Network Interface Card

Virtual Network Interface Name: private
Virtual Network Interface MAC Address: 00:16:3E:11:99:E2
Bridge: xenbr0
Rate Limit (Mbit): 100
Status: Active

Previous   Confirm

3. Click on the **Confirm** button, and your private VIF will be created:

4. You can also edit or delete an existing VIF on this page.

5. On clicking the **Delete** button, the VIF is deleted from the system.

The Storage tab

You can expand the storage capacity by either creating non-sharable virtual disks or by adding shared virtual disks. Oracle VM Manager only supports file-based disks. Physical disks are not supported.

> For HVM, you can add up to four IDE disks and seven SCSI disks. A PVM does not have such limitations, but only needs to be started in order to make the changes take effect.

Using non-sharable Virtual Disks

Let's carry out the following steps to create non-shared virtual disks:

1. Click on the **Create New Virtual Disk** option:

2. Next, we choose the disk to be an IDE disk of 1 GB or 1024 MB capacity.

3. Click on the **Confirm** button:

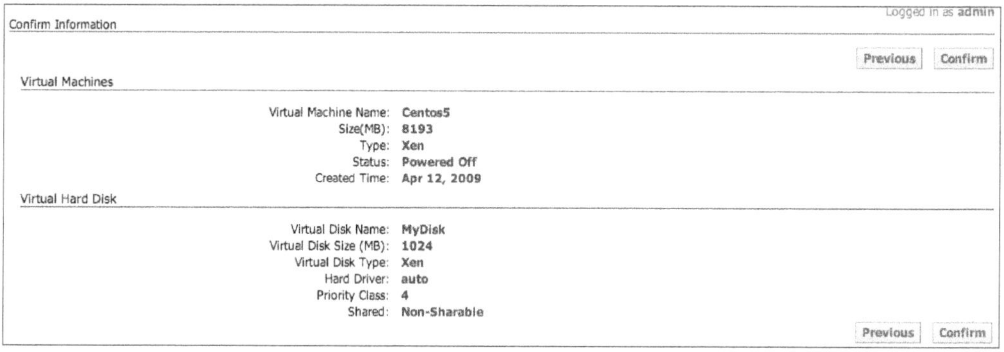

4. And as you can see in the following screenshot the disk is created and the available slots for IDE is one less than it was before we started creating the extra virtual disk:

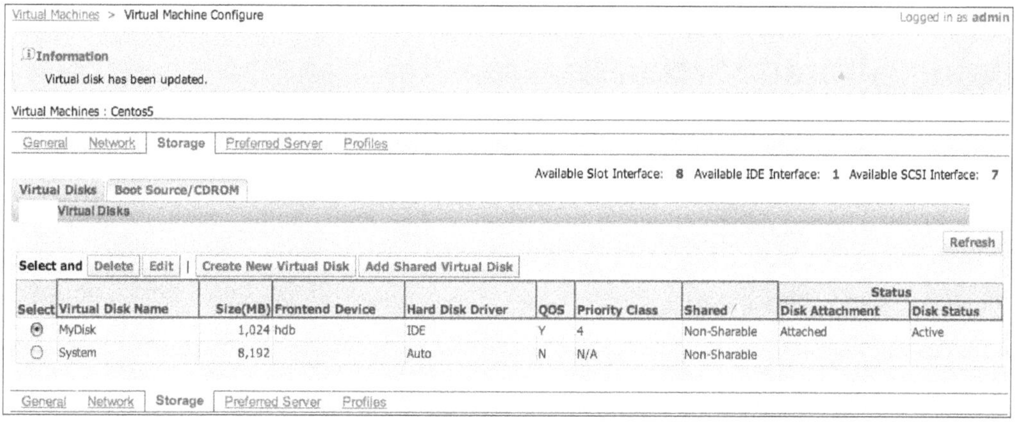

For an HVM, while selecting Auto Oracle VM Agent, first select IDE as type of the hard driver. In case the IDE has reached a maximum priority of **4**, then it automatically creates a SCSI disk. After the maximum limit of SCSI has been exhausted you cannot create extra disks anymore. This information is also available at the top right part of the **Storage** page.

> As you may have noticed that the priority of the disk runs from **0** to **7**, thus in total 8 priorities. Priority **0** is the highest and priority **7** is the least. The priority of the virtual disk is global and not just confined to the VM.

There are three IO scheduling classes, namely, idle, best effort, and real time. Oracle VM uses the real time scheduling class. The real time scheduling class is naturally given the first access to the disks, no matter what. These eight priority classes, basically, denote how big chunks of processing time the disk will get on each scheduling window.

Deleting a disk is a simple process as well:

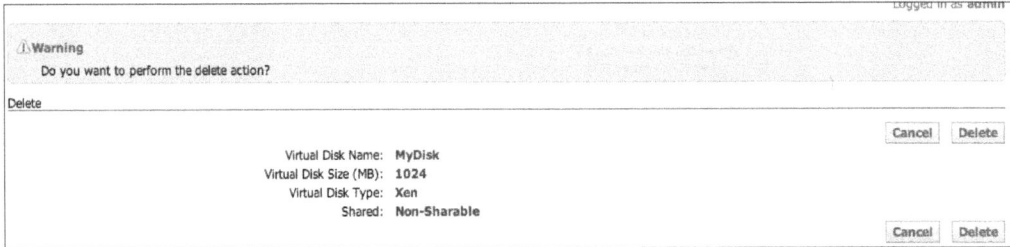

Click on the **Delete** button to permanently remove the disk from the system.

Using Shared Virtual Disks

To assign shared disk to a VM, click on **Add Shared Virtual Disk**. We were not able to create shared storage yet, but if you have done that then you'll see shared disks on the system:

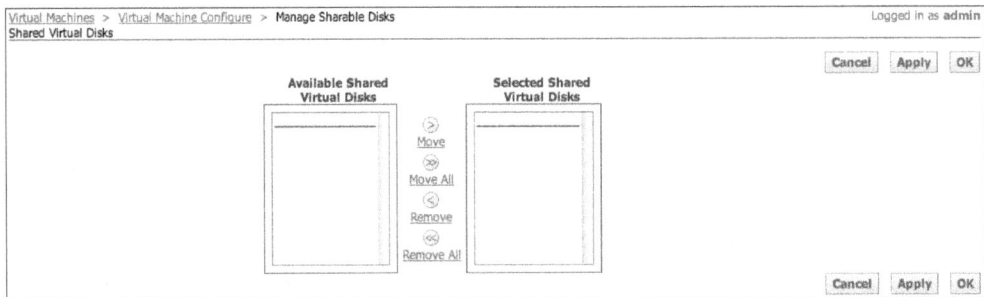

Just click on the content in the **Available Shared Virtual Disks** option and move it to the **Selected Shared Virtual Disks** option. Click on **Apply** and then click on **OK**.

Also quickly examine the parameters in the Virtual.

Column	Description
Virtual Disk Name	Your Virtual Disk's name.
Size	Size of disk in MBs.
Frontend Device	Name of disk displayed in VM.
Hard Disk Driver	For HVM it is IDE, SCSI or Auto and for PVM it will be IDE, SCSI, Auto or XVD.
QoS	Whether QoS is enabled or not. If the disk has a priority of 0 then you will see the QoS to be Y and as values get lower the QoS goes to N.
Priority Class	If QoS is enabled, the priority class will be displayed.
Shared	Whether the disk is shared or not shared.
Status – Disk Attachment	Whether the disk is attached and working well within the VM or whether due to exceeding some maximum limit the disk is not attached and the Oracle VM Agent cannot connect to it.
Status – Disk Status	Whether the disk is Active, Creating, Deleting, and so on.

Boot Source or CD-ROM

Here you can choose the **Boot Device** from **HDD, CD-ROM,** or **PXE.** HDD is needed to start the VM from the disk. CD-ROM is needed for HVM and is used to start a VM from the CD-ROM and finally the PXE is useful to boot the VM from a **Preboot Execution Environment (PXE).**

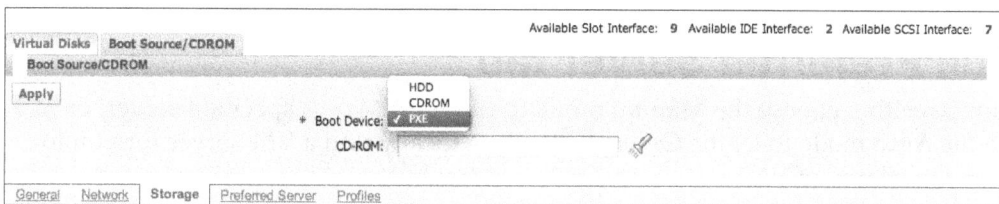

1. For CD-ROM, click on the button to choose from the available ISO files, as shown in the following screenshot:

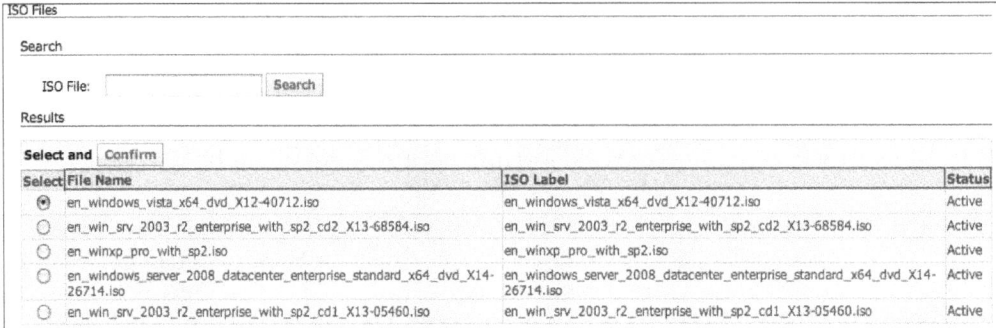

2. After selecting the correct ISO file click on **OK**, as shown in the following screenshot:

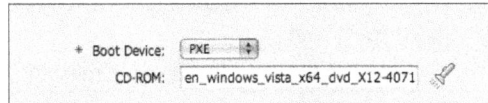

3. Finally, click on **Apply** to make the changes effective.

> This option is only possible for HVM.

The Preferred Server tab

You can either choose the **Manual** mode to run the VM on a specified server, or pick up the **Auto** mode to let the Oracle VM automatically find a VM Server for you to host your flavor of VM.

> If none of the preferred servers are found, the VM will not start and will wait until the right resources are made available to it in the form of the next preferred VM Server.

When the VM is **Powered Off** or **Suspended**, you can switch between the **Auto** mode and the **Manual** mode.

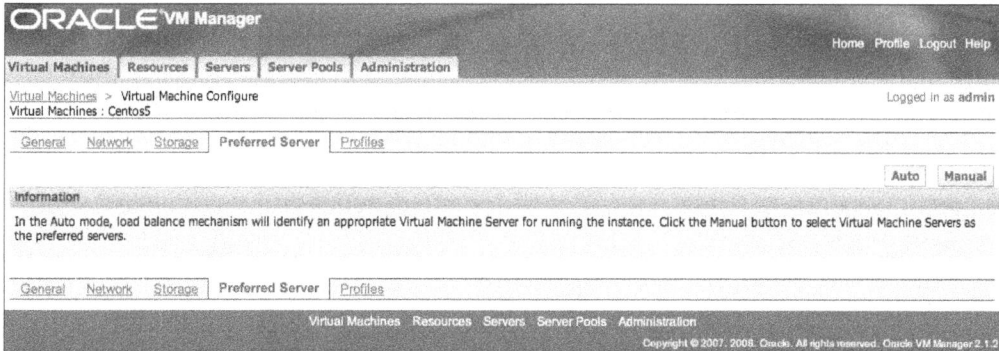

You can pick up a VM Server as the preferred server by clicking on the **Manual** button, as shown in the following screenshot:

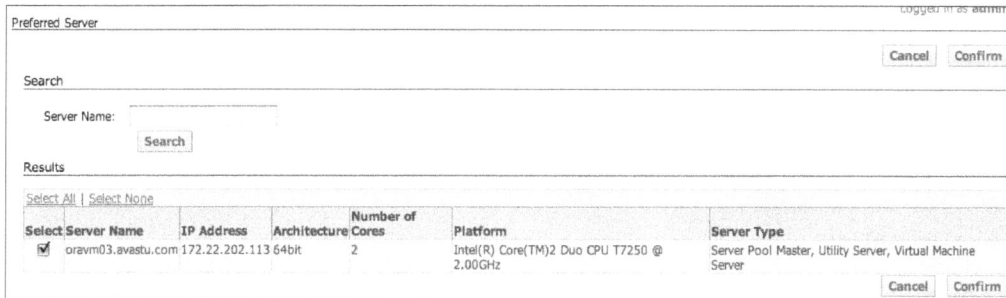

Click on the **Confirm** button to make the changes, permanent.

The Profiles tab

Here you can set up or modify the **Virtual Machine System Username** and **Virtual Machine System Password** for login, boot source, OS, and keyboard. You can also have the credentials in the first sub-pane mailed to you at your previously registered email address.

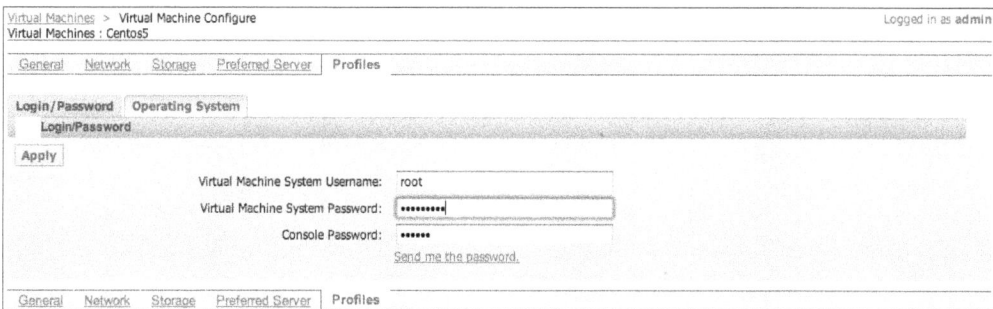

Operating System and Keyboard Settings

Here you can select an OS according to which the Oracle VM optimizes the profile of the VM, such as `vm.cfg`, fill and the timer mode for HVM. For Windows hosts, there are other behaviors such as Windows GOS, which use the **USB** tab let emulation instead of mouse emulation. Choosing appropriate settings will help you optimize and will help run the VM better. Similar choices are available for the keyboard functions.

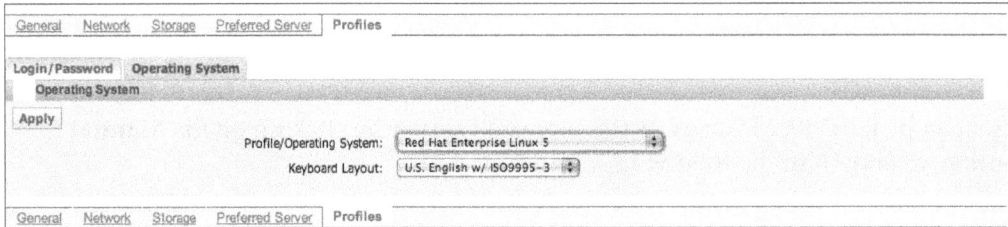

Copying Virtual Machines

Oracle VM Manager enables you to make copies of VMs based on existing working VMs. This can be done by either deploying a VM, cloning them outright, or saving a VM as a template.

Deploying a Virtual Machine

By deploying a Virtual Machine, you essentially clone a new VM to a specific server pool—that could be public and may be accessible to a larger group or you can choose to keep it private. The original VM remains in its original pool while the copy goes to its new pool. Let's have a look at how it works:

1. We take XP64Bit machine and click on **Deploy**, from the dropdown menu, and then click on **Go**.

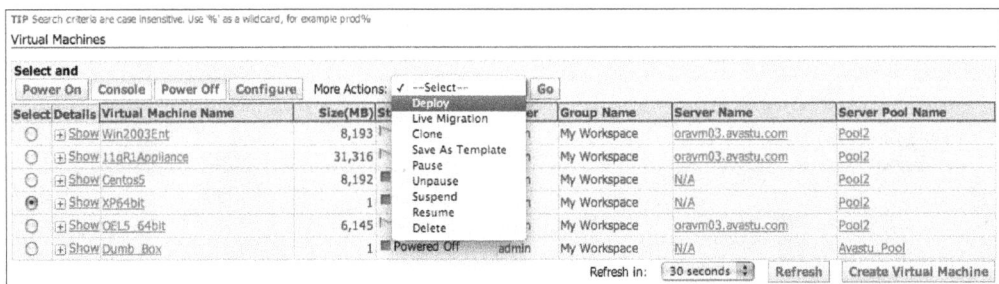

2. We name it as **temp** for the sake of testing, and change the **Group Name** to **Public Group** and then click on **Next**, as shown in the following screenshot:

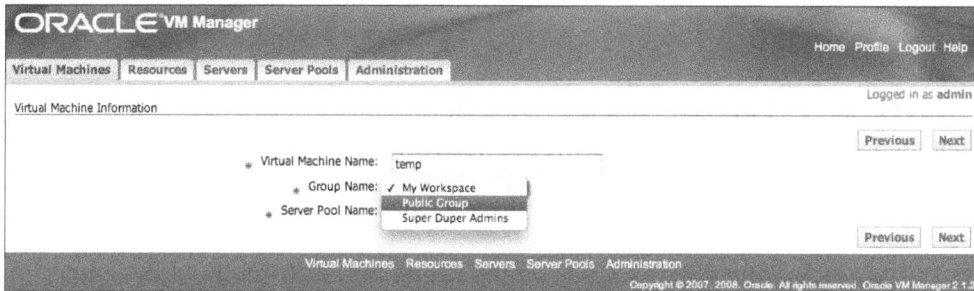

3. Click on **Confirm** to make the changes effective:

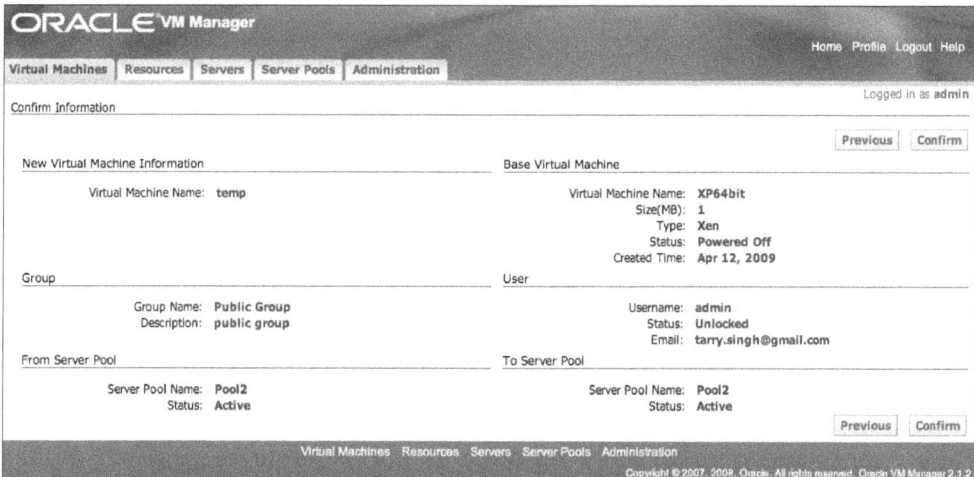

4. Your VM will now be copied and deployed. As you can clearly see in the following screenshot the **XP64bit** is **Deploying** while the **temp** is being **Created**:

[The machine to deploy must be **Powered Off** to be able to make a correct copy of its self.]

Cloning Virtual Machines

Cloning a Virtual Machine is a process to create one or more copies of an existing VM. By cloning a Virtual Machine, you can save multiple copies to another server pool and share them with other users.

Let's start a quick clone process. Click on the **Clone** button from the drop-down menu and then click on **Go**.

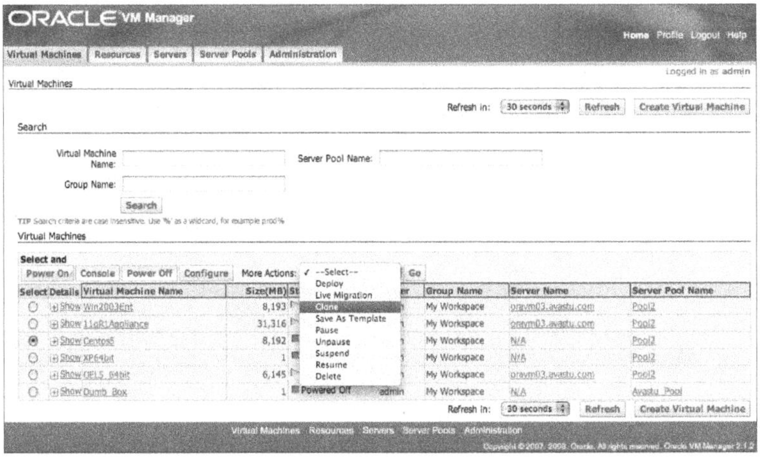

Here we want some more copies of this machine and therefore, request for **5** of them and we let another group have access to them. We fire off the cloning process by clicking on **Confirm**, as shown in the following screenshot:

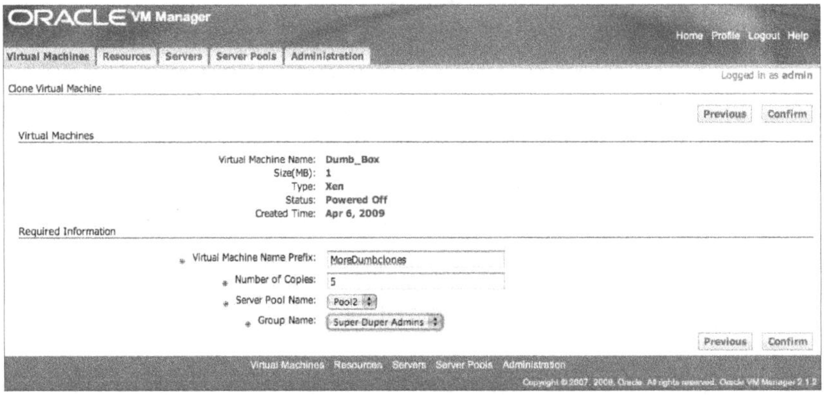

You can see five of these **MoreDumbclones** being cloned:

Select	Details	Virtual Machine Name	Size(MB)	Status	Owner	
⦿	⊞ Show	MoreDumbclones4	1	⊕ Creating	admin	S
○	⊞ Show	MoreDumbclones3	1	⊕ Creating	admin	S
○	⊞ Show	MoreDumbclones2	1	⊕ Creating	admin	S
○	⊞ Show	MoreDumbclones1	1	⊕ Creating	admin	S
○	⊞ Show	MoreDumbclones0	1	⊕ Creating	admin	S
○	⊞ Show	Win2003Ent	8,193	⊢ Running	admin	N
○	⊞ Show	11gR1Appliance	31,316	⊢ Running	admin	N
○	⊞ Show	Centos5	8,192	▦ Powered Off	admin	N
○	⊞ Show	XP64bit	1	▦ Powered Off	admin	N
○	⊞ Show	OEL5_64bit	6,145	⊢ Running	admin	N
○	⊞ Show	Dumb_Box	1	⊕ Cloning	admin	N

Saving Virtual Machine as a template

You can save a Virtual Machine as a template to enable other users to create their new Virtual Machines based on this template. This is a very straight forward process:

1. Click on the VM to save it as a template and click on **Save as Template** from the drop-down menu. Now click on **Go**.

2. We will call it an **XPTemplate**, and click on **Confirm**:

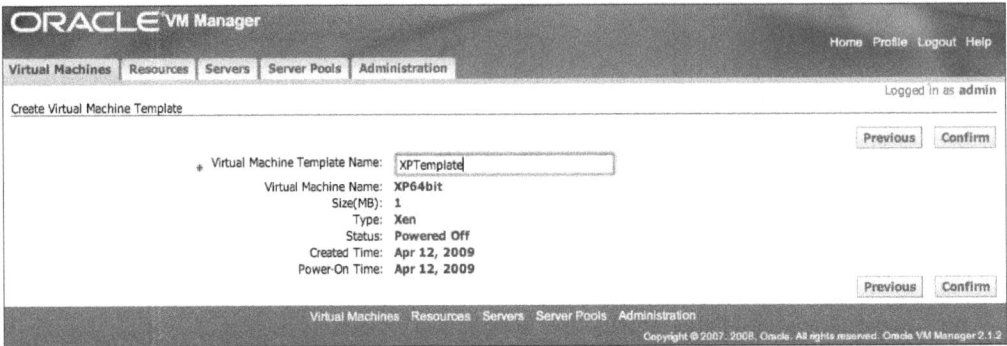

3. As you can see in the following screenshot, the **XP64bit** VM is **Saving** itself as a template:

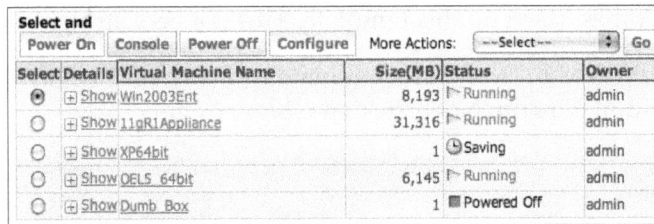

4. Going to the **Resources** page, we can find our new template has been created:

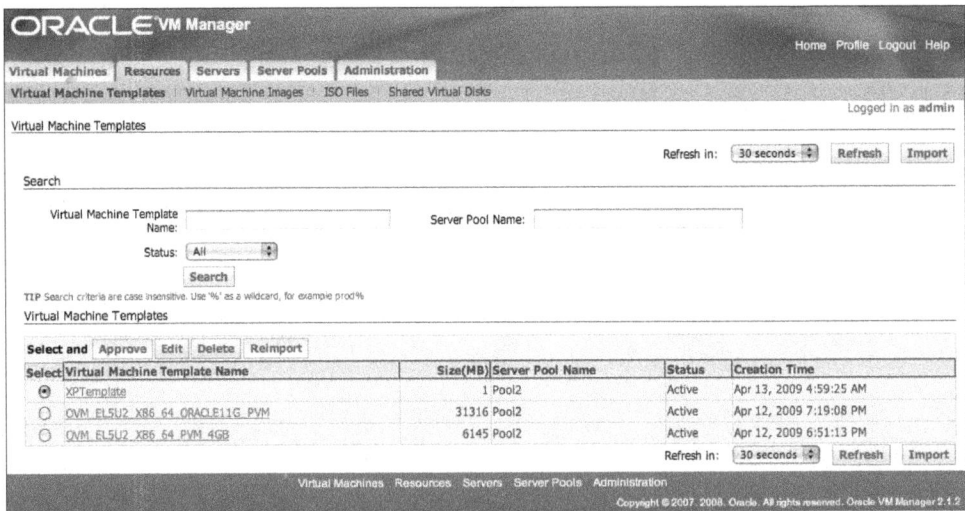

Migrating a Virtual Machine

Live migration, also known as Hot Migration, is a process of moving a running workload or VM from one VM Server to another VM Server, while all the applications and services keep running as usual. This process has minimum to no effect on the SLAs, and the consumers can keep accessing the applications while the maintenance of workload automation is taking place somewhere in the cloud. The maintenance windows and other service windows can be carried out on normal hours without any added overhead or financial impact to data center operators.

The VMs are only allowed to migrate within their own pool, thus wisely choose how you will want to create resource or server pools in advance. The servers must be identical and compatible in order to allow Live Migration.

The pre-requisite is that you must have your VMs running on shared storage. You cannot conduct Live Migration if you have VMs on local storage.

For Live Migratation, click on the **Virtual Machines** page and select a running VM. In the **More Actions** drop-down menu, choose for **Live Migration** and then click on **Go**.

Then click on the VM Server you wish to migrate to, and click on **Next**. Check the VM information and click on **Confirm** to live migrate the VM.

Deleting a Virtual Machine

This may not be one of your regular tasks but if you do delete a VM remember that all the files and data with this VM will be permanently removed from the Oracle VM Manager. Also note that your VM must be powered off to be deleted or else you will get an error.

Let's try deleting a VM that we don't need anymore. Click on the **Virtual Machines** page, click the **More Actions** drop-down menu, and click on the **Delete** option. Then click on **Go** in order to delete that VM:

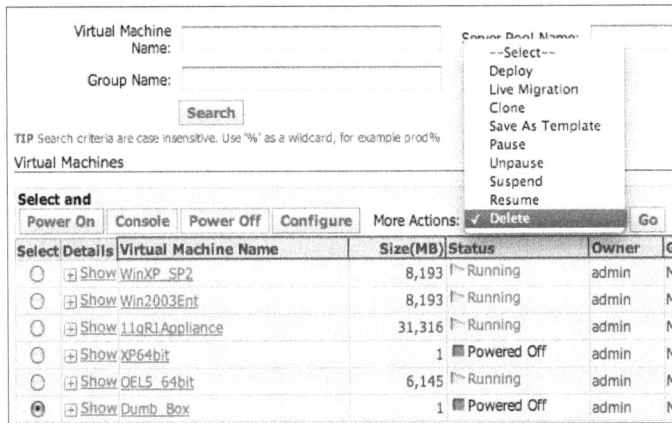

You will be asked to confirm your action, as shown in the following screenshot:

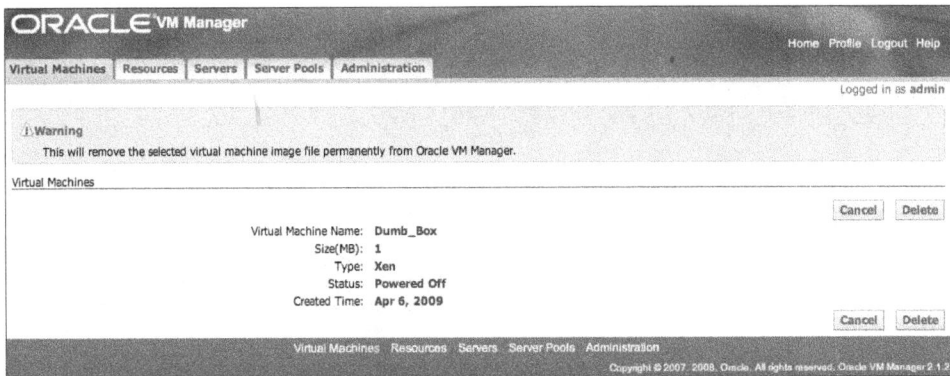

Your VM will be deleted, as shown in the following screenshot:

Summary

In this chapter we have learned yet another way to manage the Oracle VM farm. You also learned to create multiple clones to instantly fire up servers for a quick build and tear test and development platform, for instance. An elastic datacenter is the core of a true private cloud, and with Oracle VM we are getting closer to that dream.

In the next chapter, we will explore VM resource allocation within the Oracle VM IntraCloud environment.

7
Managing Virtual Machines with Oracle VM Manager: Part 3

In the last two chapters, you have seen the first two parts of the Virtual Machines management with Oracle VM Manager. Here we shall perform some typical VM resource management tasks, such as importing VMs via several methods such as templates, VM Images, ISO files, and so on. We will also look briefly at creating shared storage.

In this chapter, we will cover the following topics:

- Managing intracloud resources and VM allocation
- Importing and managing VM templates
- Importing, converting and managing VM from other VM images
- Importing and managing VMs from ISO files
- Managing shared storage

Managing intracloud resources and VM allocation

Resources within the Oracle VM environment include VM templates, VM images, ISO files, Virtual Disks, and converted VMs. Here, disk libraries could be of several formats and all you will need is to convert the disk images into Oracle formats. These could be disks from VMware *.vmdk format or other formats—which could be converted into Oracle VM format.

The VM templates are simply imported into the Oracle VM Manager and eventually used to create more VMs across the VM pool. VM images can be imported directly to Oracle VM and can be used immediately — without the process of creation.

The ISO files are imported into the Oracle VM Manager and are used to create VMs from installation media. Shared Disks will be used to not only extend the storage of the VMs but also used for extending the HA capability of the Oracle VM farm.

Let's get started with our first in the line of managing VMs in our Oracle intracloud farm.

> Only administrators or managers are allowed to approve, edit, or delete imported VMs, ISO files, and templates.

Importing templates from Virtual Machine

Virtual Machine templates are typically shared between users to create new and identical VMs. These newly created VMs inherit all the properties such as contents and configurations of the VM template. The contents could be the number of cores in the VM, memory size, virtual disk size, or Virtual NICs. A VM template can be acquired by several methods. You can get or create a VM template by the carrying out one of the following methods:

1. Saving a VM as a template, by clicking on the **Save As Template** option.

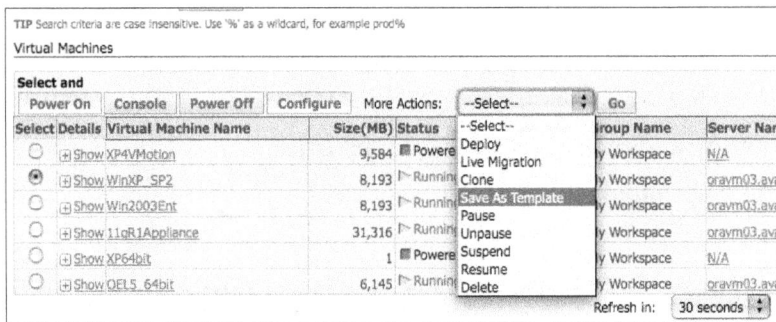

2. Downloading Oracle VM templates from Oracle's web site `http://www.oracle.com/technology/software/products/virtualization/vm_templates.html`. The root password for all the Oracle VM templates is `ovsroot` and the password account for the Oracle database VM appliances is `oracle`.

Please read the readme file to know how to use the templates. It can be found at the link `http://download.oracle.com/otn_software/virtualization/README.templates`. You have to import them into Oracle VM Manager to make them work. We have just downloaded the VM templates from Oracle's site and copied the templates into the `/OVS/seed_pool` directory. You can alternatively download them and have them copied directly from the web. It's a great way to work in the cloud while you are all connected safely to the Oracle VM Manager, and you could be sitting anywhere in the world!

Now we will go ahead and import a VM template. We will also carry out several tasks such as re-importing the VM template, checking the VM templates status, approving an imported VM template, editing the template, and finally deleting the template.

> In you are importing a VM template, it is wise to rename the configuration file of the VM to `vm.cfg`.

Importing a Virtual Machine template

As mentioned earlier, you can get or discover the VM templates from your Server Pool, from the internet, or you can convert a Linux host to a VM template by doing a P2V. Let's first copy our downloaded VM template into the VM Server. We just downloaded another copy of `OVM_EL5U2_X86_PVM_4GB`. This Oracle VM template, which we downloaded from the Oracle's web site, is an Oracle Enterprise Linux 5 Update 2 — x86 Paravirtualized Machine.

1. First let's check the status of the templates which have been already imported, as shown in the following screenshot:

2. The templates are visible from the Oracle VM Server in the `/OVS/seed_pool`, as shown in the following screenshot:

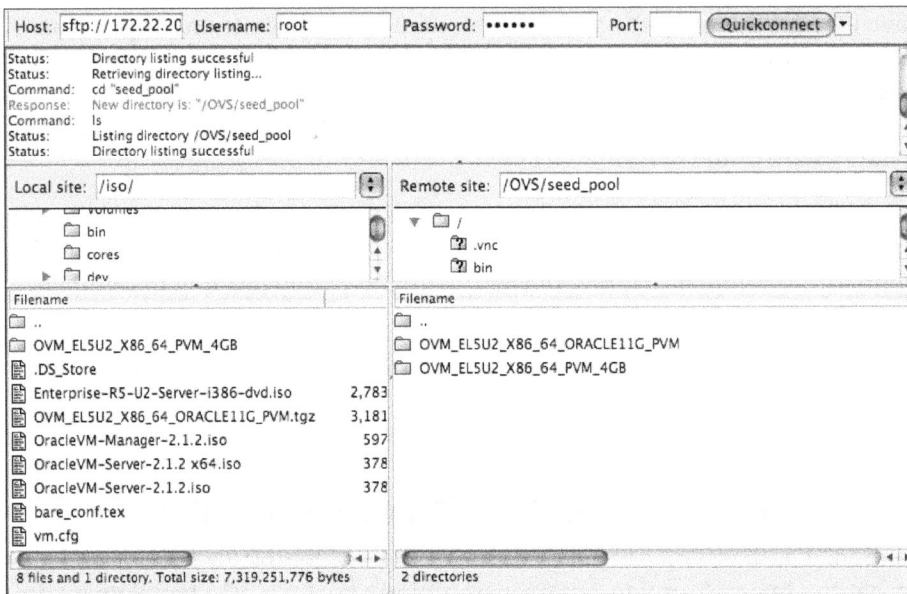

3. Let's open up FileZilla to copy the template to its `/OVS/seed_pool` directory:

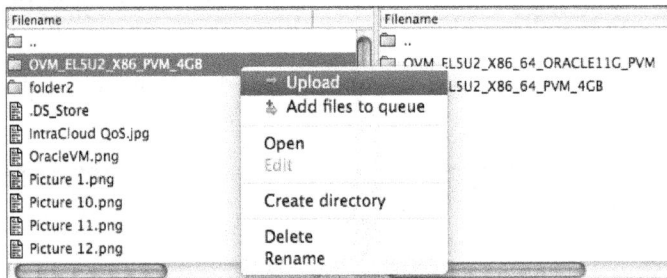

4. Then, the VM starts uploading the template:

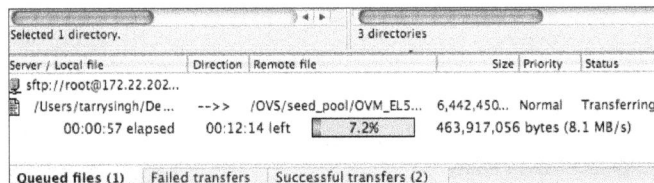

5. The template is now visible to the VM Manager. On the **Resources** page, click on **Virtual Machine Templates,** click on **Import**, and then select the **Select from Server Pool (Discover and register)** option:

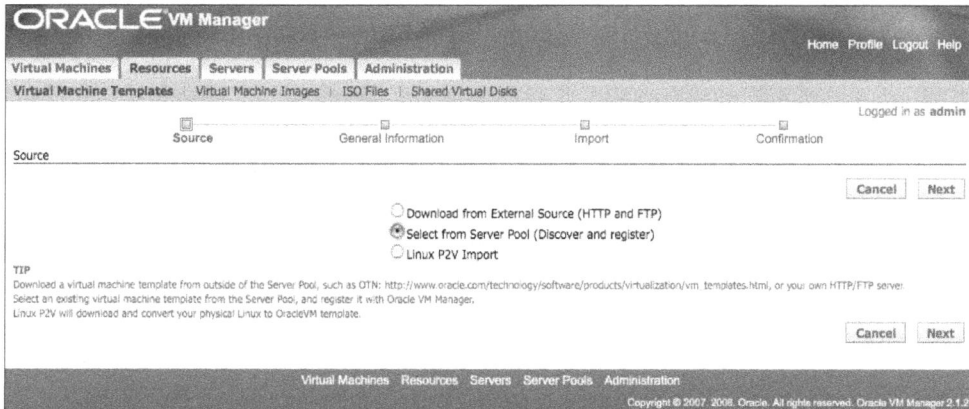

6. Click on **Next** and go to the **General Information** page—where we select our Server Pool and select the fully downloaded VM template into the VM:

7. Fill all the information, such as **Enabling High Availability**, **Virtual Machine System Username**, **Virtual Machine System Password**, **Operating System**, and **Description,** as per required and then click on **Next**:

8. Review the information, click on **Previous** if you want to make any changes and click on **Confirm** when you are ready to move ahead:

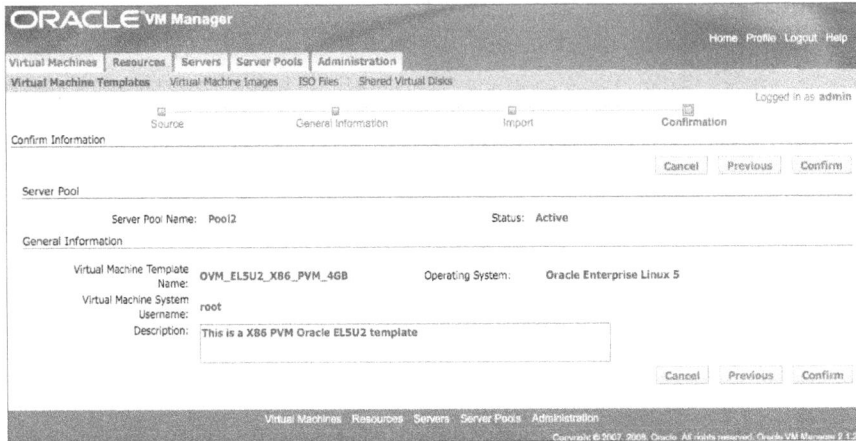

9. You can see that the template has been imported and has a **Pending** status in the VM Manager, as shown in the following screenshot:

10. So let's go ahead and approve the status by clicking on **Approve**:

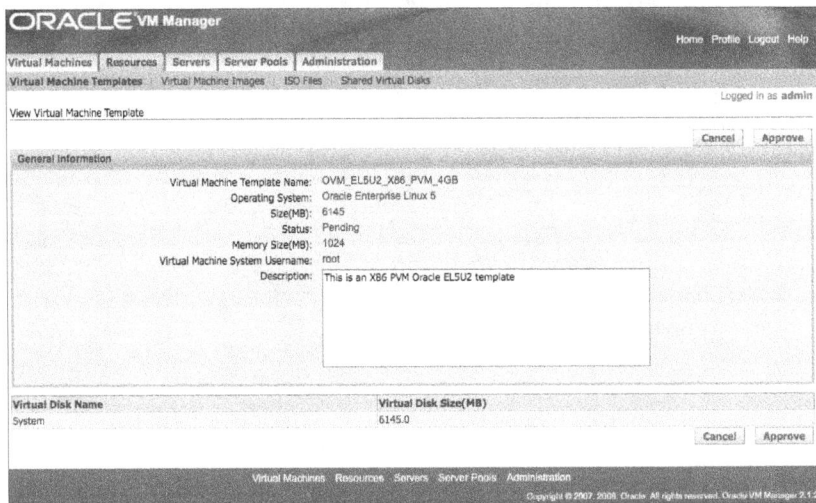

11. You can clearly see that the **OVM_EL5U2_X86_PVM_4GB** template is now **Active**.

Downloading VM Template from External Cloud

To download a VM template from the Internet web sites, such as **OTN** (**Oracle Technology Network**) or any other HTTP/FTP site, carry out the following steps:

1. On the **Resources** page click on **Virtual Machine Templates** and then click on **Import**. Click on the **Download from External Source (HTTP or FTP)** option and then click on **Next**:

2. Fill all the information, such as **Enabling High Availability**, **Virtual Machine System Username**, **Virtual Machine System Password**, **Operating System**, and **Description**, as per required and then click on **Next**:

[✎ *notes* If there is any space between the template name you might get this error:

Error: Virtual Machine Template Name may not contain spaces or other special characters except for]

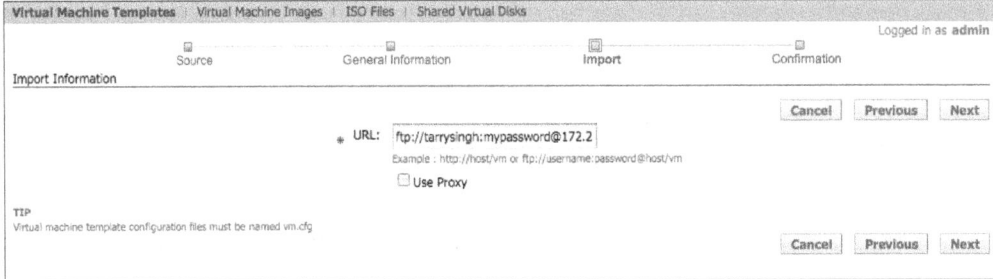

Converting a Linux host to Oracle VM

To convert a Linux host to Oracle VM environment is pretty similar to the previous actions we carried out in downloading the template from an external source. You will have to restart the Linux host with Oracle VM Server CD and use the P2V utility to prepare for the conversion.

The properties of the newly converted VM remains the same and all the virtual cores such as CPU, virtual NICs, disks, and so on, remain unaltered. You need to double check whether you have enough resources on your VM Server side to accommodate the VMs that would be converted to the Oracle VM environment. The VM templates converted will be **HVM (Hardware Virtualized Machines)**. Let's boot our Linux host with our Oracle CD, upon booting type linux p2v, in order to fire up the P2V too, as shown in the following screenshot:

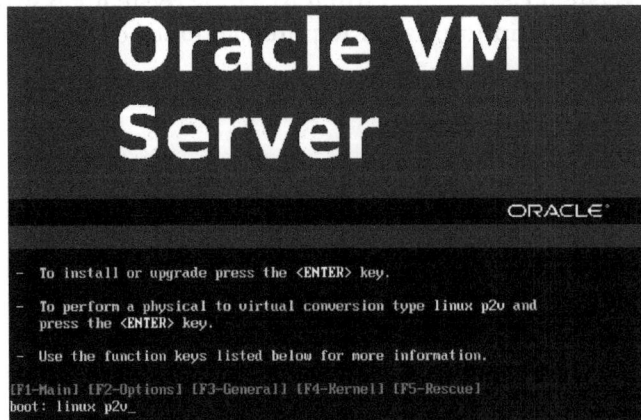

1. Give the **IP Address**, **Netmask**, **Gateway**, **Domain**, and **Nameserver** information of the `eth0` NIC. We have our Windows DC and DNS server running elsewhere in our Avastu data center and we provide that information to the utility:

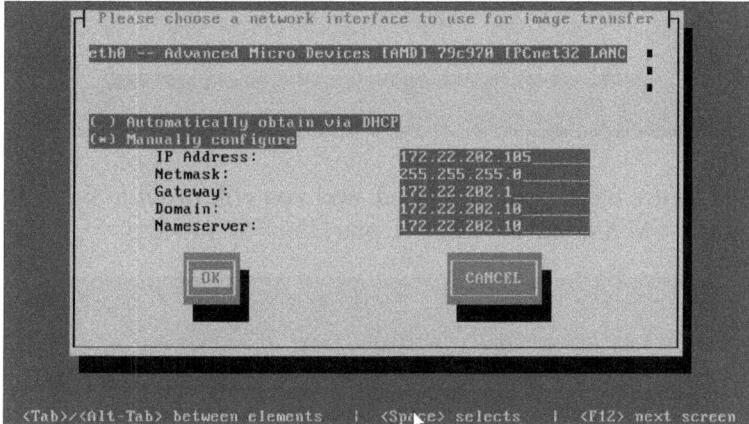

2. Select both the **sda** (boot and other file systems) and the **sdb** (swap disk) and click on **OK**.

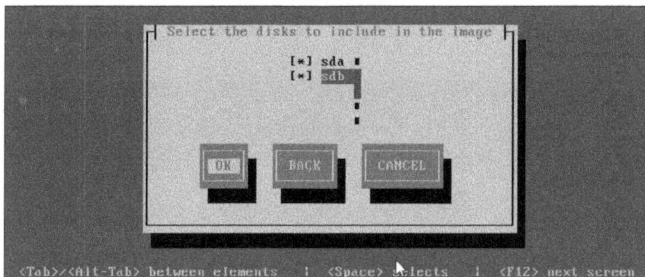

3. We also provide the **VM name**, **VM Memory (in MB)**, **Virtual CPUs**, **Console Password** and then click on **OK** to move to the next screen:

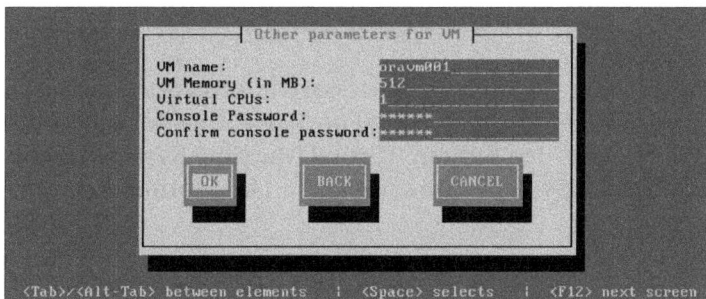

4. The information is written into the `vm.cfg` file—the VM configuration file, as shown in the following screenshot:

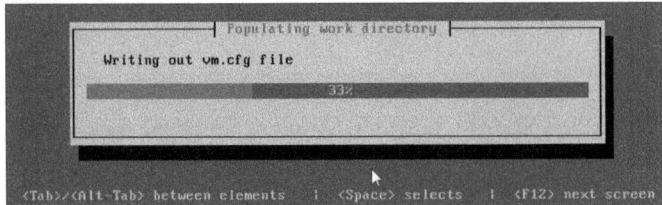

5. Then, a secure web server is started, and you will provide this information to the Oracle VM Manager while you start the P2V process:

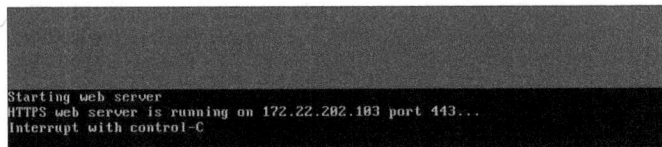

6. Now moving back to our VM Manager console, click on the **Resources** page, select the **Virtual Machines Templates** tab, and then click on **Import**.

7. Select **Linux P2V Import** and click on **Next**, as shown in the following screenshot:

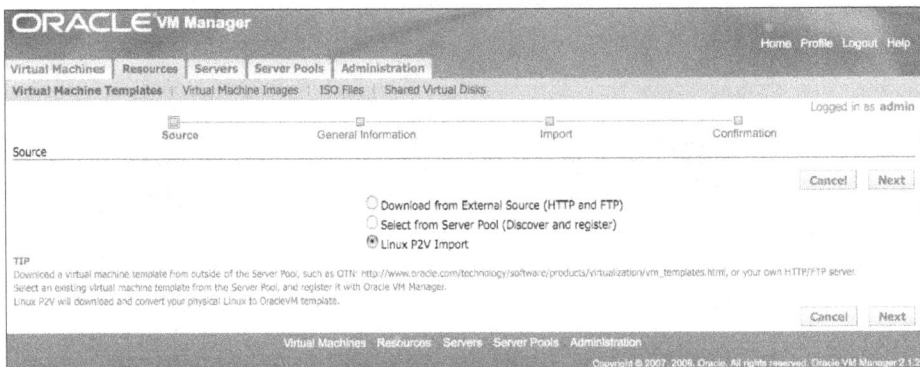

8. In the next screen, we fill in the necessary information such as Server Pool Name, Virtual Machine Template Name, Enable High Availabiliy (if possible), Operating System, **Virtual Machine System Username** and **Virtual Machine System Password** and a **Description** about the VM.

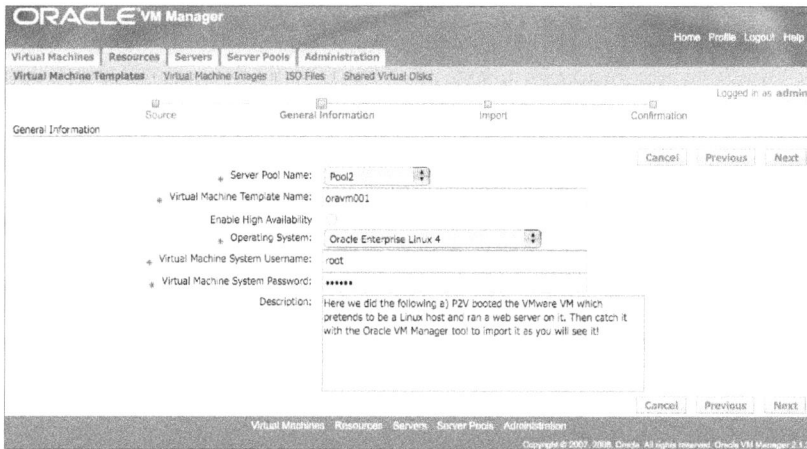

9. Type `https://172.22.202.103` as the **Hostname/IP** — the Secure URL for the Linux host we are about to migrate — and then click on **Next**.

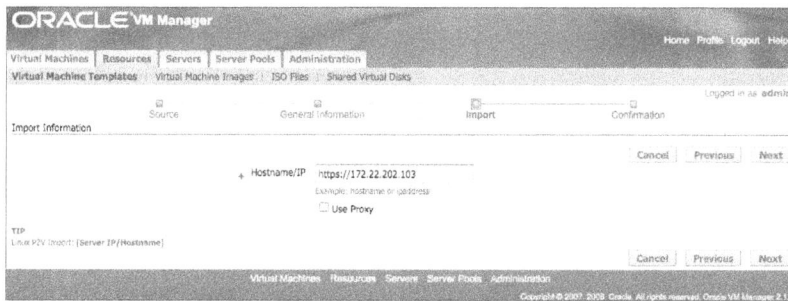

10. Click on **Confirm** to move on to the next screen, as shown in the following screenshot:

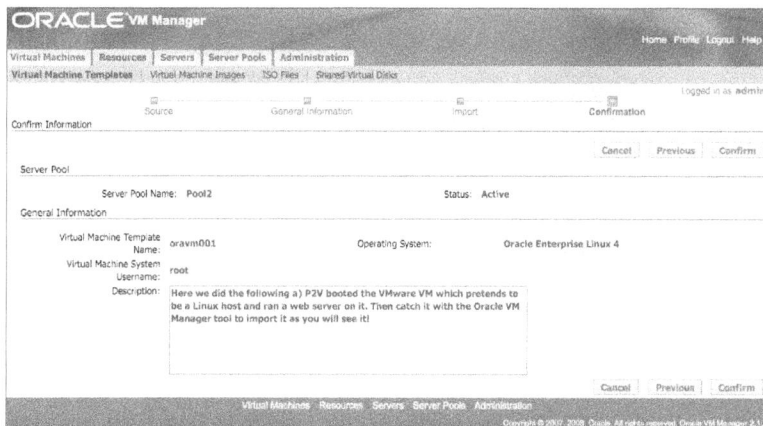

11. The Virtual Machine starts the **Importing** process:

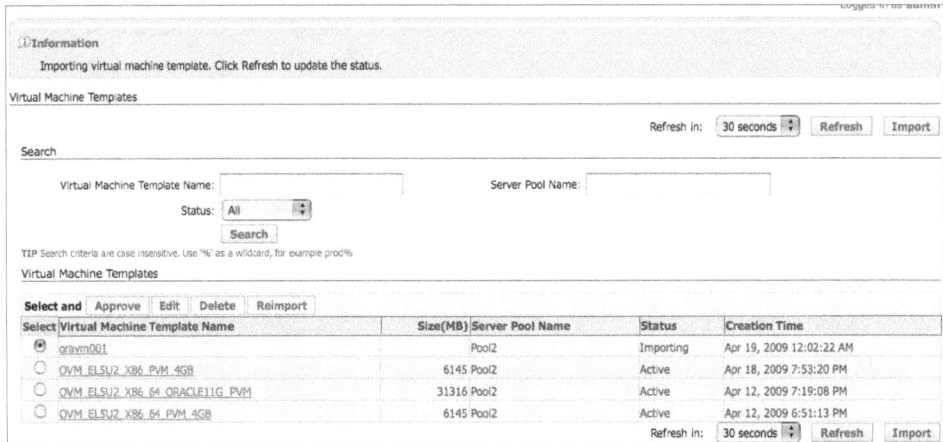

We tend to get curious to see what happens on the machine where the migration is taking place. You quickly notice that after a couple of HTTP GET calls, the VMs first image is being pulled over to the Oracle Server:

```
Starting web server
HTTPS web server is running on 172.22.202.103 port 443...
Interrupt with control-C
172.22.202.113 - - [19/Apr/2009 00:01:52] "HEAD / HTTP/1.0" 200 -
172.22.202.113 - - [19/Apr/2009 00:01:52] "HEAD /MANIFEST HTTP/1.0" 200 -
172.22.202.113 - - [19/Apr/2009 00:01:53] "HEAD /vm.cfg HTTP/1.0" 200 -
172.22.202.113 - - [19/Apr/2009 00:01:54] "GET /vm.cfg HTTP/1.0" 200 -
172.22.202.113 - - [19/Apr/2009 00:01:54] "HEAD /vm.cfg HTTP/1.0" 200 -
172.22.202.113 - - [19/Apr/2009 00:01:55] "GET /vm.cfg HTTP/1.0" 200 -
172.22.202.113 - - [19/Apr/2009 00:02:14] "HEAD / HTTP/1.0" 200 -
172.22.202.113 - - [19/Apr/2009 00:02:14] "HEAD / HTTP/1.0" 200 -
172.22.202.113 - - [19/Apr/2009 00:02:15] "GET / HTTP/1.0" 200 -
172.22.202.113 - - [19/Apr/2009 00:02:15] code 404, message File not found
172.22.202.113 - - [19/Apr/2009 00:02:15] "HEAD /robots.txt HTTP/1.0" 404 -
172.22.202.113 - - [19/Apr/2009 00:02:15] "HEAD /catalog HTTP/1.0" 200 -
172.22.202.113 - - [19/Apr/2009 00:02:15] "HEAD /catalog HTTP/1.0" 200 -
172.22.202.113 - - [19/Apr/2009 00:02:16] "GET /catalog HTTP/1.0" 200 -
172.22.202.113 - - [19/Apr/2009 00:02:16] "HEAD /MANIFEST HTTP/1.0" 200 -
172.22.202.113 - - [19/Apr/2009 00:02:16] "HEAD /MANIFEST HTTP/1.0" 200 -
172.22.202.113 - - [19/Apr/2009 00:02:18] "GET /MANIFEST HTTP/1.0" 200 -
172.22.202.113 - - [19/Apr/2009 00:02:18] "HEAD /System-sda.img HTTP/1.0" 200 -
172.22.202.113 - - [19/Apr/2009 00:02:18] "HEAD /System-sda.img HTTP/1.0" 200 -
172.22.202.113 - - [19/Apr/2009 00:02:19] "GET /System-sda.img HTTP/1.0" 200 -
```

A similar status can be seen at the VM Manager portal where the conversion is taking place, as shown in the following screenshot:

Select and	Approve	Edit	Delete	Reimport			
Select	Virtual Machine Template Name		Size(MB)	Server Pool Name	Status		Creation Time
⦿	oravm001			Pool2	Importing: System-sda.img 8192 MB(15%)		Apr 19, 2009 12:02:22 AM
○	OVM_EL5U2_X86_PVM_4GB		6145	Pool2	Active		Apr 18, 2009 7:53:20 PM

The imported VMs could have several statuses. The **Importing** status means that the VM is being imported; here you would want to wait patiently until the import process is completed. The **Pending** status simply means that the VM has been imported and is awaiting the approval of the manager. The **Active** status means that the VM template is active and can be deployed for creating new machines. The **Inactive** status means that the VM has been imported but is not yet available.

Let's explore briefly how to carry out certain tasks.

Reimporting a VM template

You can run into all sorts of errors where you might be prompted to re-import the VM template. For example, we ran into this error as our disk was full on the VM Server.

As you can see in the following screenshot, our OCFS volume was `100%` used, therefore, we cleaned up some disk space and were able to rerun the import.

```
[root@oravm03 /]# df -h -T
Filesystem     Type    Size  Used Avail Use% Mounted on
/dev/sda2      ext3    3.0G  742M  2.1G  27% /
/dev/sda3      ocfs2   100G  100G     0 100% /OVS
/dev/sda1      ext3     99M   36M   59M  38% /boot
tmpfs          tmpfs   293M     0  293M   0% /dev/shm
[root@oravm03 /]# df -h -T
Filesystem     Type    Size  Used Avail Use% Mounted on
/dev/sda2      ext3    3.0G  742M  2.1G  27% /
/dev/sda3      ocfs2   100G  103G  5.2G  96% /OVS
/dev/sda1      ext3     99M   36M   59M  38% /boot
tmpfs          tmpfs   293M     0  293M   0% /dev/shm
```

The error on your VM Manager portal will be:

Virtual Machine Templates	Virtual Machine Images	ISO Files	Shared Virtual Disks

Virtual Machine Templates > Log   Logged in as **admin**
Log

			Back To Virtual Machine Template Management
Operation	Operation Details	Start Time	Status
Importing oravm001	failed	Apr 19, 2009 12:23:07 AM	Import Error
			Back To Virtual Machine Template Management

Virtual Machines   Resources   Servers   Server Pools   Administration

Now, on the **VM Templates** page, select the VM template you want to reimport and then click on **Reimport** as shown in the following screenshot:

Virtual Machine Templates				
Select and	Approve	Edit	Delete	Reimport
Select	**Virtual Machine Template Name**			
◉	OVM_EL5U2_X86_PVM_4GB			

Approving the imported Virtual Machine template

The VMs are pending for approval after being imported. Only after the Manager, responsible for that VM or Server Pool, approves it, the VM template can be approved:

To approve a VM template, you must have a Manager or Administrator role. If you have that then on the Virtual Machine Template page click on "Approve" to approve the VM template.

Editing a VM template

To edit a VM template, click on the **Edit** button while browsing through the **Virtual Machines Template** page.

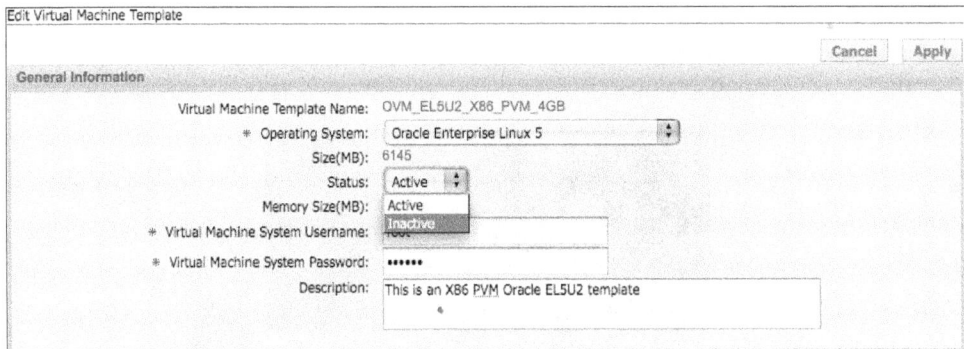

Edit Virtual Machine Template		
	Cancel	Apply
General Information		
Virtual Machine Template Name:	OVM_EL5U2_X86_PVM_4GB	
* Operating System:	Oracle Enterprise Linux 5	
Size(MB):	6145	
Status:	Active	
Memory Size(MB):	Active / Inactive	
* Virtual Machine System Username:		
* Virtual Machine System Password:	••••••	
Description:	This is an X86 PVM Oracle EL5U2 template	

Deleting a VM template

Deleting a VM template is a simple process—just click on the **Delete** button in the **Virtual Machines Template** page and your template will be deleted. Don't forget to ensure that you do have a copy of the template in case you want to use it again.

Click on the **Delete** button to remove the template from the system:

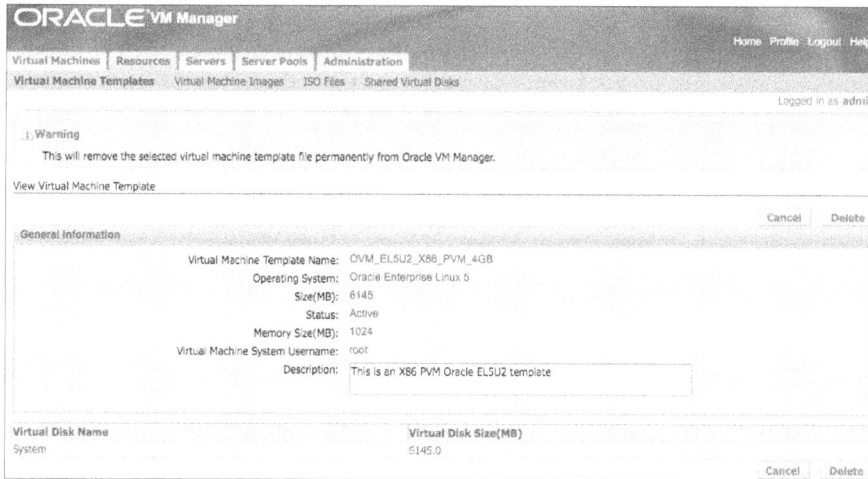

Importing Virtual Machine images

We just looked at the importing process of VM templates; now let's explore the VM images. These images are ready to be deployed the minute you have them in your Oracle VM Manager.

You can import both Oracle and VMware Virtual Machines with this utility. While importing Oracle VM Manager it is possible to convert VMware Virtual Machines seamlessly via the V2V process.

We also explore the capability of converting the VMware disk `*.vmdk` into a `*.img` file. Other formats are also supported, such as `vvfat`, `vpc`, `bochs`, `dmg`, `cloop`, `vmdk`, `qcow`, `cow`, and `raw`.

Ensure that the `vm.cfg` file has the right parameters; in our case we made sure to point it to the right disk:

```
disk = ['file:/OVS/running_pool/XP4VMotion/system.img,hdc:cdrom,r']
```

```
acpi = 1
apic = 1
builder = 'hvm'
device_model = '/usr/lib/xen/bin/qemu-dm'
disk = ['file:/OVS/running_pool/XP4VMotion/system.img,hdc:cdrom,r']
kernel = '/usr/lib/xen/boot/hvmloader'
memory = '256'
name = 'XP4VMotion'
on_crash = 'restart'
on_reboot = 'restart'
pae = 1
serial = 'pty'
timer_mode = 0
uuid = 'c9b3cd57-fbc8-dd52-8764-fc11ce31f5a0'
vcpus = 1
vif = ['type=ioemu, mac=00:16:3e:59:d5:07, bridge=xenbr0']
vnc = 1
vnclisten = '0.0.0.0'
vncunused = 1
```

Importing a Virtual Machine image

Getting the Virtual Machine images can take place in several ways. You could get them from the Server Pool, get them from the external cloud, or convert the VM from Linux VM to a VM with the P2V utility.

Don't forget to ensure that you have enough free space, as the typical Oracle VM may require twice as much space as a VMware Virtual Machine.

Selecting a VM image from the Server Pool

Carry out the following steps to select a VM image from the Server Pool:

1. Click on the **Import** option under the **Virtual Machine Images** tab, on the **Resource** page, as shown in the following screenshot:

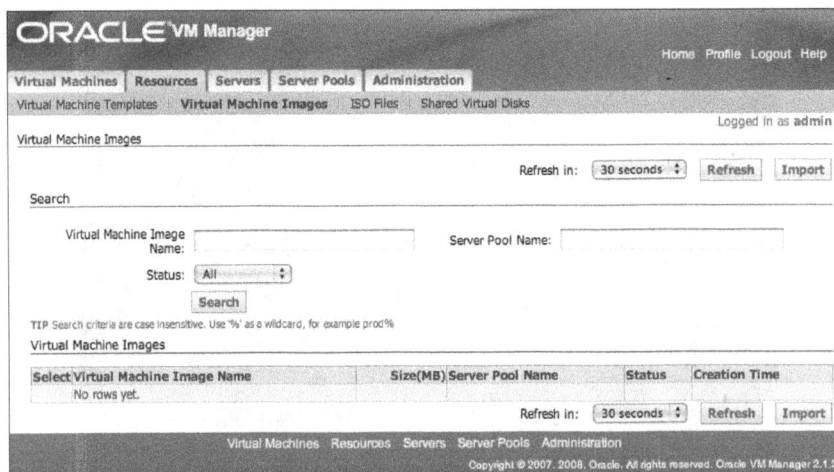

2. Click on the **Select from Server Pool (Discover and register)** option and then click on **Next**.

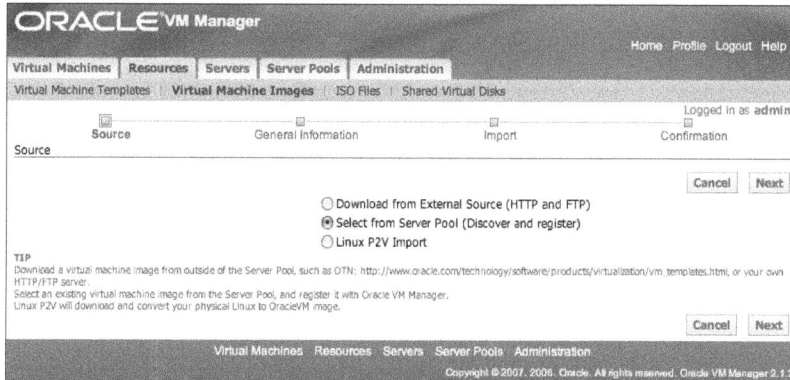

3. Select the available pool from the drop-down menu:

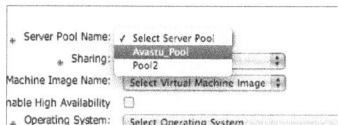

4. Select the Virtual Machine image. Later you will notice that the image is now visible to the Oracle VM Manager portal since we converted the VM and pointed it to the right disk by editing the vm.cfg file:

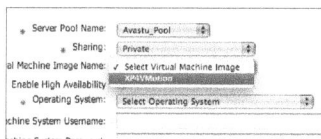

5. Select the **Operating System**:

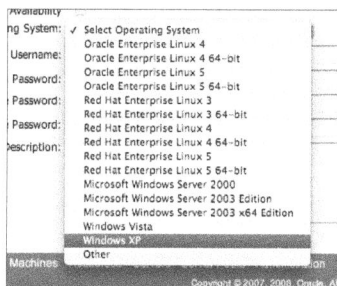

6. Click on **Next** after completely filling the **General Information** form to go to the next page:

7. Click on **Confirm** to accept all the parameters:

8. You shall get a message acknowledging the successful importation of the Virtual Machine image.

9. Click on the **Approve** button to go to the confirmation page.

10. Click on **Approve** to confirm the approval.

11. You get a successful message of the VM's approval:

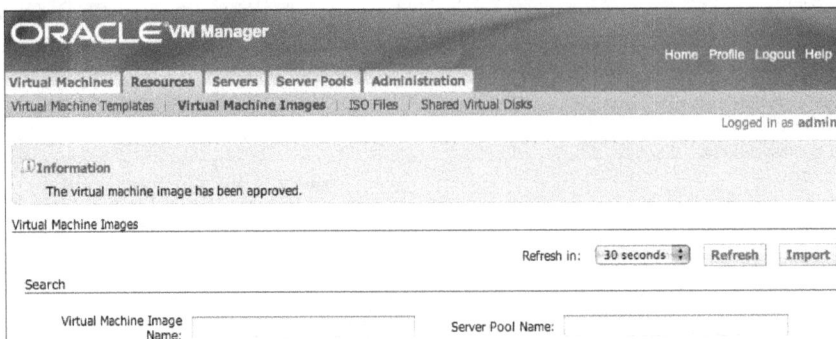

12. The state of the machine is **Powered Off**, as shown in the following screenshot:

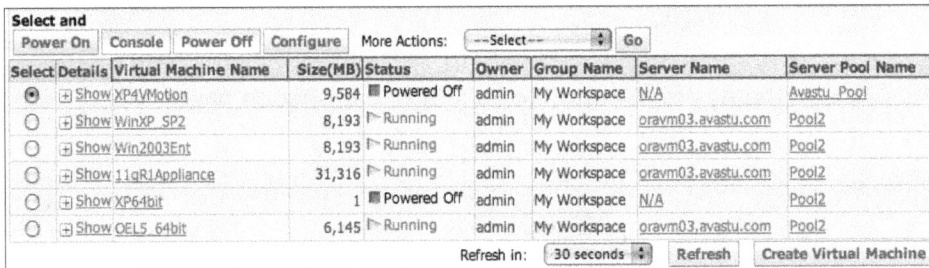

Select and

| Power On | Console | Power Off | Configure | More Actions: | --Select-- | Go |

Select	Details	Virtual Machine Name	Size(MB)	Status	Owner	Group Name	Server Name	Server Pool Name
⦿	⊞ Show	XP4VMotion	9,584	■ Powered Off	admin	My Workspace	N/A	Avastu Pool
○	⊞ Show	WinXP_SP2	8,193	⏵ Running	admin	My Workspace	oravm03.avastu.com	Pool2
○	⊞ Show	Win2003Ent	8,193	⏵ Running	admin	My Workspace	oravm03.avastu.com	Pool2
○	⊞ Show	11gR1Appliance	31,316	⏵ Running	admin	My Workspace	oravm03.avastu.com	Pool2
○	⊞ Show	XP64bit	1	■ Powered Off	admin	My Workspace	N/A	Pool2
○	⊞ Show	OEL5_64bit	6,145	⏵ Running	admin	My Workspace	oravm03.avastu.com	Pool2

Refresh in: 30 seconds | Refresh | Create Virtual Machine

13. Click on the **+** sign, located next to the **Show** option, in order to expand and see the details of the VM that was imported from the original VMware format:

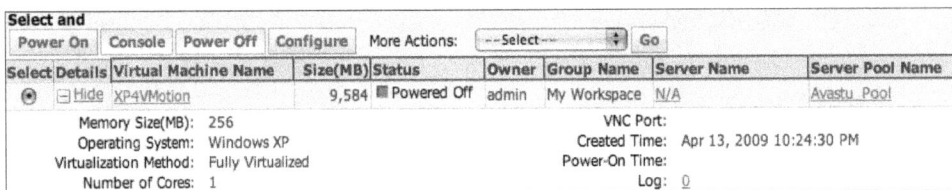

Select and

| Power On | Console | Power Off | Configure | More Actions: | --Select-- | Go |

Select	Details	Virtual Machine Name	Size(MB)	Status	Owner	Group Name	Server Name	Server Pool Name
⦿	⊟ Hide	XP4VMotion	9,584	■ Powered Off	admin	My Workspace	N/A	Avastu Pool

Memory Size(MB): 256	VNC Port:
Operating System: Windows XP	Created Time: Apr 13, 2009 10:24:30 PM
Virtualization Method: Fully Virtualized	Power-On Time:
Number of Cores: 1	Log: 0

14. Click on the **Power On** option to turn on the Virtual Machine:

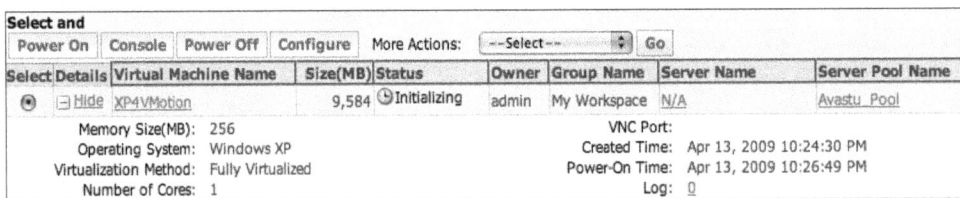

Select and

| Power On | Console | Power Off | Configure | More Actions: | --Select-- | Go |

Select	Details	Virtual Machine Name	Size(MB)	Status	Owner	Group Name	Server Name	Server Pool Name
⦿	⊟ Hide	XP4VMotion	9,584	⟳ Initializing	admin	My Workspace	N/A	Avastu Pool

Memory Size(MB): 256	VNC Port:
Operating System: Windows XP	Created Time: Apr 13, 2009 10:24:30 PM
Virtualization Method: Fully Virtualized	Power-On Time: Apr 13, 2009 10:26:49 PM
Number of Cores: 1	Log: 0

Your VM Image import will fail if the VM is not found in the `OVS/running_pool/VM_Name` directory. Also ensure that you have the right `vm.cfg` file; normally the Oracle VM Manager will create the `vm.cfg` file during the import.

Downloading from external cloud

You can also download the VM image from an external cloud, such as the VMware Marketplace or any other HTTP/FTP mirrors where VM images are being hosted. Carry out the same procedure we did in the VM template import procedure from the external cloud.

> When filling in the information for the external cloud URL, for a VM, on an HTTP mirror fill in the following details:
>
> `http://host/vm`
>
> For FTP you would fill in:
>
> `ftp://username:password@host/vm`
>
> And if you are importing a VMware VM then you would typically fill in:
>
> `ftp://username:password@host/vm/myvm.vmx` (where `*.vmx` is the config file for VMware Virtual Machines)

The conversion process which Oracle follows is pretty simple. It first copies the VM files to the Oracle VM Server and then generates the `vm.cfg` file. After the conversion has taken place, the VMware Virtual Machine will be deleted.

Doing a P2V with Linux Host Conversion

Once again, here we follow the same procedure to convert the Linux host to a VM as we did in the previous VM template import method. This method is no different than the earlier one, except for the fact that your VMs will be placed in the `/OVS/running_pool`.

Importing ISO files

You can import ISO files to provide installation media for creating Virtual Machines. We briefly covered how to import the ISO files in Chapter 5. Let's now look at how to import ISO files in more depth.

How to import an ISO file

Anyone can import an ISO file, but the administrator approves the imported ISO file. All ISO files belonging to the same image must reside in the ISO pool. ISO files reside in the same ISO group. All users in the same server pool can share the ISO files.

We have placed the ISO files in the following directory:

```
/OVS/iso_pool/install_images
```

The files are visible to the VM Manager portal, as we had imported several of the ISO images in the previous chapter.

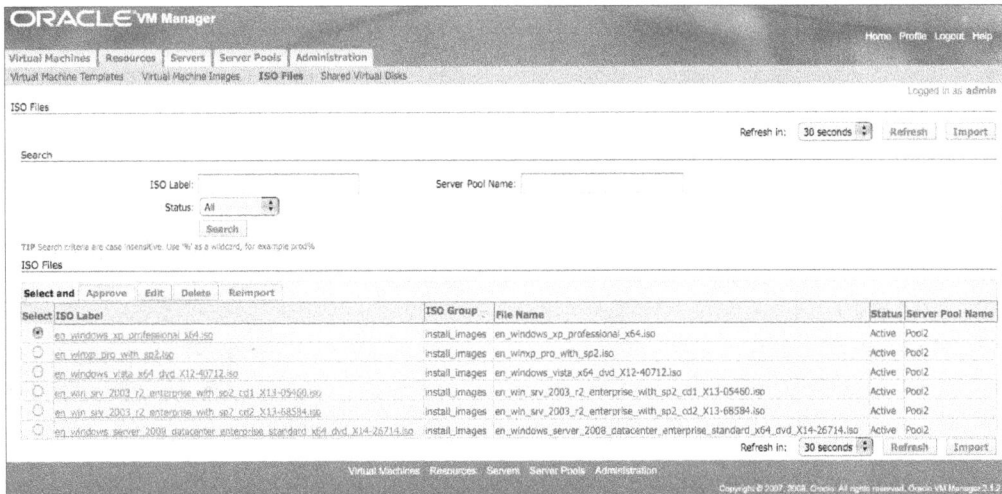

Similarly, you can either download the ISO files from an external cloud or you can select it from a Server Pool.

Selecting an ISO from the Server Pool or IntraCloud

Carry out the following steps in order to select an ISO from the Server Pool:

1. Click on the **Select from Server Pool (Discover and Register)** option and then click on **Next**:

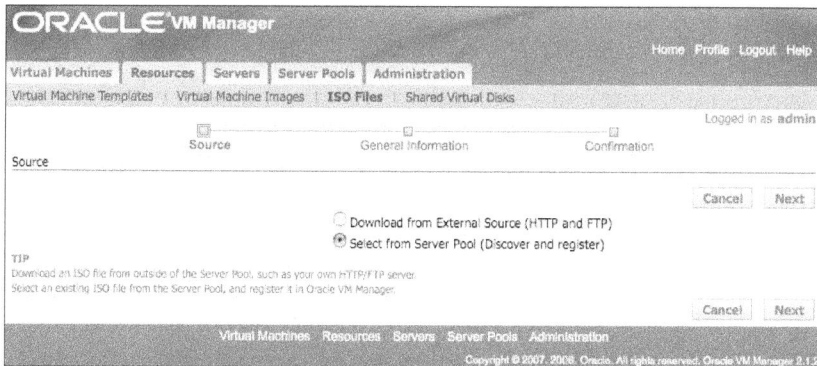

2. After selecting the Server Pool where we would like this ISO to rest, we pick up the **install_images** option from the **ISO Group** drop-down menu:

3. Then we choose the ISO file; in this case it happens to be a Windows XP x64 bit edition, as shown in the following screenshot:

4. Click on **Next** in order to move to the next screen:

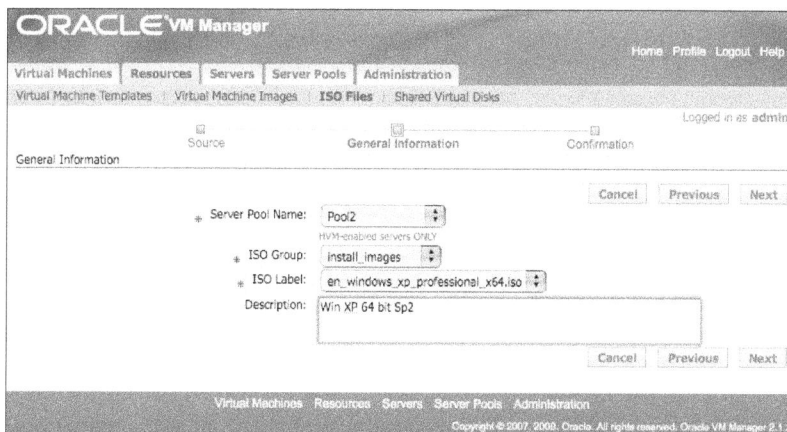

5. Click on the **Confirm** button to start the import process.

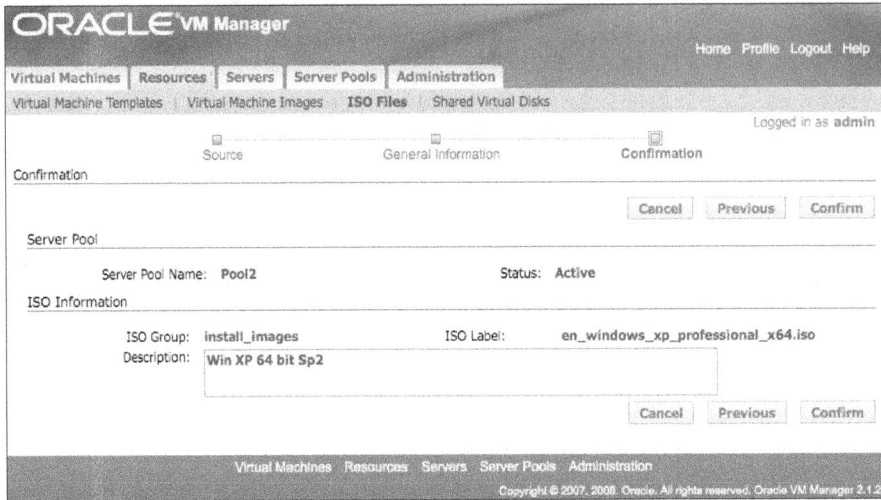

6. Click on the **Approve** button:

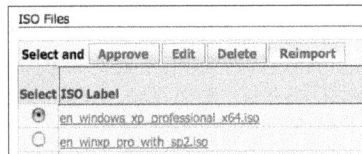

7. Click on the Approve button to confirm the approval.

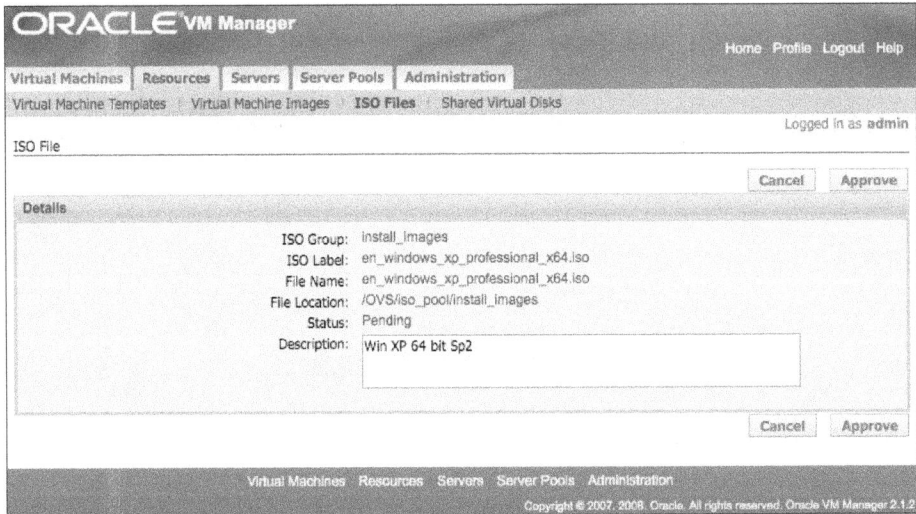

In the following screenshot, you can see a general overview of all the ISO files under **ISO Group — install_images**:

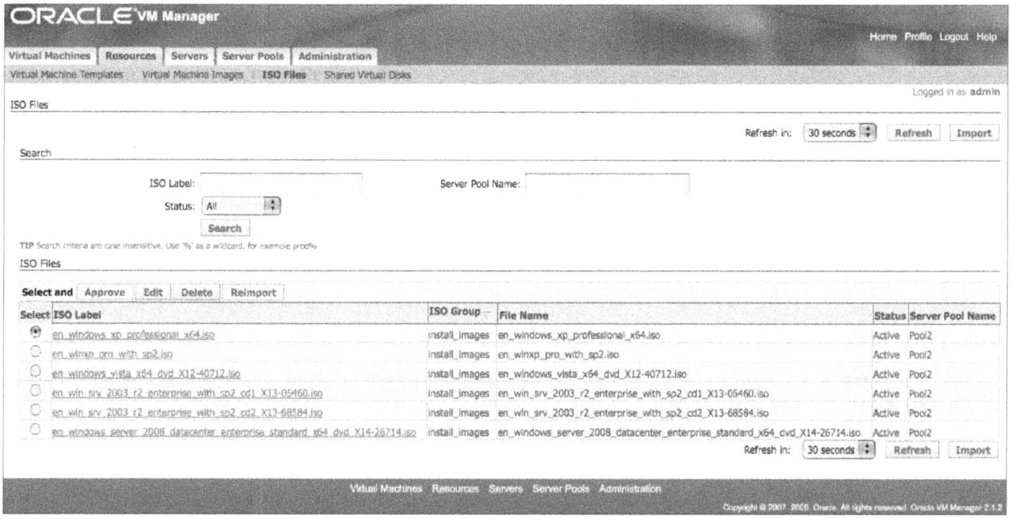

Downloading from an external cloud

Getting the ISO from an external cloud environment may be another option if you do not have the ISOs in your own IntraCloud environment.

Click on the necessary details. Here, we have filled in the FTP address of our FTP server in the **URL** option and given ourselves a new **ISO Group** and **ISO Label** name.

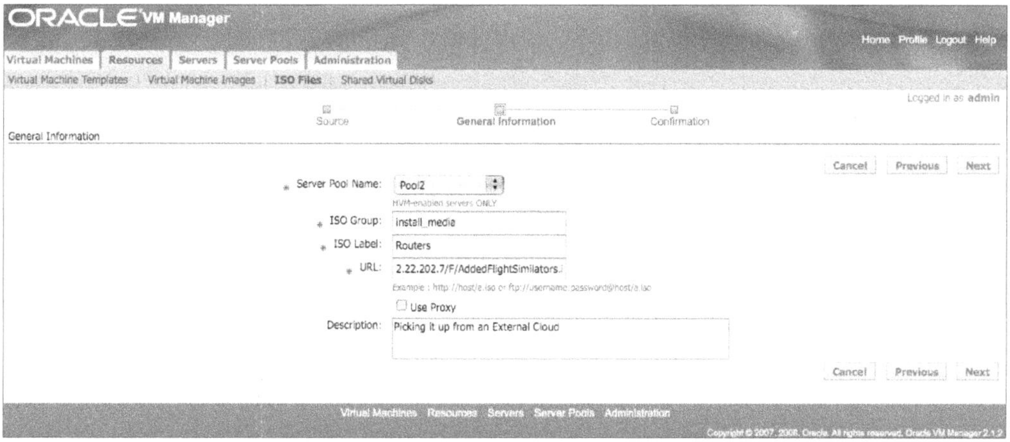

The imported ISO file can be managed by reimporting, deleting, and editing (making status active or inactive). We have covered these in the previous chapter.

Managing shared virtual disks

You can create shared virtual disks to scale up your storage capacity when needed. Oracle VM environment currently only supports virtual disks. Physical devices can be used but they cannot be managed through the VM Manager. You saw an example earlier when we converted a VMware VM to Oracle VM and the disk location was picked out of the `vm.cfg` file:

```
disk = [ 'file:/OVS/running_pool/MyVM/System.img,w']
```

Once you have configured your storage and all the VMs are resting on the shared storage substrate then all you need to do is add capacity to the infinite pool of your IntraCloud environment.

Adding shared storage has been covered in the previous chapter, as well. Other administrative tasks such as searching and deleting storage can be conveniently done from the Oracle VM Manager portal.

Summary

Thus, as we approach to the end of this book, I hope you got a good understanding of how we can manage, configure, and build VM resources—and it all can be done easily using the Oracle VM Manager.

In the next, also the last, chapter we shall take a look at troubleshooting within the Oracle VM environment.

8
Troubleshooting and Gotchas

As we approach the end of this book, we realize that the journey for us has not been without troubles and errors. I will attempt to address the ones that are bound to bother you the most in this chapter.

What will we cover in troubleshooting?

While we tackle the following issues in troubleshooting VM Manager. We are assuming that you are using the latest version of Oracle VM Manager and the Oracle VM Server version is 2.1.x:

- Oracle VM Manager login takes too much time
- HVM guest creation fails
- Not enough disk space available for ISOs and Templates
- Cannot login to the VM remotely

> As more and more users start to explore and use Oracle VM Manager, more troubleshooting and tweaks will come up. This is by no way an exhaustive list and is also not intended to be. Please do participate as much as possible in forums and contribute your tips and tricks with the community.

Oracle VM Manager login takes too much time

I have faced this issue very often and normally if you are unlucky you ought to get this type of error while installing. For instance this error message says nothing about the memory issue:

```
Failed at "Could not get DeploymentManager".

This is typically the result of an invalid deployer URI format being
supplied, the target server not being in a started state or incorrect
authentication details being supplied.

More information is available by enabling logging -- please see the
Oracle Containers for J2EE Configuration and Administration Guide for
details.

Failed

Please see /var/log/ovm-manager/ovm-manager.log for more information.

Deploying application failed.

Please check your environment, and re-run the script:/bin/sh scripts/
deployApp.sh

Aborting installation. Please check the environment and rerun
runInstaller.sh.
```

But when you upgrade your VM Manager OS with more memory you'll be able to continue with the installation.

Sometimes, you may also get all kinds of errors, such as the following one:

```
Internal Exception: java.lang.OutOfMemoryError: Java heap space
```

And they clearly point to the memory issue. This suggests that your OC4J may need more memory.

Let's run the following commands to check the log information:

```
cat  /var/log/ovm-manager/oc4j.log | grep "heap"
```

If your OC4J ran out of memory you would typically get that heapsize error. To fix this go back to the console and examine the values of the following OC4J_JVM_ARGS function in the /opt/oc4j/bin/oc4j configuration file:

```
#!/bin/sh
#
# oc4j - shell for invoking OC4J basic operations.
#
# Usage:    oc4j [Options]
#
#         Options:
#           -start                    : start OC4J
#           -shutdown -port <ORMI port> -password <password>
#                                     : stop OC4J
#           -version                  : display the version
#           -help                     : display this message
#
# Copyright (c) 2004, 2005, Oracle. All rights reserved.
#

##########################################################
######### START CONFIGURATION SECTION ##################
##########################################################

J2EE_HOME=$ORACLE_HOME/j2ee/home
OC4J_JVM_ARGS="-XX:PermSize=256m -XX:MaxPermSize=512m"
#Any persistent arguments to specify at the JVM level can be set here
#By default this will be read from the operating system environment
if [ "$OC4J_JVM_ARGS" ]
then
  JVMARGS=$OC4J_JVM_ARGS
else
  JVMARGS=
fi
CMDARGS=

if [ "$VERBOSE" ]
then
  VERBOSE=$VERBOSE
else
  VERBOSE=off
fi

ORMI_URL=ormi://localhost
ORMI_USER=oc4jadmin

OC4J_JAR=$J2EE_HOME/oc4j.jar
ADMIN_JAR=$J2EE_HOME/admin.jar
SERVER_XML=$J2EE_HOME/config/server.xml

##########################################################
#########  END CONFIGURATION SECTION  ##################
##########################################################

check_oc4j()
{
"/opt/oc4j/bin/oc4j" [readonly] 267L, 5848C
```

Edit the following OC4J_JVM_ARGS="-XX:PermSize=256m -XX:MaxPermSize=512m
function and give more memory to the OC4J.

Save the information and quit: :

```
##########################################################
######### START CONFIGURATION SECTION ##################
##########################################################

J2EE_HOME=$ORACLE_HOME/j2ee/home
OC4J_JVM_ARGS="-XX:PermSize=512m -XX:MaxPermSize=1024m"
#Any persistent arguments to specify at the JVM level can be set here
#By default this will be read from the operating system environment
if [ "$OC4J_JVM_ARGS" ]
then
```

Restart the service OC4J:

```
service oc4j stop
service oc4j start
```

HVM guest creation fails

Normally there are many actions and functionalities within Oracle VM Manager that require the host to be truly HVM-aware, which means that 64-bit (preferably) Oracle VM Servers must be running with hardware virtualization support on the chipset level. Having said that, both Intel and AMD support it and it is highly unlikely that you will come across new machines that do not support that. However, always check the compatibility within a specific family and check whether the support is turned on or off.

Nonetheless, you could be using some reusable older hardware that may or may not support HW-assist virtualization.

If you are confronted with the following message:

"Error: There is no server supporting hardware virtualization in the selected server pool. "

Then you'll have a reason to worry and check your hardware, and carry out the following commands on the VM Server that does not allow you to create a HVM:

`Cat /proc/cpuinfo | grep -E 'vmx|smx'`

Use the preceding command if your hardware is HVM-aware, then you should get some reply as shown in the following screenshot:

```
[root@oravm03 ~]# cat /proc/cpuinfo | grep -E 'vmx|smx'
flags           : fpu tsc msr pae mce cx8 apic mtrr mca cmov pat pse36 clflush dts acpi mmx fxsr sse sse
2 ss ht tm pbe nx lm constant_tsc pni monitor ds_cpl vmx est tm2 cx16 xtpr lahf_lm
flags           : fpu tsc msr pae mce cx8 apic mtrr mca cmov pat pse36 clflush dts acpi mmx fxsr sse sse
2 ss ht tm pbe nx lm constant_tsc up pni monitor ds_cpl vmx est tm2 cx16 xtpr lahf_lm
[root@oravm03 ~]#
```

If you don't get a response, then you might have a problem. For instance we pick up another VM Server which we for sure know does not have a HVM support or HW-assist virtualization:

```
[root@vmmgr ~]# cat /proc/cpuinfo | grep -E 'vmx|smx'
[root@vmmgr ~]#
```

Also ensure that the virtualization support is enabled at the HW level in the BIOS. Then run the following commands to see if the Operating System supports HVM:

```
[root@oravm03 ~]#
[root@oravm03 ~]# xm info | grep hvm
xen_caps                : xen-3.0-x86_64 xen-3.0-x86_32p hvm-3.0-x86_32 hvm-3.0-x86_32p hvm-3.0-x86_64
[root@oravm03 ~]# ssh root@172.22.202.111
The authenticity of host '172.22.202.111 (172.22.202.111)' can't be established.
RSA key fingerprint is b6:36:d8:97:b5:16:3b:04:0a:8a:26:e6:da:93:8e:89.
Are you sure you want to continue connecting (yes/no)? yes
Warning: Permanently added '172.22.202.111' (RSA) to the list of known hosts.
root@172.22.202.111's password:
Last login: Mon Apr 13 21:57:52 2009 from 172.22.202.7
[root@oravm01 ~]# xm info | grep hvm
[root@oravm01 ~]#
```

As you have seen in the preceding screenshot, we then quickly logged into the VM Server which we knew does not support HVM and did not get a reply from the 172.22.202.111 VM Server. Whereas, the x64 bit version with built-in, BIOS-enabled HVM support returns the values in the form of xen_caps.

```
xen_caps                : xen-3.0-x86_64 xen-3.0-x86_32p hvm-3.0-x86_32
hvm-3.0-x86_32p hvm-3.0-x86_64
```

> We will explain more about the mighty xm command line utility in the *Appendix*.

So if your CPU does not support HVM, use the **PVM (Paravirtualized Method)** to create your VM.

Not enough disk space available for ISOs and Templates

You are naturally bound to run into these sorts of troubles. As more and more excitement seeps in and as you start installing all the versions of Windows and Linux machines to your Oracle IntraCloud farm, the more you are bound to run out of disk space. The kind of error you might run into would be very difficult to troubleshoot. I simply ran out of space when I was pushing VM templates to the Oracle VM Server.

In any case to resolve this you will need to reduce the consumed space by either cleaning up your repository farm or your disk space. Alternatively, you can also add another repository, obviously the other disk must be available to create the additional repository.

To add a new repository, simply run the following command on your VM Server:

`/usr/lib/ovs/ovs-makerepo source shared description`

Where, source is the block device or NFS path to the file system to be added. The shared parameter could carry a value of 0 or 1. If the value of the shared parameter is 0, it means that the disk will not be shared, whereas when the value is 1, it would imply that the repository will be shared. The description parameter is displayed in the Oracle VM Manager and must be a readable value for the functional users.

You get the value of the repository you just created upon running the following command:

`cat /etc/ovs/repositories`

```
[root@oravm03 /]# /usr/lib/ovs/ovs-makerepo /dev/sda1 1 My_Repository
Initializing NEW repository /dev/sda1
SUCCESS: Mounted /OVS/19BBFF023D20424EB29497549C5C9F96
Updating local repository list.
ovs-makerepo complete
[root@oravm03 /]# cat /etc/ovs/repositories
# This configuration file was generated by ovs-makerepo
# DO NOT EDIT
19BBFF023D20424EB29497549C5C9F96 /dev/sda1
[root@oravm03 /]#
```

The makerepo script identifies the file system or shared virtual disk as a repository. It also updates the repository configuration to enable it.

It is also a good habit to occasionally check the file system using the "df" command. This command greatly helps in understanding how our volumes are doing and what the usage and mountpoint is:

```
[root@oravm03 /]# df
Filesystem           1K-blocks      Used Available Use% Mounted on
/dev/sda2              3050092    759956   2132700  27% /
/dev/sda3            112912384 108107264   4805120  96% /OVS
/dev/sda1              101086     36240     59627  38% /boot
tmpfs                  299608         0    299608   0% /dev/shm
/dev/sda1              101086     36240     59627  38% /OVS/19BBFF023D20424EB29497549C5C9F96
[root@oravm03 /]# df -h -T
Filesystem    Type    Size  Used Avail Use% Mounted on
/dev/sda2     ext3    3.0G  743M  2.1G  27% /
/dev/sda3     ocfs2   108G  104G  4.6G  96% /OVS
/dev/sda1     ext3     99M   36M   59M  38% /boot
tmpfs         tmpfs   293M     0  293M   0% /dev/shm
/dev/sda1     ext3     99M   36M   59M  38% /OVS/19BBFF023D20424EB29497549C5C9F96
[root@oravm03 /]#
```

The `df-h-T` command helps us make the values more readable. If you type the `df-help` command, you will get more information on using the `df` command effectively.

The -h argument ensures that the values are readable to us in amounts of GBs or MBs and not blocks such as –T prints the file system type as well. We have all our VMs running on OCFS and that is one place you must watch out for constantly in case of oversubscription, usage, and disk contention.

This newly added repository will have the following directories created automatically: /OVS/seed_pool, /OVS/running_pool, and /OVS/iso_pool directories. Let's take a quick look at them:

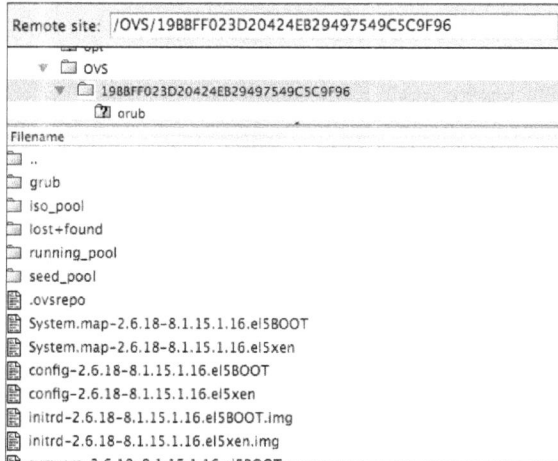

As you can see in the preceding screenshot, it's not just the directories but the other necessary binaries as well that are placed at the same location by default. Here the repository is placed under the OVS and the large value is its UUID.

Cannot login to the VM remotely

Logging into the VM can be a problem, and the best way to solve is to get **TightVNC** viewer and also install the ovs-console plugin (rpm) as we did it the previous chapter when we went ahead to manage the VMs within the Oracle VM Manager.

I have the plugin working perfectly on my MacBook Pro, another Windows machine, and also within the Oracle VM Manager.

Normally, an installation of an older version of Oracle VM Manager and Server throws the following exception when freshly upgraded.

```
java.lang.ClassNotFoundException: VncViewer.class
```

Shut down all the web pages and reload the page to bypass the error.

After the successful installation or correction of the `VncViewer.class`, you can log into the console:

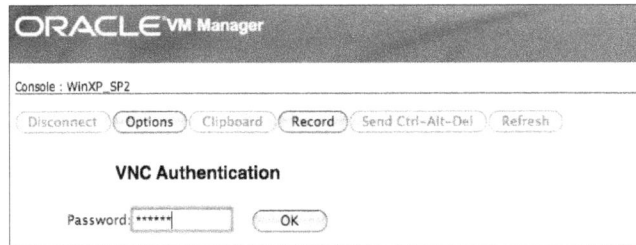

Voila! You can now work remotely on WinXP running in your Oracle VM IntraCloud environment!

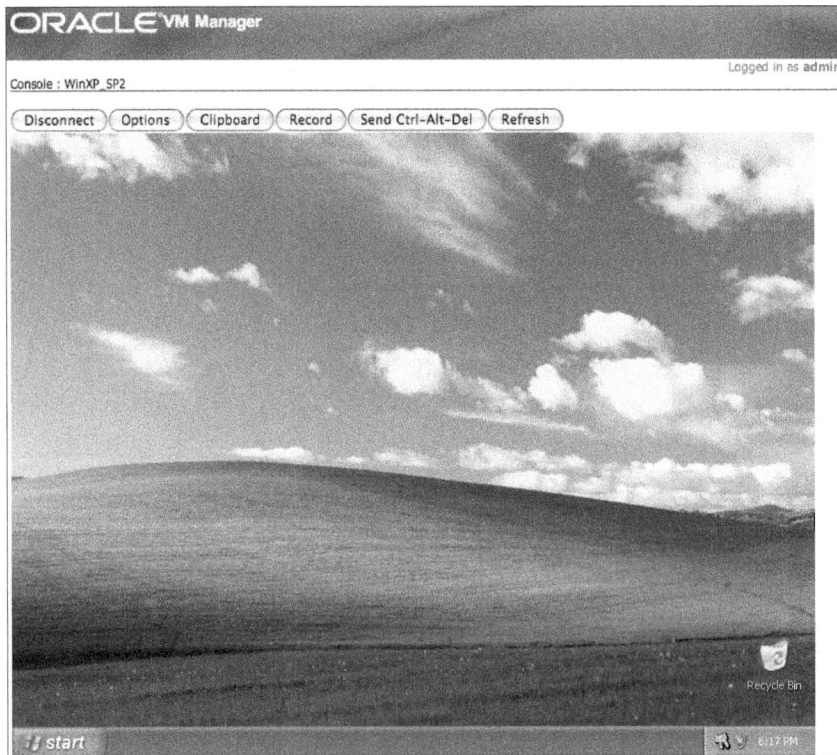

Summary

So with this chapter we close this book on a basic introduction to Oracle VM Manager. Oracle VM Manager is clearly an optimal, cost-effective IntraCoud environment which any organization can use to its advantage.

Oracle's own VM templates make a wonderful case to be tested while you can also go ahead and test all Windows flavors on it. There already are organizations choosing the Oracle VM platform, slowly and gradually. Oracle, with its careful and strategic investments in the Cloud Computing space and Virtualization, stands a better chance to go after the highly aspirational low-cost driven consumer market, and with Oracle VM Manager we have just begun scratching the surface of Oracle VM.

Command Line Tools

We will be covering some essential command line tools. I thought mentioning the top three command line tools would be a good idea. There are a lot of different directions we can go from here but let's focus on the Xen commands that I think are crucial for measuring and monitoring performance.

Once again the purpose of this Appendix section is not to give you detailed information and examples for every flag that a utility such as xm or virsh may have. We will only explore some of the important ones and leave the rest for you to exercise. There is no better way of learning than trying it all yourself. The purpose of this book is to get you excited and started.

What command line tools will we cover?

- xentop: This utility displays real-time information of VMs and VM Server.
- xm: This utility takes you a step deeper into the inner workings of the hypervisor. A lot of arguments can be given with the xm command line tool and it must be seen as a command control suite.
- virsh: This utility is yet another powerful command line tool to manage the VMs within the Oracle VM Server.

The mighty xentop command

The xentop utility is one of the **top** utility that has been very famous in the UNIX world. With Xen hypervisor we also get to view our top process and that's why we use xentop.

Let's view various arguments of xentop by typing `xentop--help`, as shown in the following screenshot:

Let's try all of the arguments one by one and see what they mean.

1. Here, we pass the `-n` argument and it gives us the output of all the Virtual NICs or VIFs.

2. Passing the `-v` argument gives us all of the vCPU output data:

Without any arguments we get all the information of the VMs running in this VM Server. As you can see in the preceding screenshot, we have a 64 bit PVM Oracle 11g Database Virtual Appliance, 64 bit HVM Windows 2003 Server, a 32bit HVM Windows XP machine, and a 64bit PVM Oracle ELU2 VM.

We also see the information such as total memory on the VM Server, amount of memory used, free memory, and the number of CPUs.

Since this is a real-time tool, you can punch in arguments on-the-fly to get results. Suppose you type b while running xentop interactively to get vbd block device data.

```
xentop - 22:17:02   Xen 3.1.4
5 domains: 1 running, 4 blocked, 0 paused, 0 crashed, 0 dying, 0 shutdown
Mem: 4192220k total, 3454532k used, 737688k free    CPUs: 2 @ 1995MHz
      NAME  STATE   CPU(sec) CPU(%)     MEM(k) MEM(%)  MAXMEM(k) MAXMEM(%) VCPUS NETS NETTX(k) NETRX(k) VBDS   VBD_OO   VBD_RD   VBD_WR SSID
112_Win2003Ent --b---    2601    0.5     401276    9.6     409600      9.8     1    1        0        0    2        0        0        0    0
129_WinXP_SP2 --b---     3151    0.6     270204    6.4     278528      6.6     1    1        0        0    2        0        0        0    0
72_OEL5_64bit --b---      598    0.1     786432   18.8     786432     18.8     1    1       25    50879    1        0    12311   130838    0
81_11gR1Appliance --b---  186    0.0    1310720   31.3    1310720     31.3     2    1        7    51057    2        0     2688    53605    0
   Domain-0 -----r      92195   30.3     599040   14.3   no limit      n/a     2    8   888886  2102988    0        0        0        0    0
```

With block device data output:

```
xentop - 22:17:02   Xen 3.1.4
5 domains: 1 running, 4 blocked, 0 paused, 0 crashed, 0 dying, 0 shutdown
Mem: 4192220k total, 3454532k used, 737688k free    CPUs: 2 @ 1995MHz
      NAME  STATE   CPU(sec) CPU(%)     MEM(k) MEM(%)  MAXMEM(k) MAXMEM(%) VCPUS NETS NETTX(k) NETRX(k) VBDS   VBD_OO   VBD_RD   VBD_WR SSID
112_Win2003Ent --b---    2601    0.5     401276    9.6     409600      9.8     1    1        0        0    2        0        0        0    0
129_WinXP_SP2 --b---     3151    0.6     270204    6.4     278528      6.6     1    1        0        0    2        0        0        0    0
72_OEL5_64bit --b---      598    0.1     786432   18.8     786432     18.8     1    1       25    50879    1        0    12311   130838    0
81_11gR1Appliance --b---  186    0.0    1310720   31.3    1310720     31.3     2    1        7    51057    2        0     2688    53605    0
   Domain-0 -----r      92195   30.3     599040   14.3   no limit      n/a     2    8   888886  2102988    0        0        0        0    0
```

So xentop provides you with real-time information of your running Oracle VM Server. Here you can see and take the right action like moving VMs to another box or allocating more resources to a VM.

The mightier xm utility

If xentop is a mighty utility, xm is the core utility within Xen. It is actually the command control suite with a huge amount of arguments which we shall learn about, soon. However, as mentioned earlier, we will not explore everything about those arguments lest we add another hundred or so pages to the book.

Running the `xm-help` command shows you why we cannot discuss every little argument here. However, I will explain on my blog the utilities associated with Xen and other versions of Xen such as Oracle VM, and so on.

```
console          Attach to <Domain>'s console.
create           Create a domain based on <ConfigFile>.
new              Adds a domain to Xend domain management
delete           Remove a domain from Xend domain management.
destroy          Terminate a domain immediately.
domid            Convert a domain name to domain id.
domname          Convert a domain id to domain name.
dump-core        Dump core for a specific domain.
list             List information about all/some domains.
mem-max          Set the maximum amount reservation for a domain.
mem-set          Set the current memory usage for a domain.
migrate          Migrate a domain to another machine.
pause            Pause execution of a domain.
reboot           Reboot a domain.
rename           Rename a domain.
restore          Restore a domain from a saved state.
resume           Resume a Xend managed domain
save             Save a domain state to restore later.
shutdown         Shutdown a domain.
start            Start a Xend managed domain
suspend          Suspend a Xend managed domain
sysrq            Send a sysrq to a domain.
trigger          Send a trigger to a domain.
top              Monitor a host and the domains in real time.
unpause          Unpause a paused domain.
uptime           Print uptime for a domain.
vcpu-list        List the VCPUs for a domain or all domains.
vcpu-pin         Set which CPUs a VCPU can use.
vcpu-set         Set the number of active VCPUs for allowed for
                 the domain.
debug-keys       Send debug keys to Xen.
dmesg            Read and/or clear Xend's message buffer.
info             Get information about Xen host.
log              Print Xend log
serve            Proxy Xend XMLRPC over stdio.
sched-credit     Get/set credit scheduler parameters.
sched-sedf       Get/set EDF parameters.
block-attach     Create a new virtual block device.
block-detach     Destroy a domain's virtual block device.
block-list       List virtual block devices for a domain.
block-configure  Change block device configuration
network-attach   Create a new virtual network device.
network-detach   Destroy a domain's virtual network device.
network-list     List virtual network interfaces for a domain.
vtpm-list        List virtual TPM devices.
vnet-list        List Vnets.
vnet-create      Create a vnet from ConfigFile.
vnet-delete      Delete a Vnet.
labels           List <type> labels for (active) policy.
addlabel         Add security label to domain.
rmlabel          Remove a security label from domain.
getlabel         Show security label for domain or resource.
```

And the remaining list of arguments.

```
dry-run          Test if a domain can access its resources.
resources        Show info for each labeled resource.
makepolicy       Build policy and create .bin/.map files.
loadpolicy       Load binary policy into hypervisor.
cfgbootpolicy    Add policy to boot configuration.
dumppolicy       Print hypervisor ACM state information.
shell            Launch an interactive shell.
```

We will run a few arguments against the xm utility powerhouse.

1. Let's start with the basics and list all of the running domains on the VM Server using the `xm list` argument, as shown in the following screenshot:

```
[root@oravm03 /]# xm list
Name                              ID   Mem VCPUs      State   Time(s)
112_Win2003Ent                    14   384     1     -b----   2611.7
129_WinXP_SP2                     19   256     1     -b----   3163.0
72_OEL5_64bit                      4   768     1     -b----    599.2
81_11gR1Appliance                  3  1280     2     -b----    187.4
Domain-0                           0   585     2     r-----  92508.4
[root@oravm03 /]#
```

2. Check the uptime with the help of the `-uptime` flag for VM ID 19:

```
[root@oravm03 /]# xm uptime 19
Name                                  ID Uptime
129_WinXP_SP2                         19 6 days,  8:22:00
```

3. Check out the network list for a VM with ID 19 by passing the `network-list`
    `19` argument.

```
[root@oravm03 /]# xm network-list 19
Idx BE     MAC Addr.     handle state evt-ch tx-/rx-ring-ref BE-path
0   0   ??                  0     1     -1    -1  /-1       /local/domain/0/backend/vif/19/0
[root@oravm03 /]#
```

4. You can get the list of vcpus by passing the `vcpu-list` argument for all VMs:

```
[root@oravm03 /]# xm vcpu-list
Name                              ID  VCPU   CPU State   Time(s) CPU Affinity
112_Win2003Ent                    14     0     1   -b-   2613.0 any cpu
129_WinXP_SP2                     19     0     0   -b-   3164.5 any cpu
72_OEL5_64bit                      4     0     0   -b-    599.3 any cpu
81_11gR1Appliance                  3     0     1   -b-    114.5 any cpu
81_11gR1Appliance                  3     1     1   -b-     73.0 any cpu
Domain-0                           0     0     1   -b-  54149.5 any cpu
Domain-0                           0     1     0   r--  38402.7 any cpu
[root@oravm03 /]#
```

5. You can print the log information by passing the `log` argument:

```
[root@oravm03 /]# xm log
[2009-04-11 14:31:29 2009] INFO (SrvDaemon:331) Xend Daemon started
[2009-04-11 14:31:29 2009] INFO (SrvDaemon:335) Xend changeset: unavailable.
[2009-04-11 14:31:29 2009] INFO (SrvDaemon:342) Xend version: Unknown.
[2009-04-11 14:31:29 2009] DEBUG (XendDomainInfo:133) XendDomainInfo.recreate([\047max_vcpu_id\047: 1, \047cpu_time\047: 14172803393L, \047ssidref\047: 0,
\047hvm\047: 0, \047shutdown_reason\047: 0, \047dying\047: 0, \047online_vcpus\047: 2, \047domid\047: 0  \047paused\047: 0, \047crashed\047: 0, \047running
\047: 1, \047maxmem_kb\047: 4294967292L, \047shutdown\047: 0, \047mem_kb\047: 599040L, \047handle\047: [0, 0, 0, 0, 0, 0, 0, 0, 0, 0, 0, 0, 0, 0, 0, 0], \0
47blocked\047: 0, \047name\047: \047Domain-0\047])
[2009-04-11 14:31:29 2009] INFO (XendDomainInfo:149) Recreating domain 0, UUID 00000000-0000-0000-0000-000000000000, at /local/domain/0
[2009-04-11 14:31:29 2009] DEBUG (XendDomainInfo:2119) Storing VM details: {\047on_xend_stop\047: \047ignore\047, \047shadow_memory\047: \0470\047, \047uui
d\047: \04700000000-0000-0000-0000-000000000000\047, \047on_reboot\047: \047restart\047, \047image\047: \047(linux (kernel ))\047, \047on_poweroff\047: \04
7destroy\047, \047on_xend_start\047: \047ignore\047, \047on_crash\047: \047restart\047, \047xend/restart_count\047: \0470\047, \047vcpus\047: \0472\047, \0
47vcpu_avail\047: \0473\047, \047name\047: \047Domain-0\047}
[2009-04-11 14:31:29 2009] DEBUG (XendDomainInfo:923) Storing domain details: {\047name\047: \047Domain-0\047, \047console/limit\047: \0471048576\047, \047
memory/target\047: \047599040\047, \047vm\047: \047vm/00000000-0000-0000-0000-000000000000\047, \047domid\047: \0470\047, \047cpu/0/availability\047: \047
online\047, \047cpu/1/availability\047: \047online\047, \047control/platform-feature-multiprocessor-suspend\047: \0471\047}
[2009-04-11 14:31:29 2009] DEBUG (XendDomain:434) Adding Domain: 0
[2009-04-11 14:31:29 2009] DEBUG (XendDomain:379) number of vcpus to use is 0
[2009-04-11 14:31:29 2009] INFO (SrvServer:108) unix path=/var/lib/xend/xend-socket
[2009-04-11 14:31:29 2009] WARNING (XendAPI:672) API call: VBD.set_device not found
[2009-04-11 14:31:29 2009] WARNING (XendAPI:672) API call: VBD.set_type not found
[2009-04-11 14:31:29 2009] WARNING (XendAPI:672) API call: VM.get_auto_power_on not found
[2009-04-11 14:31:29 2009] WARNING (XendAPI:672) API call: VM.set_auto_power_on not found
[2009-04-11 14:31:29 2009] WARNING (XendAPI:672) API call: debug.get_all not found
[2009-04-11 14:31:29 2009] WARNING (XendAPI:672) API call: console.get_other_config not found
[2009-04-11 14:31:29 2009] WARNING (XendAPI:672) API call: console.set_other_config not found
[2009-04-11 14:31:29 2009] WARNING (XendAPI:672) API call: VIF.get_network not found
[2009-04-11 14:31:29 2009] WARNING (XendAPI:672) API call: VIF.set_device not found
[2009-04-11 14:31:29 2009] WARNING (XendAPI:672) API call: VIF.set_MAC not found
[2009-04-11 14:31:29 2009] WARNING (XendAPI:672) API call: VIF.set_MTU not found
[2009-04-11 14:31:29 2009] WARNING (XendAPI:672) API call: session.get_all_records not found
[2009-04-11 14:31:29 2009] WARNING (XendAPI:672) API call: event.get_record not found
[2009-04-11 14:31:29 2009] WARNING (XendAPI:672) API call: event.get_all not found
[2009-04-11 14:31:29 2009] DEBUG (XendDomainInfo:1807) XendDomainInfo.handleShutdownWatch
```

6. Pass the `info` argument, in order to get the information about the VM Server, as shown in the following screenshot:

```
[root@oravm03 /]# xm info
host                   : oravm03.avastu.com
release                : 2.6.18-8.1.15.1.16.el5xen
version                : #1 SMP Fri Aug 1 18:27:30 EDT 2008
machine                : i686
nr_cpus                : 2
nr_nodes               : 1
sockets_per_node       : 1
cores_per_socket       : 2
threads_per_core       : 1
cpu_mhz                : 1995
hw_caps                : bfebfbff:20100800:00000000:00000140:0000e3bd:00000000:00000001
total_memory           : 4093
free_memory            : 728
xen_major              : 3
xen_minor              : 1
xen_extra              : .4
xen_caps               : xen-3.0-x86_64 xen-3.0-x86_32p hvm-3.0-x86_32 hvm-3.0-x86_32p hvm-3.0-x86_64
xen_scheduler          : credit
xen_pagesize           : 4096
platform_params        : virt_start=0xff800000
xen_changeset          : unavailable
cc_compiler            : gcc version 4.1.1 20070105 (Red Hat 4.1.1-52)
cc_compile_by          : root
cc_compile_domain      : localdomain
cc_compile_date        : Thu Aug 28 00:06:27 PDT 2008
xend_config_format     : 4
[root@oravm03 /]#
```

7. You can pass the `shell` argument to get into the shell, and pass the arguments directly.

```
[root@oravm03 /]# xm shell
The Xen Master. Type "help" for a list of functions.
xm> help
Usage: xm <subcommand> [args]

Control, list, and manipulate Xen guest instances.

Common 'xm' commands:

    console        Attach to <Domain>'s console.
    create         Create a domain based on <ConfigFile>.
    new            Adds a domain to Xend domain management
    delete         Remove a domain from Xend domain management.
    destroy        Terminate a domain immediately.
    dump-core      Dump core for a specific domain.
    help           Display this message.
    list           List information about all/some domains.
    mem-set        Set the current memory usage for a domain.
    migrate        Migrate a domain to another machine.
    pause          Pause execution of a domain.
    reboot         Reboot a domain.
    restore        Restore a domain from a saved state.
    resume         Resume a Xend managed domain
    save           Save a domain state to restore later.
    shell          Launch an interactive shell.
    shutdown       Shutdown a domain.
    start          Start a Xend managed domain
    suspend        Suspend a Xend managed domain
    top            Monitor a host and the domains in real time.
    unpause        Unpause a paused domain.
    uptime         Print uptime for a domain.
    vcpu-set       Set the number of active VCPUs for allowed for
                   the domain.

<Domain> can either be the Domain Name or Id.
For more help on 'xm' see the xm(1) man page.
For more help on 'xm create' see the xmdomain.cfg(5)  man page.

For a complete list of subcommands run 'xm help'.
xm>
```

8. The `block-list` argument without a `-l` (l for long output), as shown in the following screenshot:

```
[root@oravm03 ~]# xm block-list 14
Vdev  BE handle state evt-ch ring-ref BE-path
768    0    0     1    -1      -1     /local/domain/0/backend/vbd/14/768
5632   0    0     1    -1      -1     /local/domain/0/backend/vbd/14/5632
[root@oravm03 ~]#
```

9. The `block-list` argument with a `-l` argument, to produce the output in the SXP format.

```
[root@oravm03 ~]# xm block-list 14 -l
(768
    ((backend-id 0)
     (virtual-device 768)
     (device-type disk)
     (state 1)
     (backend /local/domain/0/backend/vbd/14/768)
    )
)
(5632
    ((backend-id 0)
     (virtual-device 5632)
     (device-type cdrom)
     (state 1)
     (backend /local/domain/0/backend/vbd/14/5632)
    )
)
[root@oravm03 ~]#
```

Xm dmesg: Read the Xen Daemon Message Buffer and if needed clean it.
Here we type in the basic syntax for the `xm dmesg` with an optional argument `-c`,
which clears the contents of the ring buffer while it displays it, as shown in the
following screenshot:

```
[root@oravm03 ~]# xm dmesg -c
 \ \/ /                   |_ /  / | | | |
  \ // _ \ \047_ \      | _ \ | | | | |_
  / /\  ___/ | | |     _) | | || |  _|
 /_/  \___|_| |_|     |___/  \__,_|_|

http://www.cl.cam.ac.uk/netos/xen
University of Cambridge Computer Laboratory

Xen version 3.1.4 (root@localdomain) (gcc version 4.1.1 20070105 (Red Hat 4.1.1-52)) Thu Aug 28 00:06:27 PDT 2008
Latest ChangeSet: unavailable

(XEN) Command line: dom0_mem=585M
(XEN) Video information:
(XEN)  VGA is text mode 80x25, font 8x16
(XEN)  VBE/DDC methods: none; EDID transfer time: 0 seconds
(XEN)  EDID info not retrieved because no DDC retrieval method detected
(XEN) Disc information:
(XEN)  Found 1 MBR signatures
(XEN)  Found 1 EDD information structures
(XEN) Xen-e820 RAM map:
(XEN)  0000000000000000 - 000000000009f000 (usable)
(XEN)  000000000009f000 - 00000000000a0000 (reserved)
(XEN)  0000000000100000 - 00000000dfe5a000 (usable)
(XEN)  00000000dfe5a000 - 00000000e0000000 (reserved)
(XEN)  00000000f8000000 - 00000000fc000000 (reserved)
(XEN)  00000000fec00000 - 00000000fec10000 (reserved)
(XEN)  00000000fed18000 - 00000000fed1c000 (reserved)
(XEN)  00000000fed20000 - 00000000fed90000 (reserved)
(XEN)  00000000feda0000 - 00000000feda6000 (reserved)
(XEN)  00000000fee00000 - 00000000fee10000 (reserved)
(XEN)  00000000ffe00000 - 0000000100000000 (reserved)
(XEN)  0000000100002000 - 0000000120000000 (usable)
(XEN) System RAM: 4093MB (4192220kB)
(XEN) Xen heap: 14MB (15072kB)
(XEN) Domain heap initialised: DMA width 32 bits
(XEN) Processor #0 6:15 APIC version 20
(XEN) Processor #1 6:15 APIC version 20
(XEN) IOAPIC[0]: apic_id 2, version 32, address 0xfec00000, GSI 0-23
(XEN) Enabling APIC mode:  Flat.  Using 1 I/O APICs
(XEN) Using scheduler: SMP Credit Scheduler (credit)
(XEN) Detected 1995.097 MHz processor.
(XEN) HVM: VMX enabled
(XEN) VMX: MSR intercept bitmap enabled
```

Attaching and detaching new virtual NICs: Show the visible NICs before attaching a virtual NIC to a domain or a VM. Here, we give an extra virtual NIC to a VM by issuing `xm network-attach 14` command. It then attaches the new virtual NIC to that VM:

```
[root@oravm03 ~]# brctl show
bridge name      bridge id               STP enabled       interfaces
xenbr0           8000.4237e7acbf89       no                vif19.0
                                                           tap19.0
                                                           vif14.0
                                                           tap14.0
                                                           vif4.0
                                                           vif3.0
                                                           peth0
                                                           vif0.0
[root@oravm03 ~]#
[root@oravm03 ~]#
[root@oravm03 ~]# xm network-attach 14
[root@oravm03 ~]# brctl show
bridge name      bridge id               STP enabled       interfaces
xenbr0           8000.4237e7acbf89       no                vif14.1
                                                           vif19.0
                                                           tap19.0
                                                           vif14.0
                                                           tap14.0
                                                           vif4.0
                                                           vif3.0
                                                           peth0
```

Deleting or detaching can be done by issuing the `network-detach` argument; we have to use a force flag and also detaching is not easy:

```
[root@oravm03 ~]# xm network-list 14
Idx BE     MAC Addr.      handle state evt-ch tx-/rx-ring-ref BE-path
0   0  ??                 0     1      -1    -1   /-1          /local/domain/0/backend/vif/14/0
1   0  00:16:3e:34:b6:59  1     1      -1    -1   /-1          /local/domain/0/backend/vif/14/1
[root@oravm03 ~]# xm network-detach 14 1 -f
[root@oravm03 ~]# brctl show
bridge name      bridge id               STP enabled       interfaces
xenbr0           8000.4237e7acbf89       no                vif19.0
                                                           tap19.0
                                                           vif14.0
                                                           tap14.0
                                                           vif4.0
                                                           vif3.0
                                                           peth0
                                                           vif0.0
[root@oravm03 ~]#
```

You have seen a few of the xm command line arguments and there are a lot of arguments which you can use when you feel the need to carry these commands out from the **CLI (Command Line Interface)**.

Always remember that a lot of actions, if your Oracle IntraCloud VM farm is configured properly, can be carried out from the VM Manager console.

The killer virsh utility

Finally, let's take a look at another fine utility called virsh. Even this utility, similar to xm, is a great tool when a CLI rescue operation is needed and one must put on their geeky gloves.

And also, similar to xm, it's huge and has many arguments which we won't cover but we will brush through the important ones for you. Let's start with the `-help` argument:

```
virsh # help
Commands:

    autostart          autostart a domain
    capabilities       capabilities
    connect            (re)connect to hypervisor
    console            connect to the guest console
    create             create a domain from an XML file
    start              start a (previously defined) inactive domain
    destroy            destroy a domain
    define             define (but don't start) a domain from an XML file
    domid              convert a domain name or UUID to domain id
    domuuid            convert a domain name or id to domain UUID
    dominfo            domain information
    domname            convert a domain id or UUID to domain name
    domstate           domain state
    dumpxml            domain information in XML
    help               print help
    list               list domains
    net-autostart      autostart a network
    net-create         create a network from an XML file
    net-define         define (but don't start) a network from an XML file
    net-destroy        destroy a network
    net-dumpxml        network information in XML
    net-list           list networks
    net-name           convert a network UUID to network name
    net-start          start a (previously defined) inactive network
    net-undefine       undefine an inactive network
    net-uuid           convert a network name to network UUID
    nodeinfo           node information
    quit               quit this interactive terminal
    reboot             reboot a domain
    restore            restore a domain from a saved state in a file
    resume             resume a domain
    save               save a domain state to a file
    schedinfo          show/set scheduler parameters
    dump               dump the core of a domain to a file for analysis
    shutdown           gracefully shutdown a domain
    setmem             change memory allocation
    setmaxmem          change maximum memory limit
    setvcpus           change number of virtual CPUs
    suspend            suspend a domain
    undefine           undefine an inactive domain
    vcpuinfo           domain vcpu information
    vcpupin            control domain vcpu affinity
    version            show version
    vncdisplay         vnc display
    attach-device      attach device from an XML file
    detach-device      detach device from an XML file
    attach-interface   attach network interface
    detach-interface   detach network interface
    attach-disk        attach disk device
    detach-disk        detach disk device
```

1. Passing the `-list` argument gives us all the VMs, including the `Domain-0`, and their states:

```
virsh # list
 Id Name                 State
----------------------------------
  0 Domain-0             running
  3 81_11gR1Appliance    blocked
  4 72_OEL5_64bit        blocked
 14 112_Win2003Ent       blocked
 19 129_WinXP_SP2        blocked
```

2. The `vcpuinfo` command can be used for VM with ID 4:

```
virsh # vcpuinfo 4
VCPU:          0
CPU:           1
State:         blocked
CPU time:      588.6s
CPU Affinity:  yy
```

3. We can get the version information using the `version` argument, as shown in the following screenshot:

```
virsh # version
Compiled against library: libvir 0.2.3
Using library: libvir 0.2.3
Using API: Xen 3.0.1
Running hypervisor: Xen 3.1.0
```

4. To get the information of the node or the Oracle VM Server, we use the `nodeinfo` argument:

```
virsh # nodeinfo
CPU model:          i686
CPU(s):             2
CPU frequency:      1995 MHz
CPU socket(s):      1
Core(s) per socket: 2
Thread(s) per core: 1
NUMA cell(s):       1
Memory size:        4191232 kB
```

Summary

As you can observe this is barely the tip of the iceberg. This doesn't mean that we should only focus on the CLI the entire time. However, it is very essential to understand the working of the master utilities within the Oracle VM servers—as all excellent Xen tools and utilities are all waiting there for you to take full advantage of them.

I hope that this humble introduction to the master class tools of the Oracle VM Server will help you get started, so that you can become an Oracle VM expert.

Index

Symbols

A

B

C

D

E

About Packt Publishing

Packt, pronounced 'packed', published its first book "*Mastering phpMyAdmin for Effective MySQL Management*" in April 2004 and subsequently continued to specialize in publishing highly focused books on specific technologies and solutions.

Our books and publications share the experiences of your fellow IT professionals in adapting and customizing today's systems, applications, and frameworks. Our solution based books give you the knowledge and power to customize the software and technologies you're using to get the job done. Packt books are more specific and less general than the IT books you have seen in the past. Our unique business model allows us to bring you more focused information, giving you more of what you need to know, and less of what you don't.

Packt is a modern, yet unique publishing company, which focuses on producing quality, cutting-edge books for communities of developers, administrators, and newbies alike. For more information, please visit our website: www.packtpub.com.

Writing for Packt

We welcome all inquiries from people who are interested in authoring. Book proposals should be sent to author@packtpub.com. If your book idea is still at an early stage and you would like to discuss it first before writing a formal book proposal, contact us; one of our commissioning editors will get in touch with you.

We're not just looking for published authors; if you have strong technical skills but no writing experience, our experienced editors can help you develop a writing career, or simply get some additional reward for your expertise.

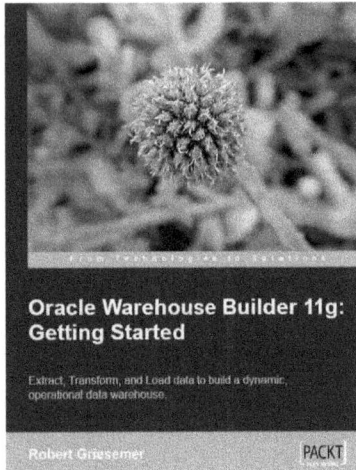

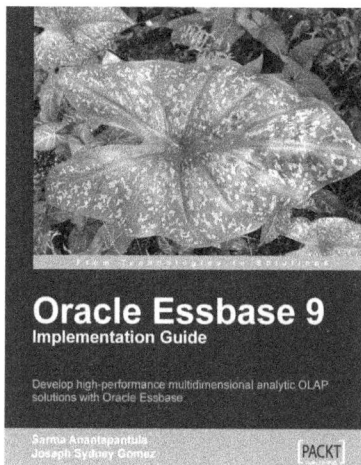

Oracle Essbase 9 Implementation Guide

ISBN: 978-1-847196-86-6   Paperback: 444 pages

Develop high-performance multidimensional analytic OLAP solutions with Oracle Essbase

1. Build multidimensional Essbase database cubes and develop analytical Essbase applications

2. Step-by-step instructions with expert tips from installation to implementation

3. Can be used to learn any version of Essbase starting from 4.x to 11.x

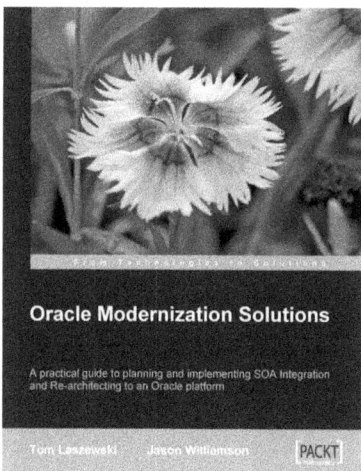

Oracle Modernization Solutions

ISBN: 978-1-847194-64-0   Paperback: 432 pages

A practical guide to planning and implementing SOA Integration and Re-architecting to an Oracle platform

1. Complete, practical guide to legacy modernization using SOA Integration and Re-architecture

2. Understand when and why to choose the non-invasive SOA Integration approach to reuse and integrate legacy components quickly and safely

3. Modernize to a process-driven SOA architecture based on Java EE, Oracle Database, and Fusion Middleware

4. Covers real-life scenarios with detailed hands-on examples

Please check **www.PacktPub.com** for information on our titles

www.ingramcontent.com/pod-product-compliance
Lightning Source LLC
Chambersburg PA
CBHW061407210326

41598CB00035B/6128